Taxing and Spei

Issues of Process

Taxing and Spending

Issues of Process

G. BRUCE DOERN

EVERT A. LINDQUIST

WAYNE R. THIRSK AND RICHARD M. BIRD

edited by

ALLAN M. MASLOVE

Published by University of Toronto Press in cooperation with the
Fair Tax Commission of the Government of Ontario

UNIVERSITY OF TORONTO PRESS
Toronto Buffalo London

Printed in Canada

ISBN 0-8020-7194-5

Printed on recycled paper

Canadian Cataloguing in Publication Data

Main entry under title:

Taxing and spending : issues of process

Co-published by the Fair Tax Commission of the
Government of Ontario.
Includes bibliographical references.
ISBN 0-8020-7194-5

1. Tax expenditures – Ontario. 2. Budget – Ontario.
3. Ontario – Appropriations and expenditures.
I. Doern, G. Bruce, 1942–   . II. Maslove, Allan M., 1946–   .
III. Ontario. Fair Tax Commission.

HJ2460.05T3 1994   336.713   C93-095575-7

Contents

3 **Earmarked Taxes in Ontario: Solution or Problem?**

Foreword

The Ontario Fair Tax Commission was established to examine the province's tax system as an integrated whole and, in conjunction with its working groups, to analyse individual components of the system in detail.

It has been many years since the Ontario tax system was subjected to a comprehensive examination. However, a great deal of research on taxation has been undertaken over the past two decades. This work, based in several disciplines, has been both theoretical and applied, and in this context the research program of the Fair Tax Commission was formulated.

The research program has two broad purposes. The first is, of course, to support the deliberations of the commissioners. The second, more novel objective is to inform public discussions of tax matters so that the commission's formal and informal public consultations can be of maximum value. For this reason we have opted to publish volumes in the series of studies as they are ready, rather than holding them all until the commission has completed its work. While our approach is more difficult from a technical and administrative perspective, we believe that the benefits will justify our decision.

The research program seeks to synthesize the existing published work on taxation; to investigate the implications for Ontario of the general research work; and, where required, to conduct original research on the context and principles for tax reform and on specific tax questions. We thus hope to add to the existing body of knowledge without duplicating it. The studies included in these publications are those that we believe make a contribution to the literature on taxation.

I would like to extend my thanks to my fellow commissioners and to the members of the FTC secretariat. I also thank the many members of the working groups and the advisory groups who have contributed to the research program and to the overall work of the commission.

Monica Townson, Chair

Introduction

Investigations of tax systems generally focus almost exclusively on the substantive aspects of taxation and rightly so. It is, after all, how the tax system affects people that is usually of greater concern. Interest in how and why the tax system works as it does is of more recent vintage.

Studies of process are of interest for two reasons. First, process is worthy of study in its own right. There is an old adage about means and ends in a democratic society – how we conduct our public affairs is as important as what we achieve. In spite of the need for confidentiality in deliberations within cabinet-parliamentary government, openness in policy processes – including the tax policy process – helps citizens to understand policies and to have input into their formation.

Second, process helps explain the structure of the tax system and how and why its desired properties tend to weaken over time. Tax reforms in Canadian jurisdictions have been infrequent. As one consequence, they tend to be major, with all the disruptions and transitional costs that that implies. It is arguable that the reason why the tax system drifts away from its "desired" position so much that it eventually requires full-blown reform is related to the tax policy process; that is, the process itself is the reason for the drift. Alternatively, one might argue that the tax system requires periodic adjustment because social and economic circumstances change over time. Whatever the reason, a policy process that could maintain the system closer to its "desired" position over time may incur lower operating costs than a system that requires major overhauls from time to time.

The papers in this volume address three important aspects of the tax policy (and spending) process. The process leading to the budget address of the minister of finance and its subsequent debate in the legislature is, of course, central to tax policy. Understanding the development of tax expenditures and how they are dealt with in the budget is essential to comprehending the ``drift'' of the tax system. Finally, the earmarking of tax revenues for specific purposes is sometimes proposed as a remedy to restore accountability to the broader budget process.

In the first study, Bruce Doern examines issues centring around the preparation and debate of the revenue budget presented (usually) annually by the provincial minister of finance. The minister assesses the changes to the process that have been introduced in the latter half of the 1980s and the early 1990s and concludes that these innovations constitute progress towards more openness and greater participation by a wide range of interests. Budget secrecy is the key issue to be faced if further advance in this direction is to be made. Doern examines the history behind the doctrine of budget secrecy and the principles that it is intended to serve. He concludes that the principles are no longer valid and, at any rate, are not served by the existing process, which makes a mockery of them whenever a lapse in secrecy occurs. Moreover, adherence to this outdated protocol prevents a number of developments that would improve the budget process. Doern provides an overview of what a budget process might look like if it were subject only to the normal confidentiality requirements of cabinet government.

Evert Lindquist's study contributes to our knowledge of how tax expenditures are dealt with in the budget and of the consequences of the asymmetries that exist between tax expenditures and direct expenditures. Generally speaking, tax structures require reform not because prevailing wisdom about ideal bases changes but because, over time, tax expenditures drive the existing bases further and further away from their ideals. How and why these tax expenditures emerge, why governments rely on them in preference to direct spending measures, and the consequences of tax expenditures for tax policy proper are thus important questions about process. Lindquist presents a review of the relatively short history of the tax expenditure literature and surveys the tax expenditure experience of a number of jurisdictions in Canada and the United States. A considerable variety of procedures has been adopted to report on tax expenditures, to evaluate their effectiveness and to foster rational choices between direct and tax spending instruments.

Lindquist develops a framework to assess a number of possible methods of reforming tax expenditures in order to generate a workable package of reforms. His proposals are intended to provide both policy makers and taxpayers with more information about the cost (revenue forgone) and effects of tax expenditures that could lead to more balanced consideration of tax expenditures and direct spending instruments.

A theme underlying much of the debate about tax policy process is the accountability of democratic governments to their electorates for the tax revenues that they raise. Earmarking of tax revenues for specific purposes has emerged as a means of restoring the accountability for spending tax revenues that many feel has eroded in recent years. In its more radical manifestations, earmarking is viewed as partial replacement of the discretion of unaccountable governments and legislatures by spending rules (earmarked taxes determine expenditure amounts). In their paper, Wayne Thirsk and Richard Bird examine the potential for earmarked revenues in Ontario. They carefully clarify the variations in meaning that surround the concept and compare Ontario's experience with earmarking with that of other jurisdictions. The paper examines the arguments for and against earmarking and the extent to which this procedure would improve budgetary performance. Their conclusion is that earmarking is not economically advisable beyond the quite limited areas in which it has traditionally applied.

Allan M. Maslove

Taxing and Spending

Issues of Process

1 Fairness, Budget Secrecy, and Pre-Budget Consultation in Ontario, 1985–1992

G. BRUCE DOERN

Introduction

The purpose of this paper is to review critically Ontario's decision making about the tax budget and to examine reform alternatives that would make the process more fair. The paper focuses on developments between 1985 and 1992 and thus covers the periods in power of David Peterson's Liberals and Bob Rae's New Democratic Party (NDP). More particularly, it begins with an effort by the Liberals in October 1985 to reform the budget process and ends with the second year of operation of an even more extensive reform initiative by the NDP.

Tax budget decision process must be defined somewhat flexibly for reasons that will become apparent.[1] In its broadest context, it contains four distinct types of process – the multi-year, through which basic federal-provincial tax and fiscal agreements are forged; annual, leading to the Budget Speech given by the provincial treasurer announcing or changing tax measures; annual and everyday, through which tax decisions are administered and revenue is collected with appropriate appeal measures for taxpayers; and periodic general tax reform, such as the current work of the Fair Tax Commission.[2] While the interactions among these four processes are important, the focus of the paper is clearly on the second – the events and dynamics of the annual process leading to the Budget Speech.

A further area of definition requiring flexible treatment is the role of the expenditure budget versus the revenue or tax budget. This paper concentrates on the tax budget. The expenditure budget process cannot, however, be left totally aside, since expenditure dynamics, especially in an era of several fiscal restraint, means that revenue is often raised through expenditure cuts. The spending side of the fiscal coin will thus be covered here to some extent, but not with a detailed account of how internal expenditures are determined internally.[3]

For the purpose of this paper, assessment of the fairness of the tax decision process involves four attributes:

- the availability of reasonable and public opportunities for interest groups and individual citizens to make known their views on tax alternatives and proposals;
- the availability of reasonable opportunities for elected members of the legislature to scrutinize the budget and to hold the government accountable for its contents, both prior to and after tabling of the budget;
- the ability of the cabinet and the provincial treasurer to make effective and timely decisions under the norms of responsible cabinet-parliamentary government within a federal system; and
- the existence of reasonable and open opportunities for independent analysis and objective data to be brought to bear on the state of the economy and scrutiny of budget options.

Fairness in this context therefore involves striking a reasonable balance among different values related to the process of making decisions. Such a process is likely to lead to fairer decisions and outcomes, but this paper does not directly assess the current method or future reformed methods against substantive, outcome-oriented criteria such as horizontal or vertical equity, redistribution and equality, and efficiency and stability.[4] These substantive values are undoubtedly brought to bear by various interests that participate in the process, but they are not the direct criteria applied here for assessing fairness. The tests are procedural and therefore more imprecise, but equally vital when compared to substantive, outcome-oriented values.

Since future reforms can be of numerous types, the paper seeks to examine alternatives primarily within the bounds of two options – continued existence of budget secrecy[5] and abolition of that doctrine. In each case, we are assuming responsible cabinet-parliamentary government. We exclude, for example, changes that might seek to emulate U.S. congressional approaches to budgeting, where executive power is shared with elected bodies not ruled by party discipline and where the government is not defeated if its budget fails in the legislative body.

The organization of the paper helps indicate how secrecy-versus–non-secrecy options will be examined. The first section examines the traditional budget process and initial efforts to reform it by Peterson's Liberals (1985–90). This period saw quite strong attachment to traditional secrecy. Such practice was intended to prevent individuals from gaining prior knowledge of budgetary measures and from profiting thereby. In this section, I outline the basic budgetary cycle and give profiles of the key players. The second section explores the NDP reforms from 1990 to 1992. These still functioned within the bounds of budget secrecy but sought to widen and alter the way in which groups participated in pre-budget consultation. The section evaluates the experiments in the 1991 and 1992 budgets.

The third section considers what would be involved in breaking the bonds of budget secrecy. What would such a system look like? What is the essential vested interest of the government, the opposition parties, and the media in retaining budget secrecy? Is there still a principled position to justify such secrecy? I then offer overall conclusions about the nature of recent reform, about whether a fairer system has been established, and about the prospects for fully breaching the budget secrecy wall.

A final caveat is also essential. In each of the two periods examined, I set the budget process in the context of the influence exerted by federal decisions. Although Ontario is Canada's largest and richest province, it is not a budgetary island. When Ottawa gets a cold, Ontario sneezes – if not first, then often loudest. Federal influence is both substantive and procedural. Ottawa has exercised substantive influence in recent years through the harsh reality of federal budget cuts, capping, or freezes, especially in transfer payments to the provinces for social programs such as health care, higher education, and social assistance. NDP budget documents drew particular attention to this factor and to the province's diminishing capacity to manage its growing deficit as the party took power in the early 1990s.[6] As will be seen, the timing of Ontario's budget is influenced by the need to consider the contents of the federal budget, usually tabled late in February. "Ontario's budgets and budgeting processes obviously can be influenced also by other federal-provincial fiscal arrangements, including periodic tax agreements and federal tax "reforms" such as flattening of the rate structure in 1987 and the 1990 changes to the GST.

The Traditional Tax Budget Process: The Late 1980s

David Peterson's Liberal government's first economic statement to the legislature in July 1985 indicated that it would seek to reform the pre-budget consultation process. In October 1985, the provincial treasurer, Robert Nixon, presented a discussion paper to the legislature outlining his proposals for reform.[7] As a long-serving opposition politician, Nixon cast his recommendations primarily in terms of the legislature's role in pre-budget consultation. He also cited the advice of the Procedural Affairs Committee (1980) of the legislature and the published advice (1985) of the federal Royal Commission on the Economic Union and Development Prospects for Canada (Macdonald Commission). Nixon also expressed his rationale for reform to his officials as an effort to open up and demystify the process. A more particular motivation was also that of trying to give the process a multi-year focus, deemed especially important for institutions that receive provincial transfer payments. Universities, hospitals, colleges, municipalities, and school boards had long been advocating that their funding be decided upon earlier in the year, and as five-year commitments.

The Nixon Reform Proposals

Robert Nixon's proposals dealt with both revenue and expenditure and centred on a recommendation that a new Standing Committee on Economic and Fiscal Affairs be struck to:

- receive the Ontario Economic and Fiscal Outlook report;
- hold pre-budget hearings;
- review all tax legislation arising from the budget; and
- prepare a recommendation on the overall level of provincial revenues, expenditures, and net cash requirements.[8]

The outlook document would provide background information on the economy and on fiscal prospects. It would be distributed widely to groups prior to their making of presentations in pre-budget hearings. Nixon hoped that participation in the hearings would be encouraged from groups "that have not previously taken part and from private individuals."[9] Hearings would occur outside Toronto as well as in Toronto and be open to the media.

The standing committee would also be asked, among other things, to prepare guidelines on budget secrecy. Nixon's discussion paper acknowledged that the "convention of budget secrecy imposes restrictions on open consultations" and that the new proposals were intended to "minimize the effects of the convention by holding open pre-budget hearings and sharing information."[10] Equally, however, "budget secrecy cannot be eliminated entirely from the budget-making process."[11]

There is little doubt that the new government saw the proposals as a genuine effort to reform pre-budget consultation. But the changes were still rooted firmly in the de facto strictures of budget secrecy, as we can see by examining the key features of the traditional budget cycle and of the roles in it of the government, interest groups, the legislature, and the media; the nature of budget secrecy and debates about it; and the role of the Budget Speech as a tactical and goal-setting occasion. These secrecy strictures continued, despite Nixon's proposals, to dominate budget making during the Liberal era.

Key Players and the Traditional Budget Cycle

The nature of the budget cycle and the key participants during the Liberal years differed little from what they had been during the four decades of Conservative hegemony.[12]

Within the government and bureaucracy, the cycle started with the quite lengthy, ten-month review and allocation of expenditures, culminated in tabling of the spending estimates in the legislature in March of each year. All departments and ministers negotiated and haggled over the level of funding for continuing programs and new initiatives. The battle over new money centred on the role of the cabinet's Policy and Priorities Board, which consisted of the premier, the treasurer, the chairman of the Management Board, and three senior cabinet members. The board was also the final decision maker on all ongoing spending. In the NDP period, the new Treasury Board has also had a key role.

Treasurer-Premier Relations and the Ministry of Treasury and Economics

In contrast to the multi-minister, multi-department expenditure process, the tax and revenue side is centred around the treasurer and within the Ministry of Treasury and Economics (MTE) since renamed the Ministry of Finance. The ministry is clearly the analytical centre of operations, both in judging Ontario's economic outlook for the coming budget and for setting out the fiscal framework (the net stimulus or restraint and deficit or surplus that will guide the budget as a whole). At various stages, the premier also becomes heavily involved, supplying a larger, political "litmus test" to the treasurer's overall economic-political judgment. During the Liberal years, David Peterson and Robert Nixon interacted frequently. They would attend meetings of the Policy and Priorities Board; chat in the legislature, where they sat next to each other; and attend several private meetings immediately prior to the budget. Peterson participated more in the budget than had Premier Bill Davis, whose long-time treasurer was Darcy McKeough. Davis supplied an overall political assessment but tended to delegate the budget task more completely.[13] The relationship between Premier Bob Rae and Treasurer Floyd Laughren is also close.

During the internal decision process, a few other ministers inevitably try to influence the content of the Budget Speech. Most such attempts are resisted by the treasurer and his officials, but occasionally political-economic pressures lead to a line minister's views being sought, albeit not usually about specific tax measures. This may not always be a good thing. For example, it is quite possible that in the design of a particular investment tax Industry, Trade and Technology (new renamed Economic Development and Trade) may have better sectoral information than MTE. During Nixon's years, on two occasions a minister sought to have the budget discussed at a full cabinet meeting, but this was firmly resisted.

Whittling Down the "Pressures"

In the internal process, participants must sift through a range of departmental and interest group demands and pressures. Often described literally as the "pressures" list, it includes primarily spending items but often tax measures as well. It typically begins as a virtual "wish list" (even in times of several restraint) and is gradually whittled down by a process of ultimate political judgment by the treasurer and the premier, aided by major Treasury officials and ministerial aides to the treasurer and premier.

The tax budget cycle culminates in presentation of the treasurer's Budget Speech in late April of each year (the 1991 and 1992 budgets were on 29 and 30 April, respectively). But it is shorter than the spending side of the operation; it arguably begins in earnest only in the late fall and early winter prior to the Budget Speech.

Revenue projections and economic analysis are occurring all the time within Treasury and Economics, but it is not until early in the new calendar year that pre-budget consultations with interest groups take place and specific tax measures begin to be seriously considered. Queen's Park likes to wait for Ottawa's budget to be tabled (usually in mid- to late February) to determine whether federal measures might alter provincial budgetary plans. A federal budget may also serve as a convenient target for political blame should circumstances warrant, as they often do.

Pre-Budget Consultation and Interest Groups

Pre-budget consultation with interest groups goes on all year: groups are constantly lobbying ministers over policies and fiscal measures. But it occurs formally in the dozen or so weeks immediately prior to the budget when it becomes fairly ritualistic. During the Liberal years, as in previous decades, the treasurer met in camera with groups that had requested consultations or that had been invited by the treasurer to offer their views. They expressed these views either through written briefs, or verbally, or both. Typically, written briefs are not made public. Robert Nixon had a strong preference for one-on-one, in-camera sessions, partly because of tradition and perhaps also as a function of his personality. Some ministers simply feel that one-on-one sessions provide a chance to engage people in real discussion.

While the treasurer can engage in general discussion with groups, he or she cannot reveal, or even hint at, possible tax changes, for fear of breaking the rules of budget secrecy. This does not mean that such consultations have no value for either side. Useful information is often exchanged, and certainly a sense of interest groups' fears and concerns can be and in obtained. The government's overall views about the economy can also be communicated to such groups, often quite frankly. Treasurers in their first years of office may also be especially appreciative of the consultations, since they truly are an education for the minister. In later years, educational ardour may diminish somewhat, either because ministers genuinely know more and/or because they are worn out by pressures and demands.

While pre-budget consultations were once confined mainly to business interest groups, by the 1980s they included both the business and the social sides of the political continuum. For the Liberals' first budget, in 1985, over 80 groups and interests, including policy institutes, were involved.[14]

The Legislature and Pre-Budget Hearings

The legislature's role in the tax budget process is four-fold. First, as a centre for partisan party politics and criticism, its main opposition parties offer no shortage of comment and criticism prior to the Budget Speech. They are also often a significant conduit for criticisms from interest groups. Second, opposition parties may occasionally suggest preferred tax alternatives (other than reduced taxes) or worst-case tax choices to avoid. The treasurer has to take some political notice of these pressures but is often disposed to think of them as just posturing by political enemies. Treasurers almost never see the views of the opposition as objective advice. Third, the legislature and its committees scrutinize and ultimately approve tax measures. The formal role of the legislature takes hold quite late in the budgetary cycle, after the government has already reached its decisions. As we see below, even the pre-budget hearings held by the Standing Committee on Finance and Economic Affairs often take place quite late in the decision process.

Fourth, the governing party's own caucus is active in the process. Treasurers such as Robert Nixon and Floyd Laughren pride themselves on never missing caucus meetings. It is a forum that often supplies the frankest and most brutal criticism, because meetings are in camera and "within the family." As well, Nixon and Laughren were viewed as "deans" of the legislature, good caucus people and "parliamentarians" who respected the role of the ordinary backbencher.

The budget, however, is also a matter of confidence, according to parliamentary rules. And thus party whips exert maximum party discipline, since defeat on a budget measure brings down the government. Debate over the budget is the main order of business of the legislature for the first few days following the Budget Speech. But it continues intermittently throughout the session until a final vote is taken, months later. Tax bills are also subject to a full process of three readings in the legislature and its committees, with the average tax bill taking two months for approval.

Since its establishment under Robert Nixon's reforms, the Standing Committee on Finance and Economic Affairs has also been a player in pre-budget consultation (see Table 1). Both the number of written submissions and the number of actual appearances by interest groups fluctuate widely from year to year. Consultations range in duration

TABLE 1
Selected Elements of Pre-Budget Hearings of the Standing Committee on
Finance and Economic Affairs

Year	Number of Written Submissions	Number of Groups That Appeared	Dates
1987	70	30	Early Feb. to late March
1988	40	20	15–23 Feb.
1989	70	41	8 Jan.–9 Mar.
1990	54	40	15–25 Jan.
1991	90	60	21 Jan.–8 Feb.
1992	*	20	10–12 Feb., but Nov. 1991 for transfer institutions

Source: Ontario, Standing Committee on Finance and Economic Affairs, *Pre-Budget Consultation*, Reports for 1987 and 1992.
*Data not available in source.

from less than a week to more than eight weeks; three years saw a fairly early January start, and three a start in February.

Legislators' views on the process become apparent from the contents of their own reports on the hearings. For example, in 1988, the hearings involved meetings on both the budget and federal tax reform.[15] The committee acknowledged that there were some groups that it wanted to hear but could not. It also recommended a post-budget review – a report from the treasurer indicating how its recommendations were dealt with. Such reports have never materialized. In 1989, the committee again noted that it was unable to hear eight delegations.[16] The hearings were preoccupied more with the recently tabled Social Assistance Review Committee Report than with the budget as a whole. In 1990, the committee for the first time heard testimony from and had discussions with firms and institutions active in economic and financial forecasting. It lamented the fact that the groups that appeared before it were overwhelmingly from the greater Toronto area.[17] Accordingly, it recommended that hearings be held in other centres. Perhaps influenced by the forecasters whom it had just heard, it also proposed that pre-budget hearings be focused on the economic outlook and the overall fiscal framework, rather than on detailed expenditures. More is written below on the committee's role in 1991 and 1992.

In conclusion, the Liberal years witnessed establishment of a committee to conduct pre-budget hearings, and an episodic hearing process evolved as the committee learned and adapted its procedures in an ad hoc fashion. Except in its first year of operation in 1987, when partisanship was resisted, the committee's reports have been quite partisan. All of the reports after 1987 contained minority reports by the two opposition parties that used them to stake out their partisan positions notwithstanding what they heard from groups and individuals that appeared before them.

Partisanship was by no means confined to the opposition. The standing committee is controlled by the governing party, and it was viewed by many as being "Treasury driven" – it rarely had any instinct for taking maverick positions such as that exhibited occasionally by its federal counterpart, which has been headed in recent years by Conservative MP Don Blenkarn.

The Media and the Budget Process

The role of the media – particularly their Toronto-based operations – in the budget process is more continuous but mixed. In the last few years, it has had three roles. First, in the run-up to the budget, the media have tended to focus on the inherent partisan conflict involved in budgetary politics. It is not an enthusiastic front-page reporter of objective budgetary data, unless such data can somehow "make news" or exemplify conflict. Second, especially through the business press, they transmit how "the market," including international markets, view the government's financial and economic credibility and soundness. This reporting is often centred in more objective data, albeit slanted to the fiscal concerns of business. Third, just prior to and on budget day, they contribute to the theatrical nature of the Budget Speech. They are especially carnivorous in their search (hope?) to find a budget leak – in short, an infringement of budget secrecy. Their assiduous coverage of real or imagined leaks can often detract from the content of the document itself.

Media coverage, mainly in print, will occasionally follow pre-budget consultations, but certainly not consistently or extensively. This is a function of limits to print space and of the perceived non-newsworthiness of the parade of interests lining up for in-camera sessions with the treasurer. This practice did not appear to change when the process became more public in 1992.

The Tax Policy Community

Another significant set of players in the tax budget process is the tax policy community[18] – primarily tax lawyers, accountants, and financial experts who represent corporate and other clients and actually understand and deal with the details of the tax system and of tax laws. Members of this group often present briefs to government, but their usual entrée is more subtle and multi-dimensional; they interact with fellow tax professionals in the government on a day-to-day basis.

The Nature of Budget Secrecy

Despite the intentions underlying Nixon's reforms, budget secrecy is still central to tax budgeting in Ontario. It follows a British parliamentary practice designed to prevent individuals from profiting personally because of privileged prior knowledge of the contents of a budget speech.[19] It is a concept forged in the nineteenth century at a time when the main revenue source was tariffs and excise taxes. The doctrine holds that when a budget leak occurs, the minister (in Ontario's case, the treasurer) must resign. This is to happen, in theory, whether or not someone has actually been able to gain financially from prior knowledge.

The concept has three major political effects. First, it protects the treasurer from excessive and unrelenting pressure. Second, it in effect excludes all but two ministers (the treasurer and the premier) from what is arguably the cabinet's most important annual decision. (To avoid a budget leak, discussion and consultation must be severely restricted within the government as well as outside it.) Third, it enhances the drama of the Budget Speech as a political occasion.[20]

Budget secrecy in Ontario has been influenced by these larger British traditions but also by developments at Queen's Park and in Ottawa. In 1983, some pages of the Ontario budget were found by a journalist in a waste bin and charges arose that a budget leak had occurred. Opposition critics called for the treasurer's resignation. This event led to a legal review within MTE to determine what the precedents said about the practical meaning of the principle. Legal advisers examined relevant cases from Britian (1936, 1947, and 1957) and Ottawa (1963 and 1983) and similar situations in Saskatchewan, Quebec, and Australia. They concluded that there was no clear tradition that the leak of any budget information must lead to the resignation of the financial minister. Accordingly, in 1983, the treasurer was advised that only in the case of improper financial gain or grave indiscretion on the part of the minister concerned is resignation appropriate.

The almost comical nature of the 1983 incident, which followed the 1983 federal leak (when a TV camera caught a glimpse of the finance minister's speech page with some data on it), prompted more discussion of budgetary reform. Subsequent federal discussion papers advocated substantial loosening of the concept and better pre-budget consultation and helped inspire Robert Nixon's reform proposals of 1985.

More will be said in later sections about budget secrecy. For the period 1985–90, budget secrecy was not growing in stature. Indeed, there was some embarrassment about it, but not yet enough to remove it as a central feature of budget making.

The Budget Speech as a Tactical and Goal-Setting Occasion

Research on federal and provincial practice has shown that budget secrecy has such staying power in large part because it helps produce a sense of drama, which allows the government to use the Budget Speech as a tactical and goal-setting occasion.[21] Like other governments in Canada, Queen's Park often sees itself as functioning amid a sea of critics, including media, opposition parties, interest groups, and financial markets. Accordingly, it covets those few occasions when it gets to present its own agenda and define, or redefine, what it thinks it stands for. The Budget Speech, along with Throne Speeches, is one such event.

If a government is in trouble, it can use the Budget Speech to rally its own troops and re-energize itself, especially if there are partisan "goodies" to be handed out. It can also articulate and communicate its key goals, values, and priorities.

Such intrinsic political functions are very useful. Moreover, for key political leaders such as the premier and the treasurer, the urge to centralize power vis-à-vis such events is virtually irresistible. Budget secrecy already centralizes power, but it may be only a marginal addition to such centralizing urges, especially in an era of televised mass media politics. I return to this point below when looking at possible processes not based on budget secrecy.

The NDP Reforms, 1990–92: Loosening Budget Secrecy?

The New Democratic Party under the leadership of Bob Rae was the surprising victor in the 1990 Ontario election. As the province's first social democratic government, it has sought to reform the budget process in the context of a deep and lingering recession and a deteriorating situation for public revenues and the deficit.[22]

The first Budget Speech by Treasurer Floyd Laughren, presented on 29 April 1991, drew attention to three elements of the budget process (expenditure and revenue) that it had set out to reform. First, Laughren announced that a Cabinet Treasury Board would be established, because the budget control system "we inherited from previous administrations simply cannot do the job."[23] Laughren said that "there was no effective mechanism for examining the structure of entire programs,"[24] nor was there any clear responsibility for management of expenditures. Second, the treasurer argued that it was important "to look for new ways to involve Members of the Legislature and the general public, as well as our employees, in contributing to the solutions needed"[25] in program review and reform.

Third, the treasurer said simply that he intended "to ask for the views of the Standing Committee on Finance and Economic Affairs on ways to open up the Budget process to involve more public participation."[26] In fact, in the run-up to the speech, Laughren had sought to widen public participation, chiefly by inviting many social interest groups – the NDP's natural constituency – to meet with the him. Many such bodies had not been participants in previous budget cycles and thus supplemented the traditional list of economic, business, and established social interest groups.

Pre-Budget Consultation, 1991

In 1991, the pre-budget consultation, despite having more participants, followed the traditional approach. In short, the treasurer conducted one-on-one, closed door meetings, focused on the sectors of the economy, or society, of concern to the particular group. Only rarely was the total economic or fiscal picture examined. No background paper on fiscal outlook had been presented by the government to serve as a basis for the meetings. About the only preparatory document that interest groups could use was Laughren's eight-page economic statement presented to the legislature in December 1990.

Laughren was frustrated, not to mention exhausted, by this process. Over 100 groups wanted to participate; about 50 were selected, but the large number involved meant that the sessions had to be numerous and short (about 30 minutes). As well, Premier Rae and his advisers in the Premier's Office expressed dissatisfaction with the overall budget process. As a government of ministers with no experience in office, the cabinet as a whole sensed that the first budget cycle was not well coordinated and did not give confidence to its supporters about the NDP's ability to govern. The result was that a report on the budget process was prepared, involving advice from both the public service and outside consultants who were NDP supporters and experts. MTE was put on notice that there had to be a better-coordinated governmental view of the budget.

Pre-Budget consultation for the 1992 Budget

The budgetary and political soul-searching after the first budget led in the 1992 budget to a process different from that for any previous budget in Canada – in the nature of the information that underpinned it; in the type of forums and meetings held with interest groups; and in the internal evaluation of the process.

Pre-budget information consisted of three documents. First, an economic outlook paper was released in December 1991.[27] Written to be "accessible," it set out the broad state of the Ontario economy and was released just as the treasurer announced his pre-budget consultation program. Second, a fiscal outlook paper was released late in January 1992.[28] It set out data on the revenue and expenditure forecasts for the government's finances, including estimates of "what would happen to the province's fiscal situation if no measures were taken to control spending and bolster the economy."[29] Third, albeit too late for actual consultations, there appeared a Budget Guidebook.[30] It included summary information on the fiscal situation, a description of the budgetary process, and a copy of the premier's television address of 21 January, which had been intended to emphasize the seriousness of the economic situation and to show that the premier was personally committed to reducing the budget deficit.[31] Unprecedented amounts of information were made available: 5000 copies of the economic outlook, 15,000 of the fiscal outlook, and 20,000 of the guidebook.[32]

The consultations differed decidedly from the previous year's. The treasurer took part in three-hour meetings attended by representa-

TABLE 2
Budget Consultations, 1992

Date	Event
29 January	Premier's Councils Roundtable
4–6 February	Briefing sessions for forum participants
18 February	Health Forum
21 February	Job Creation Forum
	Transportation/Housing/Infrastructure Forum
24–28 February	Cabinet/Caucus Retreat: Progress Report on Budget Consultations
3 March	Agriculture and Food Forum
	Forum on Training for the New Job Market
5 March	Social Services/Income Maintenance Forum
	Environment/Resources Forum
	Treasurer's meeting with labour economists
6 March	Treasurer's meeting with Fair Tax Commissioners
	Treasurer's Roundtable on Spending, Taxation and Deficit Levels
10 March	Local Business/Retail/Tourism Forum
	Social/Employment Equity Forum
12 March	Industrial Renewal Forum
19 March	Treasurer's Meeting with Ontario Business Advisory Council (OBAC)
16 April	Roundtable with major labour leaders

tives of from 7 to 12 interest groups. At each session, he would present background information. Interest group spokepersons would present their views and reactions. And there was considerable discussion among the interest groups.

As Table 2 indicates, the forums were organized on a sectoral, or thematic basis. Themes included agriculture and food, environment and resources, health, industrial renewal, job creation, local business/ retail, social and employment equity, social services and income maintenance, tourism, training, and transportation/housing and infrastructure. Sessions therefore had to deal with both the spending and the tax sides of the fiscal equation. Accordingly, appropriate line ministers chaired the gatherings, with the treasurer present at all sessions.

The treasurer held roundtable discussions with selected members of the Premier's Council on Economic Renewal and the Premier's Council on Health, Well-Being and Social Justice. He also met with organizations such as the Canadian Bankers Association, the Fair Tax Commission, the Ontario Business Advisory Committee, and the tobacco industry lobby. Some line ministers, at his invitation, also held pre-budget consultations, including Culture and Communications, Housing, and Municipal Affairs. The Standing Committee on Finance and Economic Affairs also held pre-budget hearings in both 1991 and 1992. As Table 1 above shows, the 1991 hearings received presentations from 60 delegations and about 30 additional written briefs. In addition, it heard from economic forecasters. Despite a wide range of representations, the committee felt obliged to reassure certain economic sectors that they too were important, even though they were not represented. These sectors included the environment, mass transit, the mining industry, pulp and paper, the police, and tourism.[33]

The process also generated 4300 letters and submissions from individual Ontario residents, again at the invitation of the treasurer.[34]

The hearings began in the fall of 1991 and included presentations from municipalities, universities, colleges, schools, and hospitals – the main recipients of transfer payments from the province; banks and consulting firms engaged in economic forecasting; and about 20 groups invited by the political parties. The committee issued an interim report in the fall of 1991 and a final report in March 1992. The process followed the multi-group presentation approach and thus mirrored the larger effort centred around the treasurer.

In the final report, Liberal members tabled a minority report. It brought out some sharp partisan differences over the new process. Citing a leaked government memo on consultation (not just for budgets) that stated that the process was designed "to maximize the government's profile" and "establish new support bases across Ontario," the Liberals accused the NDP of eroding the Committee's powers and downgrading the role of opposition parties.[35]

At the sessions with the treasurer, especially the thematic forums, officers took minutes. Copies were sent to those who attended and to the government's Budget Steering Committee. The treasurer promised to follow up with a post-Budget Speech letter to participants indicating the government's decisions on the recommendations made at each forum.

The sessions displayed only a limited willingness to discuss tax matters. Tax issues were certainly discussed in some meetings, such as the forum on local business, but there was a reluctance to engage the topic. First, there was concern about budget secrecy itself (because the treasurer is never able to reveal his hand); second, all groups inherently dislike taxes and are thus reluctant to suggest tax

changes in a multi-sector forum; and, third, the government's Fair
Tax Commission was concurrently meeting and doing research on tax
issues in the context of more general tax reform.

Evaluation of the 1992 Process

At the conclusion of the sectoral forums, randomly selected participants were asked to complete a six-question evaluation form to determine interest and level of support for the exercise.[36] The 18
participants, from across the spectrum of economic and social groups,
included seasoned budget participants as well as newcomers.

The first question dealt with perceptions of the process, the sub-
stance of the sessions, and what might have been done differently.
There was considerable praise for the treasurer for taking the first
step to a more participatory process. There was disagreement, however, on whether groups should still be allowed to make their presentation to the treasurer. Business groups, in particular, also wanted
confidential, frank, one-on-one sessions with the treasurer. A majority
of participants agreed that the presentation phase of the forum lasted
too long. Newcomers (mainly social groups) valued the briefing sessions more than did the seasoned participants (mainly business).
There was consensus that sessions should be held more than once a
year in order to gain input at various stages of the budget cycle.

The second question dealt with the expectations of the participants
with respect to the discussion period and whether it should be more
structured or more flexible. Some had ill-defined expectations, and
others had hoped that they would discuss trade-offs and arrive at
consensus. Many expressed fears that people would quickly tire of
the process if the goals were not better defined. Most believed that
the treasurer's role was to listen, question, clarify, and ensure that discussion did not get out of hand. They credited him with doing a good
job in these functions.

The third question asked simply whether it was essential that the
treasurer attend the session, or whether senior ministry officials alone
would be equally effective. Most individuals indicated that they
would not have attended had the treasurer not been there.

The fourth question asked how the process compared, in general,
with any other pre-budget (federal or provincial) or other policy consultations in their experience. The response was that the others were
usually one-on-one meetings with ministers and were not as well
conducted but were more specific.

The fifth question asked participants what criteria each would suggest to determine which organization or group should be invited to sessions. The responses indicated that this was a difficult choice and that participants did not envy the government in having to choose or justify the choices. Some suggested that groups had to serve some umbrella representative function for other groups. Others proposed market share as a criterion. Most groups assumed that they would not be excluded no matter what the criteria.

The sixth and final question concerned information material supplied prior to sessions. The response was reasonably complimentary, especially from the newcomers. Volunteer groups from the social sector supported greater research assistance through funding of intervenors. Participants indicated that they had met with other participants prior to sessions to discuss presentations. Most said also that they had to do additional research to prepare for the sessions.

Key players within MTE generally felt satisfied with the 1992 experiment, keeping in mind its newness and also the deep dissatisfaction with the process of 1991.

Breaking the Bonds of Budget Secrecy?

From the outset, I have indicated that the paper would examine tax budget reforms in terms of two scenarios – one that operates within the norms of budget secrecy and one that breaks away from it. Reform initiatives under the Liberals and the NDP sought to loosen the strictures of budget secrecy and, in their own ways, to broaden the pre-budget consultation process and to improve the quality of information available for such public input. I offer a more complete set of conclusions about these reforms at the end of the paper. But what would a tax decision process without budget secrecy look like?

I first review the cases for and against budget secrecy and, second, pose a few practical sample questions and speculate about how they might be dealt with in a tax decision process not governed by budget secrecy.

The Core Cases for and against Budget Secrecy

The essence of the principled case for budget secrecy is that no one should have the opportunity for private financial gain as a result of prior knowledge of specific tax decisions that is unavailable to others.[37] The finance or treasury minister must ensure that such opportunities do not arise. If they do occur through a budget leak, then the minister is obliged to resign. This principle confines decision making to a very few people – namely, the treasurer and the premier and their immediate senior officials and advisers. Therefore decisions are not discussed among a wider set of ministers, unlike the case in other expenditure and regulatory choices, nor can they be subject to full and open consultation with interest groups.

Financial gain from prior knowledge is the central concern of budget secrecy. Financial gain implies, in particular, an opportunity to buy or sell stocks of financial instruments for gain, but it could imply buying or selling other assets as well.

The case against budget secrecy tends increasingly to be three-fold.[38] First, when it occurs, or is believed to have occurred, ministers do not usually resign. Therefore the principle has no real political consequences other than embarrassment and an opportunity to score partisan points. Second, such a tattered and dishonoured principle should not be allowed to exclude many ministers from one of the most vital decisions any government must make. Third, other types of government decisions concerning matters such as expenditures, regulations, and loan guarantees may "potentially" (see more below) also create opportunities for financial gain from prior knowledge but are made much more openly and without apparent concern.

Thus far, the case against budget secrecy does not directly address prior knowledge and individual financial gain. Instead, it tends to look at inconsistencies in practice and at some of the undemocratic effects that arise from non- or selective observance. The further, logical case is argued quite rarely, partly because of the practical difficulties involved. Such a case would have to show that the ultimate culprits – namely, those who actually could and did gain from prior knowledge – were caught and made to suffer the consequences. This, however, implies a legal and investigative certainty and capacity that is simply not present, partly because budget secrecy is a convention, not a statutory rule. The core principle of budgetary secrecy is often likened to insider trading in securities markets. There are similarities in the spirit of the principles, but not at all in the legal apparatus to enforce them. In insider dealing, there is a legal regime, and person(s) giving and receiving illegal information are investigated and could, if found guilty, suffer the consequences of the law.

Budget secrecy is concerned above all, however, with public trust and the accountability of ministers. It would be the treasurer whom we would wish to catch and penalize, not private offending parties.

But this seems to be an inadequate argument and is not, in fact, the core principle, nor is it honoured in practice. And besides, such single-minded principles, designed in an earlier century for a less complex society, now face a larger set of democratic principles and comparisons.

Imagining a Tax Decision Process without Budget Secrecy

A tax decision process without budget secrecy might look much like other expenditure and regulatory decision making. In short, many ministers would be involved, but one would be ultimately responsible. Consultations would occur often, over quite detailed tax possibilities. At some point, the main responsible minister would announce the decision and table legislative bills. Outside interests and individuals would participate and be consulted both by the minister and by the legislative committee. Business and social interest groups would lobby other ministers as well as the treasurer. The tax policy community (lawyers and accountants) would continue to represent clients and interact with other tax professionals in the government. As the day of announcement of the policy or decision approached, these outside interests or individuals might anticipate what the decision might be. Some would be right, and others would be wrong. At the point of announcement, no one would, in theory, have prior knowledge. But some individuals might have actual, or what they think is prior, knowledge and profit financially from it. However, there would be no investigative process, as is the case now, to determine such gains or losses.

If this is a rough portrait of a process without budget secrecy, what is the problem with it? Does it perhaps seem too simple? What other features would have to be considered either in principle or in relation to the realpolitik of cabinet government? For example, if budget secrecy disappeared, would other notions of secrecy replace it?

We can compare various hypothetical tax decision processes that lack secrecy provisions. The two best and most comprehensive comparative books on the politics and institutions of tax policy do not even mention budget secrecy.[39] In most Western countries, it is simply not a central issue or, at least, is not thought to be as important as other democratic aspects of budget making. This is true not only in obviously non-parliamentary systems, such as that in the United States, but also in other democracies, such as France, Germany, and Sweden. British-based parliamentary democracies such as Australia,

Canada, and New Zealand do adhere to secrecy, but in the system as a whole it is not a central issue, and the same holds for financial gains from prior knowledge.

Nonetheless, even without budget secrecy, there is ample evidence that concentrations of power may still exist in tax policy making for other reasons or because of other practical needs. Consider, for example, the following realities that could circumscribe of the openness of tax decisions. In cabinet-parliamentary systems, the budget is a major feature in "want of confidence" rules – the convention whereby the government must maintain the confidence of the legislature. Defeat on any important piece of legislation, especially the budget, would result in the defeat of the government. Party discipline on its own members' voting is the vehicle through which the government maintains confidence. Therefore, regardless of budget secrecy provisions, the premier and the treasurer would undoubtedly have to ensure that the leadership's view on taxes and expenditures prevailed. In addition, tax provisions are deemed to take legal effect immediately on their being announced and tabled in the legislature. Accordingly, tax budgets have a reasonably fixed and quite consequential time of announcement, differing in this sense from expenditure and regulatory decisions. Because of these realities, and especially over an issue of confidence, the government inevitably will be somewhat secretive – it will want an orderly announcement at a specific in time. It will not want its decisions to "dribble out" in a way that would both look, and be construed to be, disorganized and even incompetent. But this is true as well of all major policy decisions.

Because of defined announcement times, some tax measures have to be considered and made public in relation to the exact kinds of economic behaviour or results that it is hoped they will produce. Thus, for example, a temporary reduction in the sales tax on automobiles should have a date of announcement that will encourage economic activity during a certain period. The intention is not to have people postpone current purchases now because they know that a tax reduction is coming later. These policy considerations may also cause a government to limit knowledge of an impending change so as to ensure that the policy has the actual effects intended for it in the period envisaged. But this is not necessarily the same issue as preventing prior knowledge for private financial gain.

There is also the issue of cabinet secrecy, as opposed to budget secrecy. The former is based upon a wider set of principles tied to the desire to promote cabinet solidarity and genuinely responsible government. Thus cabinet discussions and some cabinet information are kept secret to ensure frank internal discussion, including full airing of often sharp divisions of opinion among ministers. But, once decided, cabinet decisions are then to be defended in public as definitive government policy by all ministers, even by those who disagreed with them within cabinet. These norms of secrecy would probably also constrict the budget process vis-à-vis outside participants, though not as much as direct budget secrecy principles do.

Thus there is a solid case to be made against budget secrecy. A process without budget secrecy is hardly, in comparative terms, a radical concept. It can open up considerably the process within cabinet and for outside interest groups. But other secrecy and constricting features would still be in place, for reasons set out above.

Vested Interests in Budget Secrecy

Which interest groups and participants retain a vested interest in the current, partly discredited, somewhat embarrassing notions of budget secrecy? Those that do so have reasons that have little to do with the principle of budget secrecy.

First, secrecy gives an extra layer of protection to premiers and treasurers vis-à-vis their ministerial colleagues. It also adds drama to Budget Speeches and hence increases their role in the communication of priorities. Alas, huge deficits and persistent recessions are depreciating that factor. Indeed, it may be that more open pre-budget hearings are fast becoming the theatrical arena of budgeting to take the heat off ministers and to lower expectations.[40] Second, opposition parties have a vested interest in budget secrecy, since it creates the potential for a budget leak, which can always be turned to partisan advantage. Third, the media have a similar vested interest in leaks, as a source of newsworthy stories. The media have supported calls for budget reform but have never, to my knowledge, addressed the core issue of financial gain. Nor, in budget leak stories, have they actually pursued investigations of those individuals who might have been able to gain from prior knowledge. However, they tenaciously followed the fate of one of their own colleagues, journalist Doug Small. Small was charged (but not convicted) with receiving stolen property when he broke the story on Global television following the leak of Michael Wilson's 1988 budget. The contrast with review processes for market-insider trading could not be more stark; in these stories, both the leaker and the "leakee" are investigated. In lapses of budget secrecy, the leaker (nominally the minister) gets clobbered politically (but does not resign), and the leakee (if there is one) gets off scot free.

Another interest group may also have some vested interest in budget secrecy – namely, the business community. Business groups have often supported aspects of budget reform (such as use of discussion papers and better background information), but they are not particularly anxious to see more ministers involved in tax matters. Business interests instinctively view the tax budget process in somewhat the same way as they view the role of the central bank and the printing of money – they want the matter under the control of as few elected politicians as possible. They feel that treasury and tax decisions should not be "politicized" – opened to real or continuous influence by broader, usually social groups.

Conclusions

The analysis suggests three major conclusions about Ontario's evolving and tax budget decision process – that reforms since 1985 have made the process fairer, that the strictures of budget secrecy have been loosened but not demolished, and that the next logical step is to remove the last vestiges of budget secrecy. Each point must be related to the criteria of fairness established at the outset of the paper.

A Fairer Process

First, Ontario's budget process as a whole has become fairer over the last decade, by several criteria. More groups, representing a wider range of interests, have been able to present their views; a decade ago, business groups were the major participants. The legislature has had more opportunity to express its views and to hear those of Ontarians. Most of this improvement has come from the work of the Standing Committee on Finance and Economic Affairs, although its members, as we have seen, acknowledge that some groups in any given year are still not in fact heard, especially those outside the Metropolitan Toronto area.

Fairness has been exhibited also in preservation of the treasurer's inherent capacity to make timely and effective decisions – in short, to govern in ways that assist economic development. The notion of budgetary effectiveness goes, of course, well beyond the boundaries of this paper, in that it embraces the substantive outcomes of tax and budgetary choices. But I do conclude, on procedural grounds, that the treasurer's capacity in this regard has been kept in reasonable balance with criteria of fairness.

Greater involvement by independent analysts and forecasters, and publishing of more objective data than were the norm a decade ago, have also increased fairness. The former has occurred primarily through the legislative committee; the latter, in better government publications and in the specialized business press.

Budget Secrecy: Loosened But Not Removed

Second, these broad improvements obscure other areas of weakness and reform potential that, in turn, depend on how far the principle of budget secrecy is taken. Despite recent reforms, the bonds of budget secrecy have only been loosened, and the principle is an increasing embarrassment to the political system, rather than a principled adornment.

Recent NDP experiments with having various interest groups present briefs both to the treasurer and to each other may create a more accurate picture of both consensus and division about the economy. But they may be a particular product of the times (deficits and recessions) and of the personal styles of treasurers. Representatives of interest groups have applauded the spirit of the new format but also indicate that their support for it could evaporate. Newer social groups are likely to become dissatisfied, unless their advocacy for substantive budgetary changes in the social sphere produces favourable results.

Despite recent changes, the budget process remains distinctly partisan. At one level, this is not a liability – political parties are a vehicle for reflecting different values. But, at another level, the bedraggled state of the principle of budget secrecy is a function of "low politics," not high politics. Within the unholy trio of government, opposition, and media, each element has invited the others to kill the principle, because it is not honoured or honestly pursued; but each is locked in a game in which no one wants to be the first to admit to continuing to play a discredited game.

Taking the Logical Next Step

Third, that there is no residual principled reason why budget secrecy should continue. This is not only because of the issues discussed above, such as minister's failure to resign in the event of a leak and the media circus surrounding the budget, but also because of the relative insignificance of the problem of financial gain through prior knowledge. No institution involved makes any effort to pursue those who actually might have gained from prior knowledge, and ministers simply do not resign. There are other, more important principles that should be invoked, such as opportunities for ministers to participate in and be informed about a key decision and full discussion of actual and detailed possibilities in an era of increasingly complex economies and societies.

In short, there is little to be gained by adhering to a principle that is not only discredited but unenforceable. But, more important, there are gains to be made by normalizing to some degree the way in which tax decisions are made, so as to make it more closely resemble decision making in such matters as regulations and expenditures. The alternative to tax decision processes without budget secrecy is not a total absence of secrecy. Nor is it uncontrolled, congressional-style government by interest groups. Normalizing means that tax decisions would be treated to some extent like other types of decisions within the framework of cabinet-parliamentary government.

Such a new process could still begin in late fall, with tabling of economic and budgetary outlook papers. Before tabling of the tax budget, business groups, social groups, and the tax community would lobby and be consulted in three ways – through normal discussions with line departments and ministers whose programs affect them and who have varying degrees of empathy with and opposition to their needs and priorities; through hearings (some or all of which could be televised on cable TV and augmented by meetings held outside Toronto), held by the Standing Committee on Finance and Economic Affairs; and through hearings with the treasurer, in which tax issues are discussed directly and openly.

Within government, the process would involve broader discussion among ministers, just like that on other major policy matters. As budget day drew closer, the treasurer and the premier would stop consultations and the work of writing the budget would move to completion. The Budget Speech would then be given (it could even be tabled simply, without a speech, as more than one Ontario treasurer has contemplated). Thereafter, the normal legislative procedures would follow. To increase accountability to the legislature, the treasurer could perhaps respond in writing, either in the Budget Speech, or separately, to the standing committee's final report on its pre-budget hearings. This reply could indicate why the government was or was not accepting the committee's ideas or proposals.

The above process would be more open and fair but would hardly constitute an opening of the procedural floodgates. This is because of other features of cabinet government and of the political importance of the budget. First, cabinet secrecy (as distinct from budget secrecy) still puts strictures on ministers and disciplines them into reasonable collective choices. Second, the premier and the treasurer, as leaders, have powerful politicalimperatives that will propel them to keep the number of participants within reasonable bounds. Third, the announcement realities of tax measures will involve some significant confidentiality to ensure orderly presentation and passage of policies, including those that have economically important starting dates. And, fourth, tax increases are sufficiently unpopular to deter too many ministers from lining up within the cabinet to share "blame" with the treasurer for revenue-raising decisions.

The proposed process will not put an end to asymmetries and ine-qualities of power, nor will it address the issue of access to pre–tax budget decision making. However, it would be a fairer process than currently obtains and would build logically on the progress made in the last decade.

Notes

The first draft of this paper was prepared for the Ontario Fair Tax Com-mission and completed in January 1993. Since there is very little pub-lished independent literature on Ontario's budget process, this study has had to rely even more than is normally the case on interviews and on sec-ondary sources. The interviews with governmental and interest-group participants in the budgetary process were conducted on a confidential basis. Assurances were given that there would be no direct attribution of quotes or opinions to those interviewed. I owe special thanks to these people. A few of these individuals also read drafts of the paper and offered constructive and thoughtful comments. My debts are also consid-erable to Allan Maslove and Evert Lindquist for their constructive com-ments and suggestions. Any remaining inadequacies in the analysis remain the responsibility of the author.

1 See Doern, Maslove, and Prince (1988, chap. 3).
2 See Ontario, Fair Tax Commission (1992).
3 See Prince (1989).

4 These are central to other aspects of the research and role of the Fair Tax Commission. For discussions of the array of fairness values, see Baker (1987) and Heald (1983, chap. 6).

5 On budget secrecy, see Lindquist (1985). His analysis includes a chapter on Ontario.

6 See Ontario, Ministry of Treasury and Economics (MTE) (1992a, 13).

7 See ibid.

8 See ibid. (9).

9 See ibid.

10 See ibid. (8).

11 See ibid. (9).

12 See Prince (1989, 103–14).

13 See ibid. (111–14).

14 See MTE (1985, app.).

15 See Ontario, Standing Committee on Finance and Economic Affairs (1988).

16 See ibid. (1989, 1).

17 See ibid. (1990, 2).

18 See Good (1980).

19 For analysis, see Lindquist (1985) and Maslove, Prince, and Doern (1985, chaps. 2 and 10).

20 See Maslove, Prince, and Doern (1985, chap. 2).

21 See ibid.

22 For an overview, see Daigneault, forthcoming.

23 See MTE (1991a, 16).

24 See ibid.

25 See ibid.

26 See ibid.

27 See ibid. (1991b).

28 See ibid. (1992c).

29 See ibid. (Undated, 2).

30 See ibid. (1992a).

31 See Ibid. (1992d).

32 See ibid. (Undated, 1).

33 See Ontario, Standing Committee on Finance and Economic Affairs, (1991, 2).

34 See ibid. (1992, app. B).

35 See Ontario, Ministry of Treasury and Economics (Undated, 5).

36 The observations made below regarding the evaluation are based on interviews.

37 See Lindquist (1985).

38 See Maslove, Prince, and Doern (1985, chap. 10).
39 See Peters (1991) and Rose and Karran (1987).
40 I am grateful to an anonymous reviewer for suggesting this notion of a shift in locale for the theatrical function.

Bibliography

Baker, John. 1987. *Arguing for Equality.* London: Verso

Daigneault, Jean. Forthcoming. "Putting the Budget Secrecy Quandary Aside: Improving the Budget Consultation Process by Tapping into Policy Communities." *Policy Options*

Doern, G. Bruce, Allan M. Maslove, and Michael Prince. 1988. *Budgeting in Canada: Politics, Economics and Management.* Ottawa: Carleton University Press

Good, David. 1980. *The Politics of Anticipation: Making Federal Tax Policy.* Ottawa: School of Public Administration, Carleton University

Heald, David. 1983. *Public Expenditure.* Oxford: Martin Robertson

Lindquist, Evert. 1985. *Consultation and Budget Secrecy.* Ottawa: Conference Board of Canada

Maslove, Allan, Michael Prince, and Bruce Doern. 1985. *Federal and Provincial Budgeting.* Toronto: University of Toronto Press

Ontario. Fair Tax Commission. 1992. *Searching for Fairness.* Toronto: Fair Tax Commission

Ontario. Ministry of Treasury and Economics (MTE). 1985. *Reforming the Budget Process: A Discussion Paper.* Toronto: Queen's Printer for Ontario

– 1991a. *1991 Ontario Budget: Meeting Ontario's Priorities, Presented ... April 29 1991.* Toronto: Queen's Printer for Ontario

– 1991b. *Ontario's Economic Outlook.* Toronto: Queen's Printer for Ontario

– 1992a. *The 1992 Ontario Budget Guidebook.* Toronto: Queen's Printer for Ontario

– 1992b. *1992 Ontario Budget: Meeting Ontario's Priorities, Presented ... April 30 1992.* Toronto: Queen's Printer for Ontario

– 1992c. *Ontario Fiscal Outlook.* Toronto: Queen's Printer for Ontario

– 1992d. "Premier's Address on Ontario's Economy." Toronto: Queen's Printer for Ontario

– Undated. "1992 Pre-Budget Consultations." Internal paper, Ministry of Treasury and Economics. Mimeo. Toronto

Ontario Standing Committee on Finance and Economic Affairs. 1988. *Pre-Budget Consultation 1988.* 1st Session, 34th Parliament. Toronto: Committee

– 1989. *Pre-Budget Consultation 1989.* 1st Session, 34th Parliament. Toronto: Committee

– 1990. *Pre-Budget Consultation 1990.* 2nd Session, 34th Parliament. Toronto: Committee

– 1991. *Pre-Budget Consultation 1991.* 1st Session, 35th Parliament. Toronto: Committee

– 1992. *Pre-Budget Consultation 1992.* 1st Session, 35th Parliament. Toronto: Committee

Peters, Guy. 1991. *The Politics of Taxation.* Oxford: Blackwell

Prince, Michael. 1989. "The Bland Stops Here: Ontario Budgeting in the Davis Era, 1971–1985." In *Budgeting in the Provinces*, ed. Allan M. Maslove, 87–120. Toronto: Institute of Public Administration of Canada

Rose, Richard, and Terence Karran. 1987. *Taxation by Political Inertia.* London: Allen and Unwin

2 Improving the Scrutiny of Tax Expenditures in Ontario: Comparative Perspectives and Recommendations

EVERT A. LINDQUIST

Introduction

The purpose of this study is to describe how the Ontario government deals with tax expenditures and to identify options and recommendations for improving the scrutiny of tax expenditures. I seek also to inform the discussion of recommendations by investigating how other countries and provinces have dealt with tax expenditures.[1]

While there is considerable unevenness in the international comparative literature, there is ample experience to guide improvement of Ontario's scrutiny of tax expenditures. The U.S. experience is very rich – federal policy makers have directly addressed tax expenditures in the budget process, and almost half of the states have undertaken some form of review of tax expenditures. At the federal level, Canada is considered an exemplar among nations – during the late 1970s it integrated tax expenditure review into its priority-setting and budget decision-making system. But closer analysis reveals the many difficulties encountered by those who seek to encourage better reviews of tax expenditures. Moreover, besides Ontario, three Canadian provinces have published tax expenditure accounts, and others have experimented with "sunset legislation." Ontario has been a leader in reforming elements of its legislative budget process, creating a policy-making environment potentially more conducive to better analysis of expenditures.

This study is not a technical review of estimation techniques for calculating tax expenditures, nor does it provide details about the content of tax expenditure accounts in different jurisdictions. Rather, the study attempts to inform readers about the politics and effectiveness of tax expenditure accounting. It goes beyond reviewing the diffusion of reforms predicated on tax expenditure concepts to explore how they mesh with budgetary processes, and it assesses whether or not such reforms influence tax reform. Despite uneven knowledge about review of tax expenditures, this study reassembles fragments of evidence and experience across several jurisdictions to produce a collage of the issues that inevitably arise when reformers attempt to scrutinize tax expenditures.

Some readers will wonder why we consider developments outside Ontario. Such details should give the reader a better understanding of tax expenditure politics and often substitute for gaps in the Ontario literature – we can develop a feeling for Ontario's process and certain issues by extrapolation. For example, Good's (1980) study of the making of federal tax policy in Canada provides an excellent analysis of traditional methods of creating tax policy. U.S. literature contains a significant amount of reflection on the link between tax expenditure concepts and tax policy making that is unavailable in Canada. If we are properly to assess the efficacy and cost-effectiveness of informational, procedural, and institutional reforms, we must be aware of the politics and pressures associated with preparation of tax policy. The tax expenditure literature has been concerned too much with the need for better estimating techniques and for broader perspectives and has failed to examine closely the politics of reform. By politics, I mean not only that different political interests will disagree on what constitutes good tax expenditures, but also that tensions will arise because of the territorial reactions of tax politicians and officials to any attempt to open up tax measures to scrutiny. Shrewd recommendations for reform should be drafted in anticipation of such tensions and jealousies, because comparative analysis indicates that reforms of the tax expenditure process tend to have a precarious existence. Moreover, those advocating such changes should be clear about their likely impact if implemented; in these fiscally constrained times, we cannot afford innovations that do not add value and that perhaps harm policy making.

Readers should consider the nature of the links between an enlightened process and various types of tax reform. Accordingly, this study reviews the major tax reform initiatives launched in the United States and Canada during the 1980s. Even though these innovations were broadly consistent with the principles of tax expenditure reformers, and therefore deserve careful attention, the evidence suggests that what I call "tax expenditure thinking" had, at best, an indirect influence.

This study moves from the general to the specific and from an international perspective to increasingly more local experience. It begins by introducing in the first part the ideas associated with tax expenditure thought and reviews the international diffusion of those ideas. The second part considers how the U.S. government and several states have sought to improve scrutiny of tax expenditures. The third part analyses the Canadian experience, describing how traditional parliamentary processes for tax policy were inimical to good analysis of tax expenditure and the reforms that created Canada's status as a leader in this area, how successive Liberal and Conservative governments of the 1980s addressed tax expenditures, and whether these efforts have informed tax policy making. This is followed by a brief review of what provincial and territorial governments have accomplished, particularly British Columbia, Alberta, Saskatchewan, Manitoba, and Ontario. The fifth part describes Ontario's tax policy process and the recent changes to the larger budgetary and priority-setting process, and it then explores two brief case studies of recent tax expenditure decisions. The sixth part reviews several instruments and strategies for reform, while the seventh sets out a package of recommendations.

The recommendations seek to build on the emerging strengths of Ontario's current budgetary and related processes. Tax expenditures should be included in the sectoral program reviews undertaken by Queen's Park, which should establish some form of quasi-independent review process for evaluating tax expenditures selectively. However, comparative analysis suggests that selective review of tax expenditures is not sufficient and that constituencies for reform have to be created, which involves sensitizing policy makers and the public about the costs associated with tax expenditures. Thus a limited tax expenditure budget and aggregate totals of revenue loss should be published regularly, the expenditure estimates should use this information to indicate the magnitude of benefits and incentives conferred by tax expenditures in program areas, and the government should make selective use of sunset mechanisms. In order to create pressure on the government to act on these proposals, it is recommended that the provincial auditor be encouraged to review how well the government evaluates and scrutinizes tax expenditures.

This study and its recommendations are not intended to design a process that will make pronouncements on which tax expenditures are desirable; that depends on the disposition of a given government and the public. Such determinations are inevitably the outcome of political struggles and attitudes towards certain tax expenditures that are bound to shift over time. Rather, the intention of this study is to find ways to encourage government and public to scrutinize tax expenditures and to have those deliberations informed by sound analysis in order that public resources are used in the most effective and fair manner. As Bird and Mintz (1992, 28) have recently argued:

> Tax policy decisions should not be isolated from other government decisions. Like other policy instruments, tax policies should be evaluated in terms of the overall objectives sought by governments and not solely in terms of the reduced triumvirate – Equity, Efficiency, and Simplicity – that has dominated the subject for years. The political, social, environmental, and economic issues that confront governments today are not going to go away. Canadian tax policy analysts will therefore inevitably be called upon to provide information in order to help policy formation ... In the future, however, tax policy analysis will have to take place in a broader policy framework if it is to serve the country well.

Tax Expenditure Thinking: Ambiguous Success

The concept of tax expenditures is a highly successful intellectual construct that for 20 years has stimulated considerable academic and policy debate. Neil Brooks (1988, 19) has argued: "One of the most significant conceptual advances since [the] Carter [Commission] has been the development of the tax expenditure concept." This section shows how a concept developed in the United States rapidly diffused throughout the world and has resulted in tangible attempts to quantify and give greater exposure to tax expenditures; it also raises questions about whether or not these reforms have substantially affected tax policy making. Before examining these matters, the section briefly defines the concept of tax expenditure but moves beyond the more traditional and narrow technical understanding and identifies a larger constellation of ideas associated with tax expenditure thinking.

What Is Tax Expenditure Thinking?

The impetus to analyse tax expenditures in a disciplined and public manner can be traced back to the 1960s in the United States. Stanley Surrey, a senior official in the federal Treasury Department, was appalled at the limited repertoire of options that policy makers considered in attempting to solve pressing fiscal problems. If they wanted to contain the deficit, the prevailing reflex was to cut spending or raise taxes. But some important stones were consistently left unturned – namely, the panoply of government programs and policies delivered through the tax system, such as deductions, credits, and deferrals. Surrey realized that relinquishing revenues that otherwise would have been collected, even if they were the best means for attaining particular policy objectives, affected the deficit in the same way as an increase in programs funded through direct expenditures.

Surrey worked hard to direct more attention to these other programs, coining the term *tax expenditures* for those tax preferences that represented departures from the normal tax system and that conferred benefits on limited groups of taxpayers. He prodded his own department to produce a tax expenditure budget in 1968. Surrey also became a staunch public advocate of improved scrutiny of tax expenditures, writing papers and giving speeches about the problem and his ideas for reform. Two states (California and Wisconsin) adopted tax expenditure budgets in the early 1970s. This activity culminated in publication of Surrey's influential book *Pathways to Tax Reform: The Concept of Tax Expenditures* in 1973. Not long afterwards, the U.S. Congress incorporated tax expenditures into its reformed budget process.

The tax expenditure concept, however, has always been more than a convenient term to highlight the similarities between tax programs and direct expenditures; it also embraced a larger group of concerns about the tendency and integrity of tax systems. Advocates of the concept worried not only about policy makers overlooking tax expenditures as a possible means for reclaiming lost revenues but also about how tax policy came to be designed in the first place. They pointed to the closed, back-door nature of decision making about tax policy and the sway that special interests had over congressional committees. They argued that legislators had considerable incentive to use the tax system because decision making about it was not highly visible, tax incentives were not costed like spending programs in budget documents, and benefits could be conferred quickly. One result was an increasing resort to tax exemptions to achieve political and policy objectives, and corrosion of the tax base followed. This situation forced tax policy makers either to raise tax rates on the remaining base or search for new streams of income or activities to tax. Increasingly complex tax codes became more difficult for governments to administer and for taxpayers to fathom. To the extent that wealthier individuals and corporations could manipulate the system in their favour, progressive tax systems were subverted by a host of special exemptions not favourable to the general public. While some manipulation is hidden, eventually it leads to public perception that the tax system is unfair, inequitable, and unwieldy. This, of course, make its more difficult to levy additional taxes to finance deficits or new spending programs.

When articulated in this manner, the tax expenditure concept evokes a set of issues of clear interest to political and bureaucratic guardians who worry about the integrity and revenue-raising capacity of tax systems. Indeed, the concept has been diffused rapidly among treasury or finance departments in governments around the world and in many tax committees in U.S. legislatures. But a related set of concerns flowing from the tax expenditure problem poses challenges to the hegemony of tax policy makers. For example, many observers believe that the monopoly that these officials wield over the tax instrument has prevented thorough evaluation of tax expenditures and that measures in that area receive less scrutiny than most direct expenditures. For example, Surrey, in conjunction with P.R. McDaniel (1985, 27–8), pointed out that recipients of tax expenditures are not scrutinized for compliance with civil rights legislation. Moreover, many observers feel that existing policy processes do not allow for full analysis of the merits of using other instruments to accomplish the same objective. They see development of tax policy as cordoned off from other mainstream processes. As a result, their concern goes beyond the integrity of the tax system to whether current processes lead to the most effective and fiscally responsible policies.

Such observers (e.g. McDaniel 1988) usually see nothing intrinsically wrong with tax expenditures but believe that their comparative advantage remains to be demonstrated. In other words, they would not be content merely with explication of tax expenditures, which would delineate the normal tax structure and concomitant deviations (tax expenditures), quantify their revenue drain or outlay equivalents, create the capacity to undertake such analysis, and raise awareness of policy makers and the public by publishing a tax expenditure report or budget. To complement such steps, these observers seek to link analysis of tax expenditures to the more general budgetary process, so that policy makers or institutions other then government tax experts may weigh the benefits and costs of using tax expenditures to achieve a given policy goal. Such logic elicits some fear on the part of tax policy makers, who generally support the tax expenditure concept, because it helps them maintain or restore the integrity of the tax system. They fear that relinquishing full control over analysis of tax expenditures will undermine their own decision-making authority. However, as this study argues, opening up policy making need not imply relinquishing of such authority.

Despite this tension, reform advocates inside and outside treasuries support initiatives that eliminate unnecessary tax expenditures, broaden the tax base, protect the integrity of the system, and reduce marginal tax rates.

Rapid Diffusion of Tax Expenditure Thinking

When Surrey introduced the concept of tax expenditures, only one other country was producing an account of its tax programs. In 1959, responding to the concerns of legislators, the West German government began publishing a list of its visible and invisible subsidies, this became a statutory obligation in 1967, with the government being required to prepare a report every two years.[2] Just 15 years later, a host of countries had adopted reviews of or investigated tax expenditures, culminating in an OECD study on reporting in member countries.

During the late 1970s, several OECD countries published tax expenditure budgets or accounts, including Spain in 1978, Austria and Canada in 1979, and France in 1980. According to Surrey and McDaniel (1985, 180), in 1978, Austria followed the West German example and listed tax expenditures as part of a more general accounting of government subsidies. Ireland, Portugal, and the United Kingdom took a different tack and published lists of all tax reliefs, thereby avoiding controversy over the normative tax structure, although Surrey and McDaniel (1985, 180–81) claim that the annual British list that appears with budget documents is very close to a tax expenditure account.[3] In 1984, it was reported that Belgium and Sweden were examining the approach and Finland was considering the possibility.[4] McDaniel and Surrey (1985, 4) note that a year later Ireland, New Zealand, and Sweden were reportedly contemplating producing a tax expenditure budget and the Ministry of Finance of the Netherlands had sponsored studies on tax expenditures. Surrey and McDaniel (1985, 180) state that in Japan the Department of Finance provides the legislature with estimates of a relatively selective number of tax measures, while an Australian parliamentary committee produced a report in 1982 recommending adoption of the concept. And, according to McDaniel and Surrey (1985, 4), non-governmental lists of tax expenditures were compiled by academics in Belgium, Colombia, India, Israel, Japan, and Tunisia. Thus, by the late 1980s, 18 countries had entertained or embraced analysis of tax expenditures to some degree.

In 1984, the OECD (1984, 20–21) produced a comparative study of such practices in Australia, Austria, Canada, France, Ireland, Portugal, Spain, the United Kingdom, the United States, and West Germany. The study focused on taxes covered and estimation methods employed. Eight of the 10 countries relied on the "revenue forgone" approach; three attempted to estimate revenue gain – the revenue that would be recovered – from elimination of a tax expenditure.[5] Only the U.S. Treasury provided estimates of the outlay equivalence of the tax expenditures.[6] Canada, along with the United States, was considered a leader in "integrating tax expenditures into the normal budgetary process" – a reference to the cabinet priority-setting and budget system adopted in 1979 that had rules for costing tax expenditures as part of the allocative process – because it had produced comprehensive tax expenditure accounts in 1979 and 1980.[7]

Many countries developed keen interest in tax expenditures during the late 1970s and early 1980s. Why was the concept so rapidly diffused? One reason had to do with the economic pressures on Western governments throughout the 1970s, such as inflation, high unemployment rates, growing deficits, and movements to index income tax brackets to inflation, which, in combination with slow economic growth, reduced real increases in tax revenues. For treasury officials, the tax expenditure concept and broader tax expenditure thinking captured a good part of the problem and suggested solutions. Social policy groups saw the tax expenditure concept as another means for highlighting the unfairness of tax policy and the corrosion of ostensibly progressive tax systems and to argue for more open making of tax policy. International networks of government officials and academic scholars helped spread the idea. It was reported (McDaniel and Surrey 1985, 3) that the 1976 Congress of the International Fiscal Association, in Jerusalem, and the 1977 Congress of the International Institute of Public Finance, in Varna, Bulgaria, allowed for exchange of theories and practices. The International Monetary Fund, the OECD, the World Bank, and international academic journals and conferences also communicated the concepts.

Tax Expenditure Thinking and Tax Reform: Is There a Link?

Tax expenditure thinking emerged in the United States as a model for less constricted budgetary options for policy makers. However, the concept can also inform tax reform. Tax reform may take different forms: it may involve technical adjustments to existing measures to provide clarification for taxpayers or to remove loopholes; it may also involve selective or incremental reviews of particular tax measures in the context of budget priorities or program reviews in specific policy areas; and it may take the form of comprehensive tax reform – overhaul of tax systems in whole or in part.

The 1980s was a decade of comprehensive tax reform.[8] We have observed the proliferation of tax expenditure concepts during the late 1970s among OECD nations. Is there a connection? Advocates of tax expenditure thinking seeking to improve tax policy by means of publicized informational and procedural reforms should be persuaded that they do have an impact. It is possible to sketch out some preliminary assessments.

There were two rounds of tax reform during the 1980s. The first began during the late 1970s and culminated during the early 1980s. All OECD countries had experienced the energy crisis of the 1970s and sought to adjust tax policy as part of the larger search for appropriate fiscal policy. Several countries moved to reduce automatic tax increases caused by inflation when a given amount of real income is subjected to higher marginal tax rates in progressive systems as taxpayers slide into higher brackets. However, this problem per se did not engage tax expenditure thinking, and the reforms were adopted only as tax expenditure accounting began to be considered by most OECD countries; the shift posed technical problems for determining the normative tax base. Another strategy – one discussed in more detail below – was advocated by U.S. President Reagan. Its objective was, quite simply, tax relief. Despite deficit pressures, this approach reduced marginal tax rates and either enhanced or created many tax expenditures. A more revenue-neutral method was adopted by many countries that sought to lower marginal tax rates on income and corporate income and to raise more revenues by means of indirect taxes, such as sales and value-added taxes.[9] Again, shifting tax burdens is not a major element of tax expenditure thinking. As we shall see, however, Canada did announce a major tax reform package that lowered marginal rates, closed off many tax expenditures, and did not rely on new indirect taxes. This approach, despite the political controversy that it caused, was clearly consistent with tax expenditure thinking.

The next round of tax reform during the 1980s closely resembled the Canadian stance. Following the lead of the United States, which overhauled its tax system during 1986, many nations, including Canada, also enacted reforms to ensure that their tax systems were not out of step with a powerful trading partner. These changes included lowering personal and corporate income tax rates, collapsing the number of tax brackets while maintaining a progressive tax structure (albeit, often less progressive than before), and reducing corporate tax expenditures. Most of the reforms were designed, at least on paper, to be revenue-neutral so that governments could avoid the charge of using tax reform as another attempt to raise revenues. As a result, distribution of benefits among income groups did not change substantially, but tax systems were simplified.[10] As with Canada's tax reform during the early 1980s, this latest wave seemed to incorporate the principles behind tax expenditure thinking.

Given the evidence, should Surreyites claim victory? What was the connection between process reforms of the late 1970s and the tax reform of the 1980s? First, even though many governments had tax expenditure concepts at their disposal, few had implemented mechanisms for reviewing tax expenditures. It is arguable that Surrey and his followers produced concepts that captured the growing pressures on tax systems but that the ideas themselves did not shape reform. Rather, the pressures eventually forced policy makers into a corner, and they could respond only by broadening the tax base and reducing marginal rates in order to maintain confidence in the tax system. Another argument is that many countries followed the U.S. lead only because they had to harmonize. Why did most of them not launch tax reform before 1986? And, as we shall soon see, even in the United States – despite the fact that both the executive and legislative branches produced tax expenditure accounts – it is not clear that tax expenditure concepts significantly affected tax reform.

These observations are not meant to play down the importance of tax expenditure thinking nor to state categorically that such thinking does not shape creation of tax policy. Tax expenditure concepts, at one level, are powerful in their elegance and have travelled well as a means of conceptualizing problems with the tax system and tax policy making and for putting forth a strong argument for comparing the tax instrument with other policy instruments. However, as an accounting device, the concepts have spawned considerable debate among professionals and academics that has diminished its impact on tax policy making. When considering reforms in a fiscally constrained environment, it is essential to be aware of this ambiguity in an otherwise successful movement. The critical question is: how many resources must be invested in what are essentially informational, procedural, and institutional reforms if their connection to tax reform is indirect and difficult to discern? This question will be explored as we review experience in the United States, Canada, and Ontario.

The United States: Innovation or Avoidance of Reform?

Despite governing arrangements that differ considerably from Canada's parliamentary systems, the United States offers 51 potential living experiments on tax expenditure reforms. Although not all states have addressed tax expenditures, considerable variation and experimentation at the federal level and in roughly half the states provide an abundance of ideas and experiences for Canadian reformers to consider. Tax expenditure thinking is linked intrinsically to the hope for tax reforms, with only intermittent success. Struggles between the executive and legislatures – and, more subtly, between tax committees and tax expenditure reformers, as well as special interest politics – have impeded introduction of systematic reviews of expenditures.

This section begins by examining how tax expenditures came to be highlighted as part of the federal budget process and then reviews how and to what extent states have incorporated tax expenditure thinking into their budget processes. We then examine U.S. tax reform by the 1980s and, subsequently, consider U.S. analysts' attempts to explore the tenuous and indirect link between tax expenditure reforms and tax reform – a theoretical contribution that will help us when we look at Canadian reforms.

Creating the Capacity to Evaluate Federal Tax Expenditures

The tax expenditure concept was born amid a struggle between U.S. Congress and the president.[11] In September 1967, President Lyndon Johnson sought a tax increase to finance the Great Society programs and the Vietnam War and to reduce the burgeoning deficit. An incredulous Stanley Surrey watched as representatives on the House Ways and Means Committee scrutinized only direct expenditures as a way to offset a tax increase and never examined the many special provisions in the tax code and therefore severely constrained the options. To give such hidden programs more exposure, the Treasury Department produced its first tax expenditure account in 1968,[12] listing some 50 personal and corporate income tax provisions.[13] Congress, after pitched battles with special interests every step of the way, turned its attention to tax provisions the following year and produced the Tax Reform Act of 1969. For Congress, and for members of the tax committees in particular, it would have been far easier to request the president to make unspecified expenditure reductions.

Following that round, the Treasury Department produced a "tax aids" budget, and the conference committee (made up of senior officials from the leadership of the House, the Senate, and their tax committees – Ways and Means in the House, and Finance in the Senate) that produced the 1971 tax cut requested that the budget be submitted to the tax committees each year; later, the Joint Economic Committee (of the Senate and the House) was added to the list. But this growing interest in tax expenditures did not lead to tax reform of the kind advocated by Surrey and his followers. The Revenue Act of 1971 created or enlarged a host of tax expenditures, although some were rejected in the end. Surrey (1973, 5) described it as "one of the least creditable revenue measures in many a decade and one that considerably weakens the fairness and structure of the income tax."

The drive for more responsible budgeting produced a sea change in 1974 in how Congress constructed budgets and gave tax expenditures more exposure. Two festering conflicts led to this reform. The first was between President Richard Nixon and Congress. Nixon, worried about the free-spending proclivities of Congress, attempted to assert control over the budget by impounding funds appropriated by Congress for specific programs. While similar to the instructions that Congress had given Lyndon Johnson in 1968, this unilateral decision was viewed as a major challenge to congressional authority. However, many in Congress acknowledged that their bottom–up budget process did not produce an alternative plan nor a check on the disparate activities of committees.[14] The second conflict emerged within Congress. During the late 1960s, an increasingly younger and more liberal corps of Democratic representatives entered the House and challenged the seniority system that constrained policy development.[15] Congress was ripe for reform. There was widespread agreement that the institutional processes needed a substantial overhaul to respond to internal demands and possible external threats.

The result was the Congressional Budget Impoundment and Control Act of 1974. It sought to provide a framework that would guide the work of committees and ensure that Congress, when evaluating particular budget proposals, fully understood their implications for the macro-budget position that they had developed. Several processes and institutions were put in place. New budget committees in the House and the Senate were to produce global targets for revenues, expenditures, and the deficit. Once approved by Congress, these targets were to guide all subsequent budget deliberations. The budget committees were to monitor and cost proposals from the other committees and a new Congressional Budget Office (CBO) was to provide them with analytical assistance.

The act also established procedures for handling tax expenditures. The tax expenditure problem had been recently identified by Stanley Surrey at Treasury, and Congress was anxious to acquire its own analytical capacity. The argument that decision making on tax expenditures should be more "transparent" resonated in a Congress inclined towards more open policy making. Accordingly, the CBO and the Joint Committee on Taxation (JCT), a secretariat serving the House Ways and Means and the Senate Finance committees, were charged with producing an annual tax expenditure budget. Moreover, the president was required to submit a tax expenditure account as an annex to the annual budget submission. This meant that the Office of Management and Budget (OMB) would have to develop its own capacity on tax expenditures and work with the Treasury Department.[16] OMB's figures, like other budgetary figures, were to be accompanied by forecasts for the following five years.

By the mid-1970s, both Congress and the Executive had recognized tax expenditures as a problem and had begun introducing remedial measures to address the issue. They ignored several reform opportunities, however, such as implementing sunset legislation and mandating specific reviews of and limits on tax expenditures. Before discussing the impact of these developments on tax policy, I shall show how these ideas were diffused to state governments.

Tax Expenditures and the States

Concern about tax expenditures was not confined to Washington. Like Canada, the United States has a federal system with overlapping jurisdiction in taxation, and this situation leads to competition and interdependence in treatment of tax expenditures at either level. State governments also experienced considerable fiscal pressure during the 1970s. First, the "new federalism" initiated by President Nixon was, in part, an effort by Washington to "off-load" responsibility for many social programs to other levels of government. This initiative coincided with the tax revolt led by Howard Jarvis in California that won approval for Proposition 13, which rescinded property tax increases. Similar groundwells of public anger in other states alerted leaders at all levels to the pitfalls of calling for tax increases to finance further spending. Deterioration in traditional manufacturing brought keen competition to retain and attract employers and increasing resort to local and state tax abatements. It was in this general context that analysts noted a dramatic growth of tax expenditures. For example, it was reported that California lawmakers added 96 tax expenditures between 1972 and 1982 and that, by 1984, the value of tax expenditures each year was equal to over 80 per cent of the value of direct expenditures ($4.4 v. $5.4 billion).[17]

Several states began to explore ways and means to control the growth of tax expenditures. Several followed the lead of the Treasury Department and took steps to produce their own reports: California in 1971, Wisconsin in 1973, and Maryland and North Carolina in 1975.[18] Despite this early interest, it was not until later that decade and during the early 1980s that a significant number of states adopted some form of tax expenditure reporting: Michigan and Nebraska in 1979; Arizona, Maine, and Missouri in 1981; Hawaii and Louisiana in 1982; Massachusetts, Minnesota, and Washington in 1983; and Delaware and Mississippi in 1986. A succession of surveys indicates that anywhere from 17 to 21 states have some form of tax expenditure accounting, although the evidence suggests that 25 or more states have published one-time only, intermittent, or regular reports.[19]

States vary considerably in regularity and quality of reporting. Benker (1986, 407) observes that some mandate accounts to be produced each budget cycle, which could be every year or every two years (states that do so are evenly divided), while others had one-time only or intermittent reviews. With respect to quality (which I would define as the extent of data and analysis in the reports), she placed reports in three categories: *comprehensive* – revenue estimates and complementary information; *moderately comprehensive* – revenue estimates accompanied by lists; and *partial* – usually lists only. There were six, five, and four states, respectively, in the aforementioned categories. Gold and Nesbary (1988, 885) observe that 15 of the 17 reports that they reviewed contained estimates of forgone revenue. However, Edwards (1988, 14–15), who carefully analysed reports from 19 state administrations and two legislatures, found that only eight included statements of purpose of tax expenditures, only five analysed their effectiveness, and only two listed tax expenditures in program categories, along with direct expenditures in their budget documents.

States vary, too, in what they consider tax expenditures or provisions deserving of analysis. For example, depending on availability of data and policy makers' comfort with assessing some tax fields, states review different combinations of personal, corporate, and sales taxes. Some toyed with including local tax abatements and property tax relief but determined that it was far too complicated a task. Most states have chosen not to include in the accounts federal provisions, even those with clear consequences for the state tax system and economy. The premiss is that states should list only provisions over which they have control. This, of course, has not stopped state governments from lobbying Washington to preserve such tax expenditures. Some analysts, according to Hildred and Pinto (1990), have referred to federal provisions affecting states as "passive tax expenditures" because major federal tax reform alters both the tax base and tax expenditures, which may significantly affect particular states.

When state governments are reporting tax expenditures, responsibility for producing documents usually rests with the executive branch. While many states have published reports, only 13 have legislated their production.[20] Reports are prepared usually by revenue departments, but some are drafted jointly with state budget offices;[21] only a handful of legislatures produce alternative accounts.[22] Even in a system where legislators have considerably more policy clout and technical expertise than their parliamentary counterparts, they are clearly reluctant to take up analytical responsibility for tax expenditures.

 Although the evidence is limited, most states have allocated relatively few resources to develop and update tax expenditure accounts. Some did not allocate any new resources. For example, even though Arizona and North Carolina mandated reporting, no new funds were granted to assist the relevant state agencies to put together the report.[23] However, in 1983, Minnesota's legislators appropriated $100,000 over a period of 18 months to lay the groundwork for a report, and, even though most of the work is now done by permanent staff, approximately $45,000 per year is authorized to support one full-time staff person, one part-time person, and three summer interns.[24] In New York's Division of Budget and Finance, four or five staff members work "intensely" during November and December to produce the tax expenditure account, which goes to the legislature's fiscal committees in January. Despite these limited resources, New York has increased the number of tax expenditures that it reviews and plans, by 1995, to add three taxes to its list.[25] In short, states typically rely on existing resources and expertise to develop tax expenditure accounts. However, according to Benker (1986, 413), relatively meagre support gives agencies little incentive to produce comprehensive reports.

What happens to documents once they are completed? According to Gold and Nesbary (1988, 885), only five states (California, Maine, Massachusetts, Michigan, and Wisconsin) require their legislatures to review the documents; and in 1988 only Michigan had a subcommittee of the House tax committee dedicated to reviewing the annual report – but not as part of the larger budgetary process. Two years later, Michigan's House Fiscal Agency reported that no state "has integrated tax expenditures into the budgetary process."[26]

An alternative to ex ante review of proposed tax expenditures is review of tax expenditures every four or five years, with the incentive that if no review occurs the provision lapses. Such sunset provisions can be applied to new and old tax expenditures alike. Benker (1986) reports that the 12 states requiring reports also seriously considered sunset provisions, but none chose to go that route. Another variation is to place limits on the revenue outlays associated with tax expenditures, either in aggregate or with regard to particular beneficiaries. This approach, according to Benker (1986, 415–16), "has not been seriously considered by any state." Edwards (1988) did not mention sunset provisions. However, the Fiscal Affairs and Oversight Committee of the National Council of State Legislatures (NCSL) recommended that "any new tax expenditure legislation should include a definite 'sunset' date."[27]

The Politics of Reform in Selected States

This section briefly looks at the experiences of eight states that have tried to insert "good" ideas about review of tax expenditures into their policy processes. Their experiences highlight struggles, tensions, and innovations worthy of consideration in the Canadian context.

In 1971, California was the first state to produce a tax expenditure account. However, throughout that decade and the early 1980s, the number of tax expenditures continued to grow rapidly.[28] The Legislative Analyst's Office (LAO) was subsequently directed to recommend a legislative process for handling tax expenditures and to produce a comprehensive report biennially for the legislature.[29] In its 1984–85 annual report, the LAO submitted proposals for improving the review effort – establish a budget subcommittee in each house to review tax expenditures, allow other budget subcommittees to review tax expenditures in their policy areas; require that the governor make recommendations about eliminating or modifying tax expenditures when submitting a tax expenditure budget, and link control of tax expenditures with the budget process.[30] These proposals were not adopted by the legislature. LAO analysts directed their energies instead towards the tax expenditure report – soon regarded as perhaps the best in the country – making it replete with information on statutory basis, legislative intent, revenue estimates, and recommendations.[31] Later, as California was confronting its worst budgetary challenges ever, the LAO attempted to rekindle interest in scrutinizing tax expenditures in its 1991–92 report, as one option for mitigating severe deficit pressures.[32] The proposal was rejected, and in the ensuing attempt to cut direct expenditures and raise taxes to balance the budget, the number of tax expenditures actually increased. Legislators also made deep cuts to their own staff, dramatically reducing the number of people at the LAO and therefore lessening considerably its capacity to monitor and analyse tax expenditures.

Reformers in several other states have encountered similar difficulties when attempting to establish a credible tax expenditure process. In 1981, the Michigan budget office "selected several non-controversial tax expenditures and placed them in the appropriate functional areas in the budget proposal," but this practice was not mirrored in legislative budget documents.[33] The state government is required by law to issue a tax expenditure report, but no systematic review occurs in the legislature. In 1983, a subcommittee of the House Tax Committee was created to examine tax expenditures, but it confined its activity to developing criteria for evaluating new tax expenditures.[34] In Minnesota, early attempts to require tax expenditure reporting failed in 1979 and 1981. The reform packages sought to review all tax expenditures with respect to purpose and effectiveness and to move all tax expenditures to a sunset regime. They also called for a tax study commission to review new tax expenditures before tax committees authorized the provisions and called for laws proposing that new tax expenditures clearly state their legislative intent.[35] Constituting a direct challenge to the tax committee's authority, the relevant bills never left the committee. In 1983, the Massachusetts legislature passed constitutional amendments that would allow new tax expenditures only if a proposal received a two-thirds majority vote in both houses. Ultimately, the governor vetoed the amendments – why is not clear.[36]

The state of Washington provides another cautionary tale. In 1981, the revenue department was asked by the legislature to produce a list of tax expenditures, which was to be reviewed by a Joint Select Committee on Sunset. The committee was also to develop an approach for "sunsetting" all tax expenditures. The House's tax committee, which surely did not relish the prospect of another committee reviewing tax policy, proceeded to hold public hearings on the proposals. The hearings were extremely well attended. Naturally, any group fearing elimination of tax expenditures favouring their interests voiced strong objections. The tax committee and the legislature did not proceed with the bill. Benker (1986, 415–16) reports that the committee did, however, draft legislation proposing a review of tax expenditures without sunset provisions. Several years later, the legislature adopted a new authorizing statute for all new tax expenditures. The governor was given the option of recommending, every four years, "to repeal or modify tax expenditures." If the option were taken, then tax committees in both Houses had to hold hearings to review the recommendations and submit their own proposals. Note the underlying political gamesmanship: legislators would obviously prefer the governor to float first a proposal to modify or eliminate a tax expenditure and would not relinquish their right to legislate on tax policy. Perhaps for these reasons, this process, at last report, had yet to be used.

A 1983 reform was adopted in Minnesota precisely because it avoided the jurisdictional morass of sunset and review provisions and did not attempt to integrate the tax expenditure budget into the larger budget process. Rather, the strategy, as Salamone (1988) reported, was to cast the tax expenditure budget as purely a "fiscal tool" and to list tax expenditures that legislators could alter. Despite the obvious retreat from more ambitious proposals, Salamone argues (32–3) that the new regime nevertheless constituted a significant improvement:

> The report has replaced something that had come to be called a 'tax options' list ... prepared on request by the Department of Revenue, usually containing 20 to 50 provisions, generally focusing on items with significant fiscal impact and whose repeal posed no significant administrative or political problems. Compared to the tax expenditure report, the lists were incomplete, did not contain provisions of small fis-

cal impact, contained fiscal estimates prepared with less background work, and lacked the detail needed to make them useful to a wide audience. Worst of all, those lists tended to be viewed as being the complete menu of tax change options and, as such, they had the tendency to limit the scope of tax policy debates.

A minimalist strategy may have advantages. By not offending key parties with a stake in policy, it may be possible to encourage some regular scrutiny of tax expenditures.

Only two states require tax expenditure analysts to consider alternative instruments for achieving a given policy objective. Delaware produces a report that must include the rationale, statutory authority, and revenue loss estimates for the current and previous fiscal years. Edwards (1988) observes, however, that analysts must also assess whether existing programs are effective, are the most cost-effective means to achieve stated policy objectives, have had intended and unintended consequences to date, and have had unexpected beneficiaries. These requirements are among the most thorough of any state's. Like Delaware, analysts for Maine's legislature must review the performance of tax expenditures and consider alternative approaches for meeting stated policy objectives. Maine does not, however, attempt to review all tax expenditures every year. Rather, according to Edwards (1988, 13 and 15), its analysts review a different quarter of the state's tax expenditures each year. She further notes (1988, 13) that budget documents in Massachusetts produced by the Bureau of Analysis and Research in that state's Department of Revenue group together direct expenditures and tax expenditures by functional or program category in order to give some sense of proportion.

New York has produced two interesting ideas for giving greater exposure to tax expenditures outside state governments. First, several council members and the comptroller of New York City sought to have a tax expenditure budget incorporated into its budget process; second, the state's 1986 Economic Development Zone Act contained amendments that would require "the administrative board of each economic zone to include specified information on the cost of ... property tax exemptions, credits against local sales, income and franchise taxes, as well as credits claimed against taxes as a result of furnishing utility services to the economic development zones" (Edwards 1988, 16). Thus, responsibility for educating the public about tax expenditures was not seen as the exclusive preserve of the state government but could be delegated or mandated to other entities.

The 1980s: U.S. Tax Reform

Since 1968, the concept of tax expenditures has gained considerable currency in the United States, and several jurisdictions have implemented review processes. To inform deliberation over tax expenditure reform, we must try to assess its impact on tax policy – obviously a difficult task. The focus below is on the federal level, because we lack the space to track the tax histories of several states and because, as we shall see, federal tax reform had important implications for states.

Despite reforms to the congressional budget process, tax expenditures continued to grow in number and in total revenue loss during the late 1970s. By one account, between 1971 and 1985 they increased from 28.5 per cent to 34.6 per cent as a proportion of federal outlays.[37] So the problem remained, and it was not until the arrival of Ronald Reagan at the White House in 1980 that tax reform moved squarely onto the national policy agenda. The new president, capitalizing on a wave of popular support for lower taxation, held considerable sway over Congress. Moreover, his advisers indulged in the theory of "supply-side" economics rooted in the notion that dramatic tax reduction would "jump-start"the economy, while lost revenues would be recovered from increased takings from the remaining taxes on an expanded economy. This combination of ideas provided the momentum for significant tax cuts, encapsulated in the Economic Recovery Tax Act (ERTA) of 1981. Such tax changes, however, were a nightmare for tax expenditure reformers.

Tax cuts in themselves are not necessarily an evil for many of Surrey's followers, since they, too, desire lower tax rates. However, they seek to achieve this through reducing tax expenditures. ERTA did the opposite – it "lowered marginal tax rates and expanded tax preferences for both individuals and corporations."[38] Indeed, the CBO reported that "more than 30 [ERTA provisions] increased them" and only two tax expenditures were reduced.[39] This combination dramatically reduced the tax base. There was widespread agreement that, in the rush by legislators not to appear as if they were against individual and corporate taxpayers, the main casualties were the integrity of the tax system and any hope of holding the line on the deficit.

Even before the inevitable fiscal consequences were felt, some members of Congress called for more stringent review of tax expenditures. In 1981, the House Rules Committee considered a bill that would have integrated tax expenditures into the congressional budget process by requiring that "budget resolutions fix the level of tax expenditures each year." Similarly, the Senate considered a budget resolution that would have capped tax expenditures at no more that 30 per cent of net revenue. Another proposal sought to have all new tax expenditures referred to the pertinent authorizing and budget committees. These proposals never received more than committee hearings (Hebert 1984, 43), because of concerns about quantifying tax expenditures and, more important, territorial imperatives similar to those that prevented adoption of tax expenditure proposals in the congressional budget reforms of 1974 (Neubig 1988, 248).

When the deficit burgeoned, concerted efforts were made to raise revenues. Both the 1982 and 1984 budget agreements contained provisions to reduce tax expenditures. Congress responded first with the Tax Equity and Fiscal Responsibility Act (TEFRA) of 1982, "which directly reduced a dozen tax expenditures."[40] According to one account (Hebert 1984), Congress relinquished $82 billion during the 1982–83 and 1983–84 fiscal years. Nevertheless, by 1982, it was reported that there were still over 100 tax expenditures.[41] The Deficit Reduction Act (DEFRA) of 1984 took this strategy a few steps further by postponing several tax expenditures and other reductions associated with the 1981 ERTA initiative and by increasing the 1982 TEFRA reductions in corporate tax expenditures, including real estate shelters and sale and leaseback arrangements.

By the mid-1980s, however, there was considerable dissatisfaction about what had become an unwieldy and protracted budget process and the fact that, despite substantial political struggles, deficits continued to grow. Budget procedures, even with significant modifications over the years, did not lead to satisfactory outcomes, nor did they make it any easier for legislators to achieve tough objectives. In this environment, proposals to impose greater discipline on the process and to insulate members from "special interest" politics gained greater currency.[42] Some members supported some form of balanced-budget amendment,[43] while others called for new rules that would "sequester funds through automatic percentage cuts if the budget were not balanced."[44]

The dramatic result was the Deficit Reduction and Balanced Budget Act of 1985 (Gramm-Rudman-Hollings), which, among other things, set statutory deficit limits and required "offsets" and other procedures for budgetary proposals that would cause key budget totals to exceed or fall below established targets.[45] If an appropriations committee proposed a program that exceeded the budgetary limits and did not contain offsets, the proposal could become law only if 60 per cent of the House and the Senate approved the measure.[46] Although forgone revenues were of obvious concern, the Gramm-Rudman-Hollings legislation did not single out tax expenditures for special treatment or systematic review.[47] According to Benker (1986, 404), the CBO reported that, by 1985, there were 135 tax expenditures. The only constraint on new ones was the requirement to demonstrate that compensatory revenue gain or reduction in direct expenditures met prescribed limits.

It was in this context that there emerged the Tax Reform Act (TRA) of 1986, which eliminated or reduced a surprising number of tax expenditures while lowering marginal tax rates and collapsing several tax brackets. As one observer (Neubig 1988, 242) noted, the TRA, while not increasing revenues, "scaled back 30 tax expenditures directly, and indirectly scaled back all tax expenditures (except four tax credits) through rate reduction." It was a reversal of the "bidding war" of 1981 that led to aggressive competition between Democrats and Republicans to grant tax expenditures to various interests. Although the 1986 exercise nearly degenerated into similar spectacles at certain junctures,[48] it remained a fascinating meeting of minds by conservatives interested in lower taxes and liberals seeking a fairer tax system. President Reagan and Don Rostenkowski, a key Democrat who chaired the House Ways and Means Committee, built a coalition across parties and branches, so that the other side would not receive sole credit for reform and so that the measure would obtain the necessary bipartisan support.[49]

The very radical nature of the reform attracted many members of Congress. The reforms would have to be dramatic enough to capture the attention of the public, given that it was not demanding reform. As well, legislators had to be able to demonstrate to special interests and constituencies that there was an overarching objective and that many other interests were also losing their tax preferences. Yet, as Pearl Richardson (1988, 26) noted, the reforms did not emerge out of thin air: "TEFRA and DEFRA began the tax reform process by chipping away at preferences enacted in 1981 and earlier; TRA went much further."

Although it is beyond the scope of this study to recount tax reform at the state level, the 1986 federal changes had significant implications for state tax policy, and vice versa. By closing off certain tax expenditures, Congress affected "passive tax expenditures" in each state, albeit in varying degrees.[50] The states could have attempted to provide compensating tax expenditures, but Gold and Nesbary (1988, 888) argue that many states "followed in the footsteps of the federal government by conforming to many of these new provisions." However, the states were not "passive" when it came to lobbying against the proposal to remove the deduction for local and state taxes, which was a major drain on the federal treasury.[51]

Assessing the Impact of Tax Expenditure Thinking

Passage of the TRA seems a testament to the vision of Stanley Surrey and to the efficacy of tax expenditure informational and procedural reforms. Even the delay of close to two decades made this accomplishment no less remarkable. Observers had predicted that the push for tax reform was doomed to failure because Congress, as a decentralized institution, was susceptible to the leverage of powerful interest groups.[52] In the end, however, the appeal to higher tax policy objectives prevailed. Nevertheless, we should pause before presuming a strong link between tax expenditure thinking and tax reform. As Pearl Richardson (1988, 25) advised, any "government involved in or contemplating similar activities might appropriately ask what purpose tax expenditure budgeting serves, whether oversight and control of tax expenditures have increased, and whether tax expenditure budgeting and analysis contribute to tax reform efforts, and, if so, how."

One cluster of arguments suggests that tax expenditure thinking has had little, if any impact on the making of U.S. tax policy. First, it is suggested that policy makers usually have not followed the path recommended by tax expenditure reformers. For example, Gold and Nesbary (1988, 887) observe that "during the period of severe fiscal stress for state governments in 1982 and 1983 numerous states considered proposals to raise revenue by reducing tax expenditures. No state relied primarily on this method of raising revenue. It invariably proved more politically expedient to raise taxes than to close so-called loopholes." A similar case could be made for the reluctance of federal policy makers to attack tax expenditures during the late 1970s and early 1980s and for California legislators' more recent handling of their budget crisis.

Second, some analysts point to the failure of sunset provisions – presumably one of the more potent tools for forcing examination of tax expenditures – to change the behaviour of legislators. Their failure is attributed to the power of special interests and to legislators' willingness to renew tax measures without serious review.[53] Drawing on his federal experience, however, Neubig (1988, 242) reports that while "sunset provisions are routinely extended in the current budget situation, they subject the expiring provisions to close Congressional scrutiny, and often lead to new restrictions on the value of or eligibility for the tax subsidy."

Third, some argue that tax reform was triggered by other means, not by tax expenditure accounts and sundry review processes. Observers have attributed interest in serious tax reform not to tax expenditure accounts produced by Treasury/OMB or by JCT/CBO but rather to a relatively simple study published by the Citizens for Tax Justice in late 1984. The document identified several major corporations that had not paid taxes despite considerable profit margins.[54] By naming names, the study attracted considerable attention in Washington.

These observations suggest that enacting reforms to give tax expenditures greater exposure is tantamount to whistling in the wind. For example, as Edwards (1988, 17) noted, "several states reported that their tax expenditure report had been used for tax policy planning, but only a few claimed that issuing the report had caused an actual change in tax structure." But many observers believe that the tax expenditure concept and its concomitant tools have increased awareness about problems with tax systems. Edwards tells us also that agencies from various states that responded to the 1987 survey by New York state's Legislative Commission on Private-Public Cooperation (LCPP) "reported that the tax expenditure budgets had increased the public's and public officials' awareness of the size and importance of this issue" (17). Salamone (1988, 32) argued eloquently that such reports could be influential, even without more coercive procedural reforms:

> If we attempt to assess the impact of the tax expenditure report on the legislative process in Minnesota by looking for overt signs of integration, we might conclude that the report has not improved the state budget process. There are no sunset schedules, no required statements of intent on new legislation, and no mandatory review process. But an evaluation of the report must recognize that the quality of legislative decision making is not solely a function of process and structure. It is also a function of the quality of information provided to the Legislature, the awareness of individual legislators, and the networks through which information is disseminated. The absence of a mandatory review of tax

expenditures has not been an obstacle to the introduction of tax expenditure analysis to Minnesota public policy debates. Because the report is rich in background information, is well written and organized, and is distributed to all 201 state legislators, many libraries, and to citizens who request a copy from the Department of Revenue, it has quickly found a constituency. It has become classroom reading in a number of public affairs and public finance courses in the Twin Cities.

Pearl Richardson (1988, 27) takes this argument a step further. She notes that during the early 1980s "the consensus within the academic and policy-making communities was that the tax code contained too many unfair and unnecessary preferences. This consensus provided the intellectual foundation for political efforts to broaden the tax base and use the funds raised thereby to lower rates." In other words, increased awareness helped create the climate for tax reform. More recently, Harris and Hicks (1992, 38–40) have argued that "tax expenditure reporting may be more effective in shaping a new view about how tax systems operate than in general inputs for an instrumental decision model," and the data are more likely to be used for issue development and monitoring.

Tax reform is a complicated process, and, while many observers agree that reporting on tax expenditures may help create a disposition towards reform, few would go so far as to argue that tax reform would not happen without such reporting and review. Michigan's House Fiscal Agency (1990, 25) recently claimed that the "mounting evidence regarding the ineffectiveness and inefficiency of many tax expenditures and their bias towards growth indicate that reporting is not enough."[55] And, although Richardson (1988, 27) acknowledges that "tax expenditure analysis is part of the background of recent tax reform legislation," she argues "this does not mean that in general tax expenditure analysis is necessary to tax reform" and that the "relationship between tax expenditure budgeting and tax reform legislation is, at most, indirect." Referring explicitly to the TRA, she asserts that "tax expenditure budgeting *per se* is unlikely to bring about changes of such magnitude." A Treasury official concurs, asserting that the "tax expenditure concept ... did not play any direct role in the shaping of the U.S. tax reform ... [but] nonetheless is part of the U.S. tax policy landscape."[56]

If, as more sanguine observers believe, the path of influence is indirect, but nevertheless exists, what is the nature of that influence? How does increased awareness feed into and shape tax reform? Gold and

Nesbary (1988, 888) argue that "tax expenditure budgets are unlikely to produce any meaningful policy changes except under special circumstances. Most tax preferences are so well entrenched that their curtailment is not politically likely ... When it comes to policy innovations, however, timing is critical. Having a tax expenditure budget available increases the likelihood that curtailment of tax expenditures will be considered when additional revenue is needed." In these circumstances, tax expenditure documents provide a ready list, reasonably good estimates about the gains from reducing certain preferences, and estimates on revenue loss, and they highlight reduction of tax expenditures as a possible component of a strategy for tax reform, deficit reduction, or reallocation of resources.[57] One tax analyst in Minnesota reports that the tax expenditure account receives more scrutiny during tough economic times.[58] California, however, avoided reducing or eliminating tax expenditures as a strategy for deficit reduction. While tax expenditure concepts and documents circulated in Washington, DC, well before the 1980s, the federal tax reform of 1986, would have been inconceivable if it were not for a burgeoning deficit, the ambitions and flexibility of key leaders, and the fact that tax reform was really one pawn in a game with much larger stakes – the battle for control of the White House and the Senate in the forthcoming elections.

Are tax expenditure reports worth producing? After reviewing the results of one survey, Edwards (1988, 17) concludes that many states "apparently have found that the benefits of tax expenditure reporting are large enough to overcome the obstacles to implementing them." More recently, based on a survey of tax legislators, Harris and Hicks (1992, 42) report that "over one half of respondents strongly agree that report information would be considered or mentioned when tax policy issues are discussed." Such responses, of course, are biased, because they come from states that have adopted some sort of tax expenditure review and the officials completing the questionnaires probably drafted the reports. Even Harris and Hicks (46) note that "although proponents of reporting advocate reporting as a vehicle for focusing on the resource allocation effect of budget policy, it is unlikely that tax expenditure accounting as currently implemented motivates the combined budgetary assessment of tax expenditures and direct expenditures."

A simple statistic is often overlooked: about half of all states have no tax expenditure accounting.[59] However, as Gold and Nesbary (1988, 888) point out, the "main argument against tax expenditure budgets is that they are a waste of valuable resources. The cost of preparing a tax expenditure budget is relatively small, however, compared with the value of tax expenditures." Given the indirect and serendipitous quality of tax reform exercises, producing a budget may be a shrewd analytical investment[60] that sensitizes policy makers, interest groups, and the public to the revenue drain involved, and doing so will involve expending far less political capital on reforms that have a questionable impact, such as perfunctory tabling and reviewing of accounts, new committees or subcommittees, and sunset provisions that are honoured more in the breach.

Conclusion: Lessons from U.S. Experience

Tax expenditure thinking began in the United States with one official in the mid-1960s and is now clearly ensconced in the policy lexicon. Both the president and Congress are required to produce tax expenditure reports and have used sunset provisions to some degree. Close to 25 states have engaged in some form of tax expenditure review, and there has been considerable experimentation with procedural, informational, and institutional arrangements. The federal tax reform of 1986 reflected the principles inherent in tax expenditure thinking, and, in terms of diffusion of ideas and concepts, it has been a success.

However, the U.S. experience also illustrates the limits of tax expenditure concepts, as well as of informational and procedural reforms often proposed by advocates. Few observers, would attribute the 1986 tax reform to the presence of tax expenditure accounts. Moreover, the lack of additional institutional support for tax expenditure reports is quite telling and should lead us to consider why tax expenditure thinking does not have more influence on tax policy and budget processes.

One observer, Thomas Neubig (1988, 243–47), attributes the lack of effectiveness partly to the problems of definition and estimation plaguing tax expenditure analysis; the resulting data simply are not authoritative. Moreover, regardless of the quality of data, few governments mandate formal reviews of tax expenditure reports, and inclusion of such lists with budget documents may take place too late to engender debate on the trade-offs among instruments. Simply providing a tally of tax expenditures, no matter how comprehensive, does not mean that tax expenditure thinking holds sway over the policy process.

Another explanation focuses on institutional factors. Neubig

(1988), like some of the state observers, complains that relatively few staff members are actively engaged in analysing the efficacy of tax expenditures and possible alternatives. He notes that analytical expertise is divided between Treasury and OMB, and current processes do not lead to direct discussions. Referring to Treasury, Neubig (249) observes:

> the tax expenditure analysis staffs have not tried to quantify the effect on total compliance and simplification of switching tax expenditures to direct expenditures. One of the reasons for the lack of attention ... is that most analysts also do not view tax expenditures as perfect substitutes for direct expenditures. Before considering the merits of using tax expenditures versus direct expenditure programs, many analysts would argue for repealing or changing certain tax expenditures rather than simply switching the method of government intervention ... The Treasury Department has generally opposed refundable tax credits on the grounds of compliance and simplification concerns, but always from the narrow perspective of the tax system, not from the perspective of total government intervention.

Likewise, tax committees in Congress and in state legislatures jealously guard their control over tax policy – they have regularly deflected reforms seeking to limit tax expenditures in aggregate or to involve other legislative committees in their deliberations. The result is the same: legislators with different authorities and instruments do not have incentives or forums to evaluate tax expenditures from a broader perspective.

Finally, there are political impediments. First, the congressional style of decision making is an open political process susceptible to special interests that have great incentives to fight hard to retain and obtain special tax provisions. Their voices are more likely to be heard than those of taxpayers, whose interests are more diffuse. But Neubig (1988) argues that the problem involves more than unfavourable institutional arrangements and hard politics. He believes that political and bureaucratic leaders have been unwilling to devote time and resources to deeper reviews of tax expenditures. The result is that the "tax expenditure budget has become a revenue estimators' exercise and issue, rather than an economic, legal, budget, or policy issue" (249).

The combination of technical, institutional, and political forces inhibit diffusion of tax expenditure thinking. Why then have many governments adopted tax expenditure reporting, and why are such concepts employed regularly by policy analysts and decision makers? The concepts provide a language that captures the corrosion of taxing capacity and of the fairness of tax systems, and the associated budgets have provided, at the very least, a symbolic rallying point for reformers. If this story sounds familiar, perhaps the reader is recalling similar attempts to introduce cost-benefit analysis, program budgeting, and program evaluation into policy-making processes. Their advocates, of course, always were disappointed with how politics subverted power and attractive concepts. This is not an argument for Canadian reformers to discard plans to improve tax expenditure reporting and analysis, but it does suggest that we get our expectations in order.

The Canadian Federal Experience: Exemplary Model or Cautionary Tale?

The U.S. literature on tax expenditures contains many references to Canadian innovations in that field.[61] Aside from displaying great interest in how tax expenditures were handled under the Policy and Expenditure Management System (PEMS) adopted by Ottawa in 1979, U.S. observers often look longingly at the executive-dominated system of governance that seems more conducive to controlling tax expenditures. Parliamentary systems hold promise of overcoming institutional barriers to tax expenditure reform present in congressional models, where fractious and powerful legislatures lacking party discipline are highly susceptible to outside interests. There is prima facie support for this supposition: even though policy makers in Canada began to address tax expenditures in a concerted manner well after the United States did, Canadian federal tax reform, initiated in the early 1980s, presaged the U.S. reforms. However, similar tensions exist in Canada – different governing systems merely offer different arenas and channels for the inevitable struggles to play themselves out. Indeed, recent events suggest that the Canadian federal experience is not the model that it once was for handling tax expenditures.

The Traditional Approach: Tax Expenditures and Federal Budgets

Much has been written on Canada's tax policy and budgetary process[62] that shows how the high political stakes, as well as the convention of budget secrecy, limit policy development to a small circle of participants: the minister of finance, the prime minister, and a handful of their closest political advisers; senior officials in the Department of Finance; and analysts working on key issues. Our purpose here is to consider the implications of such processes for tax expenditures. While broader political forces create demands for insinuating tax expenditures into the tax system, and also give rise to demands for reform,traditional processes in parliamentary systems work against diffusion of tax expenditure thinking.

This section provides a glimpse of how federal tax policy was made before serious attention was directed towards tax expenditures. It draws on David Good's (1980) seminal study, which describes how several tax expenditures relating to housing policy were handled in the two budgets of 1974 – one before and one after the federal election. Writing about the first of the budgets, Arthur Drache (1978, 6) observed several years later:

> Probably no Budget document in recent years contained more attractive provisions for the majority of Canadian taxpayers. The government was fortunate in its timing in that, as a matter of fiscal policy, it wanted to reduce taxes and encourage savings. This Budget introduced such items as the interest income deduction, the registered home ownership savings plan, the spousal registered retirement savings plan, and a host of other taxpayer benefits. The government expected the Budget to be the basis of its election campaign, and these provisions were drafted as broadly as possible. It is not surprising, therefore, that by 1977, each of these three major provisions has had to be substantially revised to close up 'loopholes' which the original draftsmen knew were present, but were instructed to retain.

Although it was an election-year budget, the case, at least in decision making, was probably not exceptional. Good offers a rare and rich inside look at tax policy making in a parliamentary system, identifying many dynamics that should be at work in provincial processes at well. His study rings true over ten years later, despite a radically different economic and political climate – at the very least, many of the observed tendencies and tensions are salient to issues of reform.[63]

Tax expenditure thinking seeks to create processes conducive to comparing and evaluating the merits of tax expenditure and direct expenditure for achieving a policy objective. The practical reality throws cold water on this aspiration. Good (1980, 168) observes: "When Finance officials were asked how they analysed and selected

62   Evert A. Lindquist

between tax expenditures and direct expenditures to pursue governmental purposes we were met with surprised looks, suggesting that
the question indicated ignorance on the part of the person asking it.
Those who did reply simply noted, 'we don't.'" Noting that different
policy processes spawned their own "policy making cultures" among
central agencies and line departments, Good (181) remarks that "in
the expenditure process, contact and bargaining between spenders
and guardians is an accepted way of life and these policy concerns
are taken into account ... In the tax process, the tax community avoids
interaction with outsiders in other policy areas." The two policy-making processes were worlds apart, and the latter one was not an ideal
environment for conducting proper analysis of tax expenditures.

Aside from technical amendments to existing tax legislation and
larger efforts at tax reform, most new tax policies were analysed,
shaped, and adopted through the budget process. The imperatives
associated with producing a budget seriously constrained evaluation
of tax proposals. For example, the budget posture – the fiscal stance
adopted with respect to the deficit, unemployment, inflation, and
other variables – was adopted by the finance minister and the department's budget committee early in the process. In addition, every budget contained themes reflecting government priorities, electoral
politics, economic conditions, and attempts to have "balance" along
several dimensions (something for big business, something for the
farmers, homebuyers, and small business, and so on). The fiscal
stance and themes thus provided the framework for considering specific tax measures, such as tax expenditures.

One concern of officials was to retain control of tax policy and the
budget changes so as not to involve other departments. One strategy
was to search for "offsets" within the tax code, so that expenditures
would not be affected. Some tax expenditures were eliminated not
because of policy considerations but to achieve this balancing act.
According to Good (1980, 167), tax options were then sought that
would "minimize attentive actor attention," as opposed to making
the change based on a major policy objective. Besides the constraints
imposed by the policy framework, the budget process also proceeded
in a compressed time period and under secrecy. These constraints,
Good (169) shows, combined to create incentives for Finance officials
not to undertake fuller analysis and consultation on tax expenditure
proposals: "Deciding that escalating housing prices are to be a priority in the preparation of the Finance Minister's budget speech, substantially precludes the consideration of direct expenditures. The

hurried preparation of the speech leaves little time for outside consultation with the Central Mortgage and Housing Corporation
(CMHC) and the Treasury Board Secretariat on direct expenditures."
Good notes further: "If consultation does take place the spendingde-
partment is likely to press for direct expenditures which will expand
its budget and mandate, and the Secretariat will not be anxious to recommend supplementary expenditures to a program that, through the
normal expenditure process of main estimates, has already received
substantial increases. The greater the number of participants
involved and the more divergent their view, as is the case with direct
expenditures, the more difficult it is to reach agreement on a policy
alternative" (169).

To retain autonomy and complete their tasks, Finance officials
avoided involving colleagues from other departments, thus preclud-
ing full review of the possibilities for accomplishing policy objectives.
This attitude prevailed even when these officials knew that they
could not anticipate all factors in their analysis and that the
announced measures would substantially affect a policy sector.

That officials were constrained by the budgetary regime does not
mean that they were poorly informed about tax options. Consider
this description of how officials first responded to the demand for
housing policies:

> Although the problem of escalating housing prices was new, the alterna-
> tives searched were old. Solutions had to be found quickly. 'Several
> months before the budget, broad policy areas are set out, but by the time
> we get around to specific things (like housing prices) there just isn't that
> much time,' explained one official. Officers searched for ready-made
> solutions. They ritualistically recorded the standard litany of tax alterna-
> tives – allow a mortgage interest deduction for homeowners, reduce or
> eliminate the sales tax on building and construction materials, provide a
> $1,000 tax deduction for home purchasers, allow taxpayers to take capi-
> tal cost allowance for rental units as a deduction from non-rental
> income. Direct expenditures were also added, like a $500 grant to first-
> time homeowners and enriching CMHC's limited dividend housing pro-
> grams, not so much because they were to be taken seriously but rather
> because they 'rounded out' the list. (Good 1980, 171)

Ideas would filter into the department over the months and years
before serious drafting of a budget begins. One source was pre-budget consultations and ongoing submissions from citizens, interest

groups, and line departments. Officials also monitored the tax initiatives and practices of other jurisdictions.[64] Other tax reform proposals arrived occasionally, culled from policy reviews, royal commissions, and academic studies. Even though new options were not likely to emerge during the weeks preceding budgets – unless flashes of insight occurred or new political imperatives arose – tax officials were surprisingly aware of the possibilities. The Department of Finance was, and is, an important node of interaction and source of power in Ottawa; few serious proposals get floated and then approved without receiving scrutiny there.

Although ideas got into the departmental pipeline, the traditional tax policy and budgetary process was not conducive to the sort of analysis that tax expenditure reformers advocate. Good (1980, 169) provides several examples of how different options were handled by Finance officials: "Finance did not consult CMHC on the RHOSP because it had little effect on housing price or housing supply and it anticipated that CMHC would point out many other ways in which the money could be spent on housing. When the capital cost allowance for rental income was eliminated as an offset against non-rental income, Finance did not consult CMHC. They informed them of the change." He continues:

> One [option that] was inexpensive, in fact increased revenues and at the same time was advocated by CMHC, was to eliminate the write-off of the carrying costs of undeveloped land. In a preliminary discussion between senior CMHC officials and the Assistant Deputy Minister, Tax Policy, the latter indicated that he was generally favourable to such a change. The elimination of the write-off for carrying costs of land had a number of advantages. It did not cost anything. It was consistent with the emerging philosophy of the branch to crack down on tax loopholes. It appeared to affect only a few large developers who the public had been blaming for spiralling housing costs without exciting the vast numbers of smaller developers. And finally, the argument that holding undeveloped land off the market led to high housing costs was easy to grasp, even if the tax provision did not necessarily affect substantially the quantity of land and the speed with which it is developed. Analysis of the tax provision was undertaken by a tax analyst, not for the purposes of determining its effect upon the supply of land and subsequent housing prices (that was already assumed to occur and to be beneficial) but rather to estimate revenue effects and to prepare the arguments for the repeal of the provision. (Good 1980, 172)

And, finally, he concludes: "Sensing that some type of relief was going to be given to housing, analysts considered providing direct grants to homeowners. The proposal was put to the Assistant Deputy Minister and then 'cut down,' in part because direct expenditures raised questions which would have to be negotiated with CMHC, whereas [decreasing the sales tax on building materials] was neat and quick" (180).

The analysis at Finance was driven by budgetary and tax consider- ations, mostly revenue implications, not by whether decisions would lead to good housing policy. Good (180) argues further that "the pro- cess of making tax decisions affecting housing is divorced from con- cerns about housing policy." In order to avoid conflict, officials at Finance did not engage line departments. The result was elliptical analysis, even when officials were unsure about the effectiveness of proposals. However, Finance officials were not the only actors guilty of circumscribed analysis. Good (178) observes: "CMHC had little incentive to analyse the [capital cost allowance proposal] since it had nothing to lose by pushing for reinstatement of a tax provision which was 'free money' and did not affect its expenditure budget" (178). No actor, it seems, had incentives to take up the more fundamental ana- lytical questions.

The development of tax expenditure proposals relating to housing for the 1974 budgets stands as the antithesis to good tax expenditure thinking. However, it gives us a keen sense of the pressures that tax officials are under when drafting budgets. It also alerts us to the insti- tutional divide that prevents those at the centre from working with line departments to give tax expenditure proposals greater scrutiny and ensure that tax measures do not work at cross purposes with pro- grams already in place.

The 1970s: Ascendancy of the Tax Expenditure Movement in Canada

It is impossible to understand the emergence of tax expenditure thinking and reforms in Canada without exploring the economic and policy context of the early 1970s. Several disparate events combined to place considerable pressure on the federal treasury. First, the energy crisis in late 1973 sent the economy into an inflationary spin and created demands for a host of compensatory government pro- grams. One initiative was the effort to deindex the income tax system in 1974. Inflation led to automatic or unlegislated revenue increases as taxable incomes rose into higher brackets and therefore incurred higher real tax rates. The practical effect was to create incentives for ministers and departments to search for alternative means to achieve policy objectives. Although line departments were previously reluctant to request tax expenditures because the Department of Finance would dictate policy design, tax expenditures became a favoured alternative.[65]

Beginning in the 1975–76 fiscal year, there was a dramatic increase in tax expenditure programs. One example that Savoie (1990, 162) gives is the liberal expansion of the investment tax credit to embrace regional development and transportation. Ottawa effectively employed the same strategy when it granted tax points to help pay for Established Programs Financing (EPF) payments and childcare tax credit outlays, as opposed to cash transfers.[66] The resort to such arrangements had similar effects on tax expenditures. All of these decisions lowered revenues and rapidly increased the deficit. As Richard French (1980, 74) so pithily observes: "Among the most important sources of the deficit were decisions to index personal income tax, increase transfers to the provinces, and institute tax expenditures targeted on the corporate sector in the name of growth, jobs and competitiveness."

It was against the backdrop of this economic and fiscal turmoil that several strands of thinking coalesced. First, Stanley Surrey's tax expenditure concept, as well as the 1974 reform of the U.S. congressional budget process, received attention in Canada. Second, a critique from the Canadian left focused on the unfairness of the tax system. David Lewis, as leader of the New Democratic Party, used the slogan "corporate welfare bums" to great effect during the 1972 federal election campaign. In 1976, the National Council of Welfare, an advisory body attached to Health and Welfare Canada, published *The Hidden Welfare System*, which argued that tax expenditures skewed an ostensibly progressive tax system in favour of higher-income groups.

These concerns and ideas, in turn, stimulated a considerable volume of systematic research. Allan Maslove (1979) attempted to provide rough estimates of the revenue drain associated with tax expenditures and recommended publication of a tax expenditure account and adoption of sunset provisions. Roger Smith's (1979) monograph for the Canadian Tax Foundation delineated and estimated tax expenditures. These ideas resurfaced as part of a larger set of proposals by Tom d'Aquino, Bruce Doern, and Cassandra Blair (1979) to reform parliamentary democracy and improve the budgetary process in Canada. In his ground-breaking study of federal tax policy making, David Good (1980) called for the process to be ventilated but expressed concern about the ability of a tax expenditure account to improve the process. A journal, *Canadian Taxation*, was established in 1979 to provide a progressive forum to probe the tax system and recommend reforms. Finally, the Department of Finance began work on a tax expenditure account in 1977, informed by the activities of analysts in other countries, particularly the United States.[67]

These financial pressures and ideas eventually led to action, but not under the Liberal government. As so often happens, the ideas gestated, travelled, and gained currency within the federal bureaucracy and the larger policy community, but it fell to Joe Clark's minority Progressive Conservative government (1979–80) to convert them into tangible initiatives. There were two important measures. First, the government released Canada's first official tax expenditure account with the budget of 11 December 1979;[68] another followed in 1980. The approximately 200 listings related to taxation of personal and corporate income and to sales and excise taxes.[69] Second, the government unveiled a cabinet decision-making and budgetary system called the Policy and Expenditure Management System (PEMS), which featured rules and procedures designed to constrain the proliferation of tax expenditures. While much has been written on the many facets of this complicated innovation, the focus here is limited to tax expenditures and pertinent features of the larger system.[70]

PEMS was an elaborate attempt to return control over the budgetary and priority-setting process to cabinet ministers without overloading the centre. Rather than have the minister of finance and the Treasury Board attempt to make detailed decisions on resource allocation for particular departments and programs, PEMS sought to have the priorities and planning committee determine government priorities and its fiscal stance and then make broad allocations to several "envelopes." Resource allocations within these envelopes were to be made by cabinet policy committees.

PEMS was designed to create incentives for departments to weigh the implications of their demands in the context of government priorities and fiscal pressures. Once a sector, or even a department, was granted an allocation, it was expected to find ways to live within its means; if it wanted to launch a new, more effective program, it was to find resources and make trade-offs within its allocation. This logic was extended to tax expenditures: if departments convinced Finance and the cabinet that a tax expenditure made good policy sense, an amount equal to the lost revenues would be deducted from their envelope allocation. In other words, tax expenditures were no longer "free" programs for spending departments.

However, Finance did not relinquish control over the tax policy instrument and reserved the right to introduce tax expenditures as part of fiscal policy making. When the latter obtained, the envelopes were not to be docked for lost revenues. The logic could have been extended further: if departments believed that a tax expenditure pertinent to their policy domain had outlived its usefulness, or the lost revenues could be redirected towards more effective direct expenditures, then they should have been able to recoup the resources from the reduced or eliminated tax expenditure. The rules, however, were surprisingly ambiguous in this regard. They left open the possibility that Finance would see fit to "scoop" such funds, therefore providing less incentive for line departments to identify such opportunities.

In a relatively short period, Ottawa developed means for identifying and analysing tax expenditures. PEMS and its approach to control of tax expenditures is often cited in the international literature on tax expenditures, but few observers outside Canada have tracked the system's performance during the 1980s and its effect on tax expenditures and tax reform. The sections below consider the initiatives associated with successive Liberal and Conservative governments.

Tax Expenditures and the Liberals, 1980–84

The Liberals' record on tax expenditures during the early 1980s is contradictory, to say the least. On the one hand, they launched the most substantial tax reform of any government, clearly consistent with Surrey's principles, since the late 1960s. On the other hand, they were responsible for one of the most insidious tax expenditures (taken up in a later section), which undermined the integrity of PEMS as it related to tax expenditures, and they backed away from regular publication of the tax expenditure account.

The first major initiative of the new government was the National Energy Program (NEP), unveiled as part of the October 1980 budget. The NEP entailed radical transformation of the energy sector and relied on a battery of direct expenditures and regulations, as well as elimination, modification, and introduction of several tax expenditures. New tax expenditures included exploration incentives, super-depletion allowances, and equipment write-offs. The magnitude of the intervention also served to corrode, early on, the integrity of PEMS and its efficacy in dealing with tax expenditures. Because the tax structure was altered so dramatically, no one could determine what the base-line tax structure should be for delineated tax expenditures.[71] It was partly for this reason that a separate "energy" envelope was created, but this served only to insulate energy policy makers from the very competition and trade-offs that PEMS was supposed to encourage. Other ministers and departments learned that securing special treatment was possible if they had the support of the prime minister and the priorities and planning committee of cabinet.

If the 1980 budget was a setback for the tax expenditure movement, then Allan MacEachen's budget of November 1981 was a triumph for its principles. Quite simply, the budget introduced large-scale tax reform. According to Irwin Gillespie (1991), the proposals were "at least as substantial as" and "more comprehensive" than those made by finance minister Edgar Benson's White Paper of 1969 in response to the Carter Report (Canada, Royal Commission on Taxation, 1966) and predicated on a "commitment to horizontal and vertical equity" (198). The reform, Gillespie notes, aimed to reduce marginal tax rates for middle- and upper-income taxpayers, to eliminate or reduce a host of personal and corporate income tax expenditures, and to broaden the tax base by replacing the manufacturer's sales tax with a wholesale sales tax. Taken as a whole, the package was not revenue-neutral, since Ottawa hoped also that the reforms would reduce the deficit (197).

The triumph, however, was short-lived. The budget came as a surprise to the business community and the public, even though it was obliquely anticipated in the 1980 budget. Rather than evaluate the essence of the policy package, special interests and the media focused on the specific damage that certain provisions would allegedly cause and more generally pointed to the lack of consultation, which called into question the legitimacy of the entire budget. That the economy had entered into a major recession in late 1981 and went into a tailspin in 1982 did not help the cause. Moreover, the Department of Finance itself was not prepared either to market the reforms or to deal with the onslaught that followed. There was no concerted communications strategy for identifying the winners and benefits of tax reform – in other words, creating a constituency to counter the vocal special interests – and there was no attempt to pre-empt the legitimate concerns of the business community by announcing transition rules.[72] Perhaps these oversights were attributable to the appointment of a new deputy minister and assistant deputy minister for tax policy, but they may have reflected also the considerable turnover in the upper echelons of the department over several years.[73] The government responded by modifying many measures, retreating on others, and appointing a committee to review the merits of the proposed whole-sale sales tax. The Canadian Tax Foundation was asked to form an independent committee to review and make recommendations on how to improve the tax policy process, and the Department of Finance responded with its own discussion paper.[74] A major business research organization, the Conference Board of Canada, also initiated a study on budget secrecy.[75]

The November 1981 budget is usually labelled an abject failure, a botched attempt at tax reform. But this must be put in perspective. Many observers were willing to acknowledge that its policy under-pinnings were sound. Moreover, while the conventional wisdom, according to Doern and Phidd (1983, 304), holds that "the Budget was virtually replaced six months later," Gillespie (1991) argues that most of its provisions – such as the reduction in the number of tax brackets and lowering of marginal tax rates – eventually became law, follow-ing consultation and low-key amendments to the Income Tax Act.[76] He quotes a leading tax expert, Harvey Perry, as saying that the finance minister "achieved 90 per cent of his objective" (208). Finally, although many observers point to parallels between Canada's tax reform package of 1988 and the U.S. Tax Reform Act of 1986, MacEachen's package contained the principles underlying both.

This, of course, was not recognized in 1982. The concept of tax expenditures and words such as "fairness" and "equity" disap-peared from the Department of Finance's lexicon. The government lost interest in a tax expenditure account; the next one would not be produced until another party took power. The public pounding that the minister of finance took following the budget reduced the department's credibility, led to the cabinet's priorities and planning committee shaping the June 1982 budget, and shattered morale in the department. Rectifying this state of affairs was an important con-sideration in the prime minister's next cabinet shuffle. His most capable minister, Marc Lalonde, was given the Finance portfolio along with an experienced deputy minister. Lalonde, obviously try-ing to mollify business concerns about his role in orchestrating the NEP as energy minister, adopted a pro-business posture and sought to improve the department's capacity to undertake consultations and strategic planning by creating a new branch led by an assistant deputy minister.[77]

While the NEP of 1980 and the tax reform budgets of 1981 had clear ramifications for tax expenditures, PEMS was still in place. How did it perform in terms of controlling tax expenditures during the early 1980s? Savoie (1990, 322) reports that when "tax expenditures were placed in the appropriate spending envelope at the time PEMS was introduced, we saw the fewest number of tax expenditures introduced since they became a popular policy instrument in the mid-1970s." However, it is not clear that PEMS ever prodded departments and the government as a whole to examine carefully the trade-offs between tax expenditures and other policy instruments, particularly direct expenditures. Savoie points out that the practice of deducting the value of new tax expenditures from envelope allocations ended "largely as a result of spenders attempting all kinds of end-runs to gain support for new tax expenditures or because Finance feared that it was losing control over the approval of new tax expenditures" (322). Spending ministers with clout could persuade or press cabinet colleagues to accept their tax proposals, and even Finance could not block such political determinations,[78] particularly if regional considerations were at play.[79] In the 1982–83 fiscal year, tax expenditures cost about $23 billion (Savoie 1990, 323).

Although PEMS would not officially die until 1989,[80] much of its procedural integrity was undermined during the early 1980s. During his brief period as prime minister in 1984, John Turner removed key structural features – namely, ministries of state for Social Development and for Economic and Regional Development, as well as the "mirror" committees of deputy ministers. Other features, such as envelopes and multi-year operational planning, would linger on.

Tax Expenditures and the Conservatives, 1984–92

The NEP, the November 1981 budget, and the 1982 recession provided ample ammunition for Brian Mulroney and his Progressive Conservatives during the 1984 election campaign. And, to a surprising extent, the new government's response to tax expenditures was linked to many of its most important initiatives.

One of the government's first initiatives was the Nielsen Ministerial Task Force Program Review, launched in September 1984. Its objective was to find ways to reduce unnecessary and ineffective pro-grams.[81] According to Savoie (1990, 134), several task forces made up of public- and private-sector representatives reviewed close to 1000 government programs and made recommendations about whether they should be cut, modified, or retained. There were 19 program areas, with some embracing both direct expenditures and tax expen-ditures (133). However, none of the central agencies per se, such as the Department of Finance, was the object of review in the manner of line departments and their programs. Savoie notes that, at this time, there were over 300 tax expenditures, with close to two-thirds going to business (94), and the task forces examined 20 tax expenditure pro-grams worth about $7 billion per year (304) and recommended that several be cut. It was in this context, and perhaps flowing out of the program reviews, that Finance produced its first tax expenditure account in five years.[82] Study team reports were returned by Decem-ber 1985, and a final report was issued in March 1986. While few rec-ommendations were translated into policy,[83] the government did claim that savings "amounting to $500 million in on-going direct and tax expenditures" emerged from the reviews.[84] Roughly $215 million of those savings was attributed to reducing tax expenditures such as investment tax credits.[85]

The government's reluctance to move quickly on tax expenditures reflected its sensitivity to two external pressures. The business com-munity sought lower tax burdens, either through general rate reduc-tions or through special incentives. Social groups called for elimination of tax breaks favouring wealthy individuals and corpora-tions and for greater reliance on credits.[86] Moreover, although the government was determined to control expenditures on social pro-grams – considering the principle of universality too expensive and as transferring too many resources to middle- and higher-income groups – the prime minister pledged, during 1984, to preserve social programs as a "sacred trust." Tax expenditure thinking was soon reflected in the government's approach to social policy, which sought to focus resources towards those most in need. Where the tax system was concerned, one way to accomplish these objectives was to rely, where possible, on tax credits rather than tax deductions. Another method was to make some credits refundable, so that individuals without taxable incomes could benefit.[87] This approach was sup-ported by the Business Council on National Issues (BCNI) and by many social groups that would have preferred increased funding for social programs but saw a credit-based method as a second-best alternative; given that the Conservatives were unlikely to impose such programs.[88]

The government also sought tax reform. While it had campaigned on tax reform, the matter rose to the top of the policy agenda only when it became clear that the United States would revamp its tax system. Like policy makers in many other countries, those in Canada believed that they had to harmonize the tax system in a similar fashion. The finance minister issued two discussion papers on tax reform in 1986 and 1987 and held consultations.[89] The reforms occurred in two stages. The first stage, following the U.S. example, focused on personal and corporate income taxation and involved collapsing 10 personal income tax brackets into three, lowering many marginal rates, shifting several tax deductions to credits in order to favour lower-income taxpayers, and reducing several tax expenditures.[90] The second stage sought to broaden the base further and to reform the manufacturer's sales tax by introducing a goods and services consumption tax – the successor to MacEachen's proposal for a wholesale sales tax – that was intended to finance the net revenue loss associated with the first stage, since the entire tax reform was to be revenue-neutral.[91] To compensate lower-income taxpayers for increased outlays caused by the consumption tax, a refundable tax credit was introduced.

These reforms were informed by tax expenditure thinking and linked to the government's social policy stance. As Irwin Gillespie (1991, 208) has pointed out, it was surprisingly consistent with MacEachen's 1981 tax proposals, though not as substantial, perhaps because some of those earlier proposals had been enacted. While the changes just reviewed may cast the Conservatives as tax expenditure "angels," tax expenditures reportedly cost the federal treasury at least $30 billion per year during the late 1980s – close to the size of the stubborn deficit.[92] The Tories also introduced the incredible life-time capital gains exemption of $500,000 to show that Canada was "open for business," although tax reform reduced the exemption to $100,000 (small businesses and farmers, however, retained the original exemption). The same government announced the Cape Breton Development Tax Credit in order to replace a regional subsidy program.[93] Moreover, it lost hundreds of millions of dollars by failing to eliminate quickly the infamous Scientific Research Tax Credit.[94] This debacle led to creation in 1987 of the Tax Measures Evaluation Unit within the Department of Finance. Since this complicated story involves both Liberal and Conservative governments and introduces a different set of issues, it deserves further discussion.

Tax Expenditures, the Auditor General, the Public Accounts Committee, and Finance Canada

The Scientific Research Tax Credit (SRTC) was announced in November 1983. A 50 per cent credit was intended to encourage investment in research and development. The anticipated annual cost, as estimated by Finance, was $100 million. However, the instrument could be traded – eligible investors could sell the credit to investors not engaged in research activity. The scheme worked too well. Early concerns were expressed by Revenue Canada officials about the take-up rate; even private-sector tax professionals were incredulous that the rules were so liberal and open to abuse. When pressed for clarification, the minister of finance, Marc Lalonde, being anxious to curry favour with the business community, stood by the original design and interpretation. By the time the Conservatives swept into power, the tax credit had already cost well over one billion dollars. In October 1984, Lalonde's successor, Michael Wilson, quickly announced that the program would be halted at the end of 1985, but investors still took advantage of the opportunity, and, in the end, the tax credit cost about three billion dollars.[95]

This episode is important for several reasons. First, it demonstrates how quickly tax expenditure can lose revenues for any government and the horrendous implications of not having adequate monitoring procedures in place. Indeed, the SRTC now serves as a cautionary tale for tax analysts in all Canadian governments. Second, while this episode again led to questions about the competence of tax policy designers in the Department of Finance, the concern of outsiders gravitated towards evaluation of tax expenditures that were already in place. And third, as will be discussed below, the SRTC highlights institutional tensions that may arise in the making of tax policy and the ensuing problems for those seeking to audit and reform tax expenditures.

The SRTC rekindled the interest of the Office of the Auditor General (OAG) in tax expenditures. In 1977, the OAG had expressed interest in evaluating tax expenditures on the principle that they were another form of government program. Doern (1989, 84) reports that the OAG pulled back because such inquiry would be too political and, presumably, because it did not want to wrestle with the powerful Department of Finance. The OAG established an audit team in 1983 to explore the SRTC and other tax expenditures. The team's work became a centrepiece of the OAG's annual report for 1984, which demanded greater accountability for tax expenditures and called on the Department of Finance to create its own capacity to evaluate tax expenditures.[96] The Senate's National Finance Committee (NFC) recommended that analysts conducting the evaluation be separated from those undertaking policy work. In addition, the OAG – as well as the House of Commons's Public Accounts Committee (PAC) and the NFC – recommended "regular publication of a tax expenditure account."[97]

Cooperation was not readily forthcoming from Finance, which considered itself first among equals in Ottawa and answerable only to its minister. Its view was that it did not deliver conventional "programs" but rather provided the framework within which *other* programs operated. In other words, programs such as debt financing, fiscal policy making, and tax policy design were not conducive to traditional program evaluation. (Many observers would argue that the real reason was that Finance officials never brook second-guessing by outsiders, even though they never hesitate to scrutinize the proposals and programs of other departments.) While agreeing that the SRTC should be monitored closely, the department's only concession was to work with the Office of the Comptroller General and to develop a suitable approach to program evaluation – a selective tax expenditure account was published in 1985. However, no progress was made on the evaluation front for two years. To be fair, the delay might have been attributable to the change in government, which resulted in a new minister and may have led to an oversight by the PAC, which monitors government adherence to the OAG's recommendations.

The OAG published another report in 1986, which claimed that tax expenditures had cost $28 billion in 1983,[98] and again called on Finance to evaluate tax expenditures. In 1987, the department responded by creating the Tax Measures Evaluation Unit, perhaps motivated by the fact that tax expenditures were to be reviewed as part of the government's tax reform initiative. The unit was located within the Tax Policy Branch and had its own director. The plan was to allow the unit to grow to 10 staff members over a three-year period (the branch had approximately 100 people on staff). An important step was to develop criteria for selecting which tax measures to evaluate. It was decided to give priority to certain measures: those with sunset clauses, those with potentially high revenue costs, those of concern to the PAC, those that were innovative and whose impact were difficult to gauge, and those that might inform evaluation of other measures. Using these criteria, a three-year plan was set out. The reviews were to be undertaken by staff analysts or consultants, and their work was to be subjected to peer review by external reviewers, usually from academic institutions. Although this approach did not separate the evaluation function wholly from the Tax Policy Branch and did not embrace other programs managed by the department, it was commended by the OAG and the PAC.

A director was appointed, and the unit soon began its work. In November 1988, with the John Deutsch Economic Policy Roundtable at Queen's University, the unit sponsored a conference on tax expenditures and government policy, bringing together government officials and academics from Canada and elsewhere. The proceedings were published in a substantial volume of studies.[99] Over the next three years, the unit commissioned studies on the Cape Breton investment tax credit, tariff remissions, the exploration tax credit, the disability tax credit, and the revenue elasticity of tobacco excise taxes.[100] However, the unit was suddenly disbanded in July 1991, ostensibly for cost-cutting reasons.[101] This decision immediately raised the ire of the OAG and the PAC. Both were concerned that evaluation within Finance would be compromised. They were incensed at the department's audacity and the affront to their authority and miffed about not being informed directly. The PAC's chair demanded an explanation and extensive documentation.[102] The committee then held hearings in October 1991 to receive testimony from representatives of the OAG, the OCG, and Finance.

Finance officials argued that they had found a way to reduce overhead while maintaining the integrity of the tax evaluation function. Responsibility for analysing particular tax measures would be spread among analysts within the Tax Policy Branch, and analysis would still proceed on the basis of a three-year plan and the original selection criteria. However, this activity would be coordinated by a Tax Expenditure Advisory Committee, to be chaired by a senior official from outside the branch, with representation from the OCG and Revenue Canada and subject to peer review. During the hearings, members of the PAC reiterated their interest in a tax expenditure account, but officials said that they were not able to produce one because of resource constraints.[103] The testimony somewhat mollified the committee. However, the PAC recommended that the advisory committee have additional representation from Revenue Canada and instructed the

OCG to report on whether the new arrangements met the Treasury Board's guidelines for program evaluation. The committee demanded to be informed about annual evaluation work plans and to have the right to submit its own priority measures for consideration. It also reiterated its desire for an annual tax expenditure account to be published as part of the budgetary process.[104]

However, days later, another round of questioning and correspondence between the committee and the deputy minister was precipitated by the perceived mishandling of a study commissioned on the disability tax credit. The already suspicious PAC soon followed up on a previous request for clarification from the deputy minister, gaining yet another opportunity to request a tax expenditure account.[105] After responding to the more specific requests, the deputy minister expressed his reluctance to produce a tax expenditure account because of insufficient data on GST-related items and because of the difficulty of analysing tax expenditures when transition and carry-over provisions from tax reform were still in force. Nevertheless, Gorbet (1991b) wrote that "in order to demonstrate the Department's commitment to improving the timeliness of the information made available to Parliament and the general public, a personal tax expenditure account, covering both 1988 and 1989, has been included in the work plan for 1992. A comprehensive account covering personal, corporate and sales taxes will be undertaken on a regular basis beginning in either 1993 or 1994 depending on data availability."

The PAC persisted.[106] In April 1992, it requested that the OAG examine the finance department's "new tax measure evaluation method, in light of the events that occurred during the examination of the disability tax credit, and using the evaluations called for in the Department of Finance's 1992 workplan ... and [that it] submit a detailed report to the Public Accounts Committee in early 1993."[107] More than ever, the PAC's members must have doubted whether the department would ever deliver on its earlier commitment to produce any of the promised tax expenditure accounts, particularly with the appointment of a new deputy minister. However, in late December 1992, the department released a tax expenditure account outlining personal income tax provisions.[108] Revenue estimates were provided for the 1988 and 1989 fiscal years, as well as detailed discussion of criteria for delineating tax expenditures and how the estimates were calculated.[109] Every effort was made to cross-reference tax expenditures with those covered in the 1985 account, even though many had been altered or eliminated as part of the 1988 tax reform. That the 1992 account was released before schedule suggests that Finance sought to appear more responsive and responsible than it had been in the past.

Conclusion

For many who think about tax expenditures, Canada stood out as a leader in reporting and integrating reviews of tax expenditures into the more general decision-making process. But, as this overview indicates, these impressions are out of date. Not only did PEMS never work according to plan, but only a shadow remains of the original system. Moreover, tax expenditure accounts have appeared only intermittently.

A more informed perspective provides grounds for both pessimism and optimism. On the one hand, we have encountered sobering and cautionary tales: arrival of tax expenditure thinking in Ottawa did not stop the design of an ill-conceived tax expenditure, which led to a terrible drain on the treasury; tax officials resisted attempts to subject their analytical products to the same standards as other government programs; and, as with the reception accorded the Carter Commission's proposals in 1966, the tax reform proposals of 1981 received a terribly rough ride in the political domain. On the other hand, two different governments launched serious reform efforts consistent with tax expenditure thinking, and this is no small accomplishment. Moreover, the incoming Conservative government in 1984 included tax expenditures as part of its program review, and the Department of Finance has responded, in some measure, to demands that it more carefully scrutinize tax expenditures already in place.

The Canadian case also confirms some of the tendencies and tensions found in the United States associated with promoting better tax expenditure analysis. First, the Department of Finance, like tax committees in many U.S. legislatures, jealously guards its monopoly on making tax policy. While many would agree that the tax policy instrument should be buffered to some extent, the resistance of tax officials to any kind of outside scrutiny smacks of over-protectiveness. Second, PEMS was intended to subject tax expenditures to greater scrutiny, but, like U.S. sunset provisions, it was easily subverted when political will was lacking. Third, there also seems to be considerable reluctance to go beyond supplying information on tax expenditures. In short, the concentration of power in the Canadian parliamentary system does not neutralize the territorial imperatives and political temptations that can subvert a more sensible and practical approach to scrutinizing tax expenditures.

Canada: Little-Known Provincial Experiments

The Canadian literature on tax expenditures has focused almost entirely on the experience of the federal government. However, like U.S. states, several provinces have produced tax expenditure accounts and have found other ways to improve scrutiny of tax expenditures. Only one province has published an account on a sustained basis, although others have done so occasionally. This section briefly reviews the experience of British Columbia, Saskatchewan, Manitoba, Ontario, and Alberta with such reporting (the order is determined by the date at which a province first published an account), considers what other provinces and the territories have done, and then draws some conclusions for weighing reform options in Ontario.

British Columbia

British Columbia was the first province to produce tax expenditure accounts, as part of background papers in the 1980, 1981, and 1982 budgets at the behest of the minister of finance, Hugh Curtis.[110] In his 1980 Budget Speech, Curtis said that the government wanted to "communicate effectively and be accountable" and that one way to do this was to pay "increased attention to tax measures, such as complex deductions and credits that do cost money, but are somehow lost in a maze of fine print" and provide "expenditure equivalents" for such measures.[111]

The first account provided estimates of revenue forgone through provincial tax expenditures (exemptions from social services and corporation capital taxation, and natural resources royalties) and under the federal-provincial tax collection agreements (personal income and corporation income taxes). Estimates were provided not only for the 1980–81 fiscal year but also for tax expenditures introduced since 1976. Most surprising, the account, without explanation and against standard tax expenditure practice, provided totals of revenue forgone. While precise figures are not available, it has been estimated that it took about two months for one tax policy analyst to pull together the account using available data. The analyst would have drawn on the expertise of about 10 analysts in the tax policy group.[112]

In subsequent years, the documents grew in size and sophistication. Tax expenditures were classified in various ways: by legislative authority, by revenue source, and by function. They contained special boxes that explained why "A Tax Expenditure Is Not a Loophole" and offered calculations of the value of implicit subsidies in interest rates and energy price subsidies. The documents also offered a defence for the heresy of totalling revenue forgone. While admitting that it was "not appropriate to add the cost of all tax expenditures and conclude the total is the combined revenue effect, ... totals of tax expenditures are presented ... not to provide estimates of aggregate revenue forgone, but to indicate the pervasiveness of tax expenditures implicit in various provincial taxes."[113] The later documents even included charts that calculated the percentage of revenue forgone against specific categories of taxation as well as in total. So, for example, it was estimated that tax expenditures led to over 44 per cent of tax revenue forgone in 1981–82.[114]

Controversy over estimates of the imputed revenue forgone because of a renter tax credit that was eliminated in late 1982 helped kill the tax expenditure accounts – apparently a political decision. A similar tax with sunset provisions introduced in 1989 reduced the value of the credit by 20 per cent a year until it was eliminated. The government kept delaying the sunset procedure, however, until it worked up the nerve to have it repealed in the 1993 budget. More recently, the NDP government introduced a fuel tax in the 1992 budget with sunset provisions whose effectiveness will be reviewed by officials in the Ministry of Finance after five years.[115]

Saskatchewan

Since 1981, just a year after British Columbia first published its account, Saskatchewan has produced a tax expenditure account with virtually every budget. However, in contrast to British Columbia, the practice was instigated by officials within the Ministry of Finance. There is no legislative basis for the account; the department has continued to produce the data purely for informational purposes.

In 1981, the account consisted of one page of preamble and two pages of tables listing 23 tax expenditures and estimates of revenue forgone. Both the preamble and the number of tax expenditures listed (46 in 1993) have grown over the years, but the document remains only four pages in length.[116] The account is usually pieced together in the weeks just before the Budget Speech (the about-to-be-announced tax measures are factored into the estimates) and employs only two or three analysts (there are only 12 officials in the Taxation and Inter-governmental Affairs Unit). Perhaps as little as one-fifth of a person-year equivalent is required to produce the account: officials developed an income-tax simulation model and are willing to make do with rough estimations for sales tax measures. Moreover, since the account is produced each year, it has become a routine activity that can benefit from calculations and methods used in previous years.[117]

It is reported that the account is used throughout the year as a reference document and is useful as a policy tool for the minister, but, apparently, neither the opposition parties nor the press draw much attention to the figures. The tax expenditure account was dropped from the last Progressive Conservative budget document because it reportedly did not fit the context of the budget. Some thought was given to releasing the account as a separate document, but the 1991 estimates eventually appeared with the 1992 estimates in the subsequent budget.[118] Related to the 1991 aberration was appointment of the Financial Management Review Commission in 1992 by the incoming NDP government to assess the province's financial affairs. In its report, the commission broached the subject of tax expenditures, but only to note its dissatisfaction with the secrecy and lack of reporting of the impact of forgoing revenues to particular individuals and corporations, and it observed that had any of the transactions been a direct expenditure it would have been reported to the legislature. Aside from insisting that such transactions receive more public exposure, the commission had little to say about how to remedy such abuses.[119]

Manitoba

Manitoba's government, like British Columbia's, produced three tax expenditure accounts in sequence, with the 1986, 1987, and 1988 budgets. The accounts were contained in the third section in Appendix C of the budget papers, following reports on tax adjustments and inter-provincial comparisons of major levies. Like the Saskatchewan document, these accounts simply identified specific tax measures (52 in 1988) under the broader categories of personal income tax, corporate income tax, retail sales tax, fuel taxes, health and post-secondary education levies, and corporate capital tax. The entire account took up only four pages[120] but was difficult to produce, particularly the first time, since sales tax data were hard to gather and several methodological issues had to ironed out. The exercise involved approximately six staff members over a one- or two-month period – roughly equivalent to half a full-time person-year.[121]

There were two budgets in 1988; an account appeared in the first, but there was more in the second one delivered by the new Conservative government. Apparently, the government was inclined to streamline documents and to focus text on anticipating the most likely concerns and queries of the public. When the account failed to appear in the second 1988 budget and in subsequent budgets, there was no public outcry. Prior to that, the tax expenditure accounts received little attention and never elicited public controversy. Estimates of the revenue forgone through tax expenditures are still produced for internal use, however, usually in the run-up to a budget.[122]

Ontario

Despite having a tax analytical capacity superior to most of its provincial counterparts, Ontario produced only three tax expenditure accounts – two for public consumption (1986 and 1988), and one from the Ministry of Revenue for internal consumption.[123]

During the mid-1980s, Queen's Park had two opportunities either to employ tax expenditureconcepts or to address issues associated with tax expenditures. The first was in its 1983 Budget Paper produced by the Ministry of Treasury and Economics on the province's revenue structure and how it had evolved since 1970. The paper did not identify tax expenditures as an issue or try to quantify any as such. However, some sections listed and costed rebates and exemptions (associated with "short-term sales tax stimulation" for the economy)[124] and depreciation allowances, tax rate reductions, and small business exemptions (as "investment and employment tax incentives"). The total cost of the latter incentives was put at $740 million for 1982–83.[125] There was no invocation of the tax expenditure concept.

The second opportunity was in a 1985 discussion paper issued by the treasurer setting out proposals for reforming the budget process. The paper noted how little public scrutiny revenue and expenditure measures receive and that specific expenditures tended to be examined in detail only following reports of the provincial auditor that had highlighted those items. It made no finer distinctions with respect to revenue measures that could have introduced discussion of tax expenditures. The paper recommended creation of a new standing committee in the legislature on economic and fiscal affairs to receive

preliminary budget documents, hold hearings, review budget legislation, and make recommendations on global fiscal targets. No special
mandate was suggested with regard to scrutiny of tax expenditures.[126]

Reluctance to invoke the tax expenditure concept ended abruptly
when a tax expenditure account was published in May 1986. The
paper (Ontario 1986) began by identifying the subject as "the controversial and frequently misunderstood subject of tax expenditures."
The preamble noted the advantages and disadvantages of the policy
instrument, outlined some of the conceptual and estimation problems, and warned against adding up all the estimates in order to
arrive at a total. The categories under which more than 60 estimates
of revenue loss were presented included taxes on personal income
(under the tax collection agreements with Ottawa as well as those
specific to Ontario), on corporate income, and on retail sales. The document had 18 pages and contained more information on the specific
nature of each exemption than did other provinces' accounts.[127]

The discussion paper elicited a reaction from the provincial auditor
in 1987. In a curious and cryptic response, the auditor observed that
while direct expenditures had to appear in the Public Accounts and
be approved by the legislature, and that new tax measures also
would require such approval, changes to tax measures by the government may not be debated if they do not entail a change in legislation
and, moreover, the financial consequences do not appear in the Public
Accounts. The auditor noted the difficulties in estimating the costs of
tax expenditures and the lack of formal accounting of those costs; this
situation created incentives to accomplish policy objectives through
tax expenditures rather than through direct expenditures if there
were spending ceilings in force. However, the auditor criticized the
authors of the discussion paper for not providing "an estimate on the
aggregate of those tax expenditures related to specific programs or
policy areas" and for not "adding up individual cost estimates to
arrive at a grand total."[128]

Seemingly echoing the rationale offered by British Columbia's minister of finance just a few years earlier, the auditor outlined the rationale for his preferred approach: "We believe that while aggregation of
estimated tax expenditures may well be an imperfect and at times
misleading measure, such aggregation is helpful in portraying the
magnitude and overall significance of tax expenditures in the Province's financial picture. In this regard, annual tax expenditures are in
excess of $7 billion. Direct expenditures for the 1987 fiscal year
totalled $32 billion."[129] The auditor also chided the authors of the

paper for not factoring in tax remissions. However, unlike their federal counterparts, neither the provincial auditor nor the Public Accounts Committee has pursued this matter further. The auditor's mandate is restricted to reviewing raising of revenues and disbursement of those funds. So, while the auditor and the committee have investigated how well the government collects taxes, the auditor's mandate technically precludes examining tax expenditures, which involves *relinquishing* revenues.[130]

It was not until 1988, almost two years after release of the paper, that the concept actually crept into an Ontario budget. The 1988 budget contained two small tables detailing specific changes to a handful of tax expenditures, and there was no aggregation of the figures. However, it was not clear how these tables related to those that summarized all the revenue changes contained in the budget, and no attempt was made to explain the link or the distinctions which certainly would have been lost on the public.

A full-fledged tax expenditure account was included as an appendix in the Economic Outlook and Fiscal Review document released in December 1988 as part of pre-budget consultation. Though containing information similar to the May 1986 document, it was organized differently. Like Saskatchewan's account, it presented estimates of revenue forgone in easy-to-absorb tables for expenditures on personal income tax, corporate tax, and retail sales tax, followed by a brief description of each measure. Moreover, the main part of the document also included a table listing the "ten largest tax expenditures within Ontario's sole jurisdiction" (Ontario 1988a). The Economic Outlook was used as a vehicle for the tax expenditure account once more, in late 1989 (Ontario 1989b), and a small account of tax expenditure changes was retained in the 1989 and 1990 budget papers. But, without explanation, the tables disappeared in the subsequent budgets and economic outlooks of the NDP government.[131]

Alberta

While Alberta has not published a tax expenditure account, it has apparently made public the cost of tax expenditures in a variety of ways. Since the late 1970s, provincial budget documents have listed in an appendix the cost of some personal and corporate tax measures (such as the renter assistance credit, the royalty tax credit, and the Alberta Stock Savings Plan) as part of a larger table delineating major sources of budgeting revenues, and some estimates have appeared in the Public Accounts. Beginning with the 1981 budget (Alberta Treasury 1981), these figures were also given in a separate table entitled "Deductions from Income Tax Revenue." This latter practice ended with the 1990 budget, which, ironically, featured the government's concerted effort to reduce, eliminate, or allow to "sunset" several tax expenditures. These measures, which emerged as a special focus of larger program reviews, were estimated to save $350 million (Alberta Treasury 1990). Apparently, the auditor general had called for more attention to be directed to tax expenditures and may soon revisit the issue.

During the mid-1980s, the auditor general took a sustained interest in tax expenditures. In forthright language, he wrote: "Budgeting and reporting certain program costs as tax expenditures [distort] the Province's reported revenues and expenditures. Furthermore, the control exercised over these costs by the Legislative Assembly is significantly weaker than the control exercised over normal government expenditures ... For 1983–84 and 1984–5, the Province incurred tax expenditures through the tax collection system amounting to $739 million and $550 million, respectively" (Alberta Legislature 1985, 68).

The auditor argued that deliberately listing such programs as tax expenditures, not as conventional expenditures, kept total expenditures and revenues lower. Moreover, tax expenditures "do not receive the in-depth budgetary review and debate that other expenditures receive ... [and] are disbursed without direct government pre-approval because they are usually deducted by the recipients of the benefits, from revenues paid to the government under self-assessment systems ... [Accordingly, it was recommended that] tax expenditures be treated in the same manner as normal government expenditures for both budgeting and financial reporting purposes" (68).

However, the treasurer had responded: "There is no general agreement amongst governments that tax expenditure programs should be provided for in budgetary appropriations and disclosed as expenditure in the financial statements. There is no clear distinction to determine which of these programs are 'tax expenditures' and which are truly 'revenue abatements.' It can also be said that these tax credits and deductions relate to the generation of tax revenue and should, therefore, be applied to reduce this revenue" (84).

The auditor reiterated his concerns in three subsequent reports. The 1985–86 report estimated revenue forgone for seven tax expenditures and noted that the government lost tax revenues whenever Ottawa unilaterally created a new tax expenditure. The auditor also referred to a joint study undertaken with the U.S. General Accounting Office and published by Canada's Office of the Auditor General (1986), which indicated that most users (the population surveyed was unclear) wanted tax expenditures to be listed in some form, but he acknowledged that many users felt that such information was "too conjectural" (Alberta Legislature 1986, 84). Reacting to the treasurer's remark that tax expenditures "are disclosed in accordance with legislation," the auditor retorted: "While it is true that present legislation does not require tax expenditures to undergo the same budgetary process as normal expenditures, it is equally true that present legislation does not require tax expenditures to forgo this process"; further, "in 1986–87, expenditures amounting to nearly 8% of the Province's consolidated expenditures escaped the full rigour of legislative and pre-disbursement expenditure control" (Alberta Legislature 1987, 83). In the final report that broached tax expenditures, an exasperated auditor again declared his concerns but declined to repeat his brief recommendation for a fourth time, resolving instead to "monitor debate and research across Canada on the subject of tax expenditures" (Alberta Legislature 1988, 72).

Other Provinces and Territories

None of the other provinces and territories has published formal tax expenditure accounts, although tax officials produce estimates when required. The smallest of these jurisdictions simply do not have many tax expenditures. The territories administer little more than a political contribution tax credit. Prince Edward Island is now experimenting with its first economic incentive – an investment tax credit announced in the 1992 budget. Another issue for all but the largest provinces is the number of people available for tax policy analysis. Nova Scotia and New Brunswick, for example, have no more than three members of staff working on tax issues; the territories, even fewer. As well, the smaller the population of a jurisdiction, the less useful are any data from Statistics Canada as a basis for cost estimates. The samples drawn from smaller provinces are simply not large enough to engender confidence.[132]

Despite this, there are practices worthy of note. Nova Scotia has experimented with sunset provisions (for example, the Nova Scotia Stock Savings Plans was introduced in October 1987 and eliminated in December 1992) and, more recently, introduced two new tax expenditures (employee share ownership and cooperative tax credits), which terminate on 31 December 1995.[133]

Finally, Quebec issued a discussion paper in early 1993 that examined in detail its financial options. One section considered different stances for confronting the province's enormous fiscal challenges. It contrasted a revenue strategy of increasing consumption taxes and tax burdens on individuals and businesses with one of cutting tax incentives for businesses and individuals. The document listed several key tax incentives put in place to encourage economic growth and estimated the cost for 1985, 1987, 1989, and 1991. It also outlined federal-provincial incentives and the revenue gains and losses associated with harmonizing Quebec's system with the 1988 federal tax reform.[134] Most of the recommendations for reform involved careful scrutiny of direct expenditures, and little was said about whether there were appropriate mechanisms in place for evaluating the merits of tax incentives versus other policy instruments; the tax system was presumed to be effective and not out of step with those of other provinces and nations.[135]

Conclusion: Implications for Ontario

We can draw several lessons from provinces' experience, some of which reinforce what we gleaned from Canadian federal and U.S. practices. First, provinces much less populous than Ontario have produced tax expenditure accounts regularly and relatively inexpensively. Second, there are advantages to producing such accounts regularly, and, once the initial investment is made, it becomes easier to generate subsequent accounts. Third, the experiences of British Columbia, Saskatchewan, Manitoba, Ontario, and Alberta affirm a lesson from the Canadian federal and the U.S. cases: tax expenditure accounts have only tentative footholds in most budgetary processes. The accounts do not seem to develop a strong constituency. Instead, they tend to be used in a subtle fashion; they have a low profile in budget documents and can be eliminated at the whim of a finance minister. Nevertheless, we must recall the potency of the instrument and the fact that, as the BC government and the Ontario auditor have emphasized, tax expenditures constitute a considerable portion of government involvement in the economic and social affairs of any jurisdiction.

Ontario: On the Cutting Edge?

The Fair Tax Commission has commissioned several studies relating to tax expenditures and to tax policy making more generally. One study (Doern, this volume) reviews recent developments in the tax policy and budgetary process; another (Block and Maslove, forthcoming) develops a list of tax expenditures administered by the province. The purpose of this section is to indicate how the budgetary process in Ontario deals with tax expenditures. It begins by providing some historical context and examines how the process has changed during the last decade. It then reviews how two new tax expenditures were arrived at – conversion of the Ontario Tax Grants for Seniors to a tax credit and implementation of the Ontario Investment and Worker Ownership Program. Based on this evidence, the concluding section ventures an assessment of the strengths and weaknesses of the current process. The final part of the paper offers several recommendations for reform.

An Evolving Budget Process

Until recently, there has been little detailed analysis of the process by which Ontario's budgets are made. There is no equivalent to David Good's (1980) in-depth study of federal tax policy making, which was informed by scores of interviews with officials and politicians. The literature indicates that, during the early 1980s, Ontario's budget making was an exemplar in the traditional process. Insulated by the convention of secrecy, it was guarded closely by the treasurer and his officials. Limited consultations were held in advance of budgets, but Treasury officials were unable to discuss openly what proposals were under consideration. And, as in Ottawa, line ministries were informed about budget measures that might affect their policy domains only after decisions had been made.[136] During the Davis era (1971–85), the premier usually was not informed about the contents of the budget until the day before it was presented to the legislature.[137] One surmises, then, that tax expenditures were entirely the concern of the Ministry of Treasury and Economics, and specifically of the Tax Policy Branch. There is no evidence suggesting that tax expenditures received any different treatment at Queen's Park than they did in Ottawa.

The budget process soon began to receive greater scrutiny. In 1983, the province experienced its first ostensible breach of budget secrecy (budget documents were found in a garbage can). Moreover, events at the federal level – controversy over the 1981 tax reform budget, the 1982 discussion paper, and the 1983 "leak," when a page of Marc

Lalonde's budget was inadvertently photographed – led officials in Ontario to re-evaluate the appropriateness of strict interpretations of budget secrecy.[138] This rethinking culminated in release of a discussion paper in 1985 by the new Liberal treasurer, Robert Nixon, exploring ways to improve the budget process. It announced, among other things, the government's intention to expand the range of groups invited to pre-budget consultations and to establish a Standing Committee on Economic and Fiscal Affairs to receive pre-budget documentation, hold pre-budget hearings, review tax legislation contained in budgets, and provide recommendations on the fiscal stance. For its part, the government would endeavour to present a fiscal and economic outlook in advance of the budget. The committee was also to review budget secrecy and determine when conventions could be relaxed.[139] Nevertheless, the budget process was still guided largely by the precepts of budget secrecy, which, in turn, buffered the tax policy process from change. The government, however, began to take greater interest in publicizing tax expenditures, releasing accounts in 1986, 1988, and 1989.

Changes with considerable potential for allowing tax expenditure thinking followed arrival of the NDP in power in September 1990. The new government presented its first budget in late April 1991. Even before then, key ministers and advisers were dissatisfied with the process. There was a feeling that decision making was not linked to government priority setting, that time-consuming pre-budget consultations did not inform final decisions, and that the budget was not accompanied by a good communications plan.[140] Internal reviews were launched, and efforts were made to modify the process.

The first change, announced with the 1991 budget, was formation of a cabinet committee called the Treasury Board. Its purpose was to focus on budget policy and to review programs from a corporate perspective. A complementary reorganization shifted the bureau responsible for managing expenditures from the Management Board Secretariat to the Ministry of Treasury and Economics (MTE). That was a promising development for those interested in improved scrutiny of tax expenditures, because the same ministry would oversee both tax expenditures and direct expenditures. The second change transformed budget consultations.[141] Rather than simply broadening the types of groups invited to discuss budget issues, the plan was to have roundtable consultations to get group representatives talking to each other as well as to the treasurer and other ministers and to provide them with as much documentation as necessary. To encourage constructive discussions, it was decided that the roundtables should proceed on a sectoral basis, so that groups would have common policy interests, and that line ministries would be there to listen and field questions. Although these reforms were not intended specifically to deal with tax expenditures, they are conducive to exploring tax expenditures more fully. They bring ministers and officials responsible for both tax expenditures and direct expenditures to the table to respond to theconcerns of outside groups about the merits and deficiencies of existing programs.

A final outcome of the first budget cycle, and the rapidly deteriorating economy, was the decision to launch program reviews. The reviews were part of the new Treasury Board's mandate to get beyond incremental adjustments to established programs. The intention was to determine whether programs were relevant to the priorities of the government, were focused properly, were the most efficient means for accomplishing the policy objective, and offered good value for money.[142] The cabinet approved reviews of over 20 program areas, covering almost 80 specific programs and spanning 14 ministries. A lead ministry was designated for each program review, and a team of officials was appointed with representation from MTE, the Cabinet Office, pertinent line ministries, and the Management Board Secretariat. Responsibility for coordinating reviews fell to MTE's Office of Economic Policy. The reports, containing options and recommendations, were to be sent from the line ministry for review by the Treasury Board and subsequently to the Priorities and Planning Board. Along with the normal estimates and new initiatives, these recommendations were to feed into the 1992 budget process.

These program reviews allowed evaluation of tax expenditures alongside other programs in functional areas. However, few of the reviews encompassed tax expenditures. Two exceptions were Ontario Tax Grants for Seniors, discussed below, and the province's Research and Development superallowance, because it was integrated into the allocation for the Technology Fund. Other tax expenditures related to business assistance were not investigated, perhaps because the Fair Tax Commission had initiated a review of Ontario's tax system and because of the confidentiality of tax-related information.

All these developments – creation of the Treasury Board, administrative reorganization, sectoral consultations, and program reviews – were attempts to grapple with difficult fiscal challenges and to ensure that the government's priorities were reflected in program and budgetary decisions. While not designed specifically to address tax expenditures, they offered a climate potentially more receptive to the kind of analysis advocated by tax expenditure reformers. To get a closer look at the implications for tax expenditures, I examined two recent policy initiatives by the Ontario government. The first involved conversion of Ontario Tax Grants for Seniors to a tax credit. This social policy program has existed, in one form or another, for two decades. The impetus for change emerged out of a program review. The second case reviewed establishment of the Ontario Investment and Worker Ownership Program. It complemented the first case because it dealt with an economic and regional policy issue, received impetus from outside MTE, and concerned an entirely new program. In both instances, tax expenditures were handled differently from what the literature on traditional tax policy making would have led us to anticipate.

Case One: Ontario Tax Credits for Seniors

Ontario governments have sought to provide relief for the property tax and sales tax for over 20 years. In order to deliver the benefit, they have shifted back and forth between tax expenditures and direct expenditures. Even though MTE always had responsibility for policy development in this area, policy on the structure and delivery of benefits changed, in response to evolving economic and demographic pressures, as well as political calculations about the visibility of the benefit. This case also illustrates that tax expenditures do not always reduce the progressivity of the tax system but can be employed to increase it.

The antecedents to the seniors tax credit emerged as a solution to what Queen's Park considered key deficiencies of federal tax reform during the late 1960s and early 1970s. The province felt that Ottawa had focused on national tax issues and had failed to assess the combined impact of municipal, provincial, and national tax systems on lower-income households. Ontario had in 1968 put in place a basic-exemption shelter grant calibrated to average municipal taxation and a supplementary grant for recipients of the guaranteed Income Supplement (GIS), but it sought to ease the burden of property and sales taxes on those with lower incomes through tax credits, for which people would not need incomes in order to benefit.[143] In 1972, the government introduced its property tax credit after Ottawa agreed to collect taxes while the province provided financing. Ontario rightly claimed that this innovative system would be more progressive and simpler to administer. The tax credit replaced the basic exemption; both homeowners (in principal residences) and renters were eligible. Pensioners would continue to receive their supplementary grants.[144]

Queen's Park planned also to extend the approach to the retail sales tax and health premiums, once the "kinks" had been worked out during the first year or so.[145] From 1973, a new tax credit alleviated the burden of higher energy taxes and sales taxes on lower-income households. At the same time, property tax credits increased and a pensioner tax credit replaced supplementary grants. The latter credit was taxed back at a rate of 1 per cent of taxable income. Reflecting the inflationary spiral, the amount allocated to the tax credit system increased from $305 million to $375 million.[146] By the mid-1970s, then, Ontario had a fully elaborated system of tax credits. An internal study in 1977 indicated that the reforms had indeed provided tax relief to lower-income households (Ontario, Ministry of Treasury, 1977). While Queen's Park had not persuaded Ottawa to adopt a similar approach, it launched and institutionalized the innovation within its own jurisdiction.

Despite the apparent success of the program, treasury officials soon began to consider alternatives. Seniors got benefits after a year's delay, caused by reliance on the income tax system, and seniors, though making up only 11 per cent of tax filers, claimed 40 per cent of the credits. Moreover, the credit provided only partial offset, reducing property tax by just over half. Meanwhile, the province continued to consolidate municipal and provincial programs. It increased the basic credit and the maximum amount that seniors could receive, partly to replace a school tax credit and municipal elderly residents assistance.[147] Just two years later, it dramatically overhauled its delivery of benefits to seniors. While not rejecting the larger tax credit system,[148] it converted seniors' tax credits for property and sales taxes into direct grants, at a cost of $214 million.

This reform had clear political advantages – seniors would receive benefits twice a year, as soon as they were eligible. As well, seniors without taxable income would not have to file income tax forms each year. The changes defused growing anger among seniors who felt that they should not be paying taxes for education. While the government could not overtly agree to this position, since it believed that funding education was a responsibility of all taxpayers, the reforms increased the exemption, effectively lowering the tax burden on seniors. On a completely different level, the treasurer, Frank Miller, was increasingly irritated by Ottawa's resistance to provincial proposals to modify the tax system; it claimed that such changes would violate the tax collection agreements. He commissioned a study on revamping and/or withdrawing from the agreements, and perhaps conversion of seniors' tax credits to grants reflected this thinking. However, there were costs to administering grants – a bureau was needed to compile the list of eligible seniors, receive applications, calculate benefits, and mail cheques twice a year.

The seniors program remained intact until the early 1990s. Several developments, including pressures that had been building for some time, combined to press Bob Rae's government to reconsider the program. First, with over 80 full-time members of staff, administrative costs associated with delivering grants increased to over $3 million and, during peak periods, to more than $100 million. Second, inflation and rising municipal taxes reduced the offset provided by the grants to one-third rather than one-half of the typical senior's property tax bill. Third, the government was feeling financially squeezed and had to reconsider all programs. The first program reviews in late 1991 evaluated seniors' tax grants.

The program review meant that, for the first time, MTE did not have a monopoly on analysis of the problem and weighing of options. Although MTE was designated the lead ministry, rethinking grants engaged several line ministries, the Office of Seniors Issues, and the ministries of Community and Social Services, Municipal Affairs, and Revenue. The value of broader participation was demonstrated by some of the issues addressed. For example, how would the reform interact with the provincial drug plan and health care system, and how should the province factor in seniors' steadily rising retirement incomes? Several options were considered, including making the benefits taxable,[149] granting tax credits if an income test were met,[150] and adopting a refundable tax credit. In the end, after numerous briefings by officials to the Cabinet Committee on Social Policy, followed by more to the Treasury Board and the Priorities and Planning Board, the government decided to replace seniors' grants with refundable property and sales tax credits delivered to seniors after they completed their income tax returns. Lower-income households would receive increased benefits, while higher-income households would cease receiving benefits – the province projected $100 million in savings overall.[151]

These reforms were announced in the April 1992 budget. The extensive briefings reflected the controversial nature of the decision for a social democratic government – a move away from a de facto universal program. For treasury officials used to working solely with the treasurer and buffered by secrecy, these briefings must have seemed interminable. However, one participant noted that the process helped build broad support for the reforms inside the public service and among ministers. Had the treasurer acted unilaterally on the issue, the initiative probably would have been rejected.

Case Two: Ontario Investment and Worker Ownership Plan

One of the first issues to test Bob Rae's government was the prospect of major industries closing in several small communities. In November 1991, Queen's Park announced its Ontario Investment and Worker Ownership Plan (OIWOP). The purpose of this tax expenditure was to provide incentives for workers to invest in labour-sponsored investment funds, to allow labour organizations to set up those funds, and to permit workers to purchase shares in the enterprises in which they are employed. At first, MTE resisted these ideas and questioned the ability of outside analysts to inform government policy. While the policy initiative was a response to threatened closures of steel mills, the idea had had a long gestation period. Earlier versions of the policy had been broached but rejected within MTE. The impetus for the new proposal came from politicians, and the early analytical push, from the Ministry of Labour (MOL); OIWOP consisted of two programs and implementation involving two ministries – Labour, and Industry, Trade and Technology.

Under David Peterson's Liberals, the Premier's Council on Industrial Strategy sought ways to assist employees to invest in their workplaces and communities. The government indicated that it would support an initiative if labour groups coalesced around a proposal. A study was commissioned, but the inability of key labour groups to agree on a common approach killed the project. At the same time, representatives from the Toronto Stock Exchange lobbied MTE to consider a regime modelled on the Quebec Solidarity Fund. However, MTE officials saw that approach as expensive, inefficient, and potentially regressive vis-à-vis the tax system. Another strand of thought emanated from a small research group supported by labour groups and cooperatives – the Worker Ownership Development Foundation (WODF). During the late 1980s, WODF began exploring cooperative forms of ownership and gravitated towards loan guarantees and subsidies. Finally, the Federal Working Ventures Fund had been recommending labour-sponsored investment vehicles for some time.

Despite growing interest in worker ownership, these ideas did not gain much currency in the government.[152] Nevertheless, one treasury official reported that worker ownership had been considered in every budget process since 1985.

This all changed under the NDP. The Cabinet Office wanted to explore worker ownership as part of a larger attempt to encourage ministries to work cooperatively and investigate partnership models for industrial renewal and promoting investment. The Office of Economic Policy was instructed to work with MOL on this issue. Although research was commissioned, the project lost momentum, in part because of MTE's lack of interest. Crises involving Algoma Steel and Spruce Mills, however, rekindled interest in worker-owned options. MOL hired a former WODF analyst to study worker ownership and lay-off policies, while MTE assigned a junior analyst. (Advocates outside the ministry took this as an affront, but central agencies tend to work in a relatively non-hierarchical manner, and it is not unusual for a junior person to be *the* expert on an initiative.) It was not until May 1991 that treasury officials began asking questions in a concerted fashion, having been prodded by the Premier's Office, and a month later MTE announced publicly that it was considering a policy on worker ownership and would produce a discussion paper by mid-August.

A working group was formed with representatives from MTE's Office of Economic Policy and the Tax Policy Branch and from the ministries of Financial Institutions, Industry, Trade and Technology, Labour, and Revenue. The group analysed different parts of the proposal collectively and communicated with home ministries for comment. Disagreements were not attributed to an overbearing MTE style, even though it was the lead ministry. A discussion paper and draft legislation were prepared by early August, circulated within the government for comment, and then released for public discussion.[153]

The proposal had two parts. The first sought to provide tax credits similar to conventional mutual funds to individuals investing either in investment funds sponsored by labour organizations or in employee groups purchasing a majority interest in an employer's business. Queen's Park proposed a 20 per cent tax credit on the first $3500 invested in any year and further that the federal government match the credit, raising it to 40 per cent. (Ottawa had supported similar programs in other provinces and nationally.) The second part proposed that an employees' group establish a Labour-Sponsored Venture Capital Corporation (LSVCC) to invest in an employer's business. For individual investors, the tax credit was similar to the above, except that they could receive an additional 30 per cent credit on the next $11,500. Again, the government hoped that Ottawa would support the program.

There were several reasons why a tax solution was favoured over subsidies. First, there were strong Canadian precedents, and it seemed that the federal government would support the first part of the proposal. Second, it was difficult to conceive of other ways to encourage individuals to invest, unless one resorted to subsidies. However, trade realities meant that selective grants could be the object of "countervail," and tax incentives were less susceptible to this threat. While the government could have adopted the model of the Quebec Solidarity Fund and could have contributed seed capital, this approach would have required support from the federal government and labour – not likely, given the economic circumstances. The Ontario government chose not to modify or eliminate either the Small Business Development Corporation, which provides equity financing for small business, or the Employee Share Ownership Plan, which assists employees to buy small numbers of shares in companies. Each provides tax-free grants. Queen's Park argued that while the programs ought to be reviewed, and although they have broad objectives similar to OIWOP's, they "operate differently and appeal to different client groups."[154]

Release of the proposal naturally led to lobbying. The deadline for receipt of comments was 26 September 1991. Additional meetings were held with groups after briefs were submitted. Representatives from the financial community advocated relying more heavily on the approach of the Employee Share Ownership Plan, which enabled workers to invest in company shares but effectively left power in the hands of owners and management. While the government kept to its position, one official described the consultation process as "well-focused and helpful" – unlike others in which he had been involved – because the proposal was well-defined and because groups were willing to discuss specific aspects of it. Another official complained about the severe time constraints but acknowledged that if this effort had been attempted within the budget process, there would have been less consultation and the government would have had to use consultation to modify the legislation after the budget. A bill was submitted to the legislature in early November. Many amendments were made to the proposal during the legislative process, but these flowed from the earlier submissions and consultations. For example, the minimum requirement of 50 per cent ownership for LSVCCs was reduced to 40 per cent.

Implementing the program was complicated: MOL was to monitor the operation of funds and regulate individual contributions; Financial Institutions was to monitor funds' adherence to financial regulations; and Industry, Trade and Technology was to determine the extent of labour's ownership in a business. Moreover, the federal government had a key role, too; it sweetened the proposal in February 1992 by matching Ontario's share of the basic tax credit for individuals. However, it did not support the larger tax credit associated with worker ownership funds. Ontario announced enhancements to the program in the budget of 30 April 1992, increasing the maximum credit from $700 to $1000 and raising the asset limit for businesses eligible for LSVCCs. The ownership side ran into difficulties. Except at Spruce Falls, few unions have invested in employers' businesses. One factor could be controversy over the board's role in reviewing applications for establishing LSVCCs. Early data show substantial numbers of workers taking up the investment tax credit.[155] There obviously was a market that had not been tapped into by other investment vehicles. But aside from aggregate number of workers and average take-up falling within predicted range, will labour-sponsored investment plans differ significantly from other investment funds? Are there other, possibly more effective instruments for encouraging ownership and savings by workers? How will the program be evaluated in future? This case thus underscores a key deficiency in policy development for tax expenditures – there is typically little ex ante concern expressed, except superficially, about how the program will be evaluated.

Conclusion: Ontario Practice in Perspective

These cases affirm that tax expenditures rarely command political attention of their own accord. There is always a surfeit of ideas; it takes key problems and political initiative to move one of them high on the policy agenda. But, in stark contrast to how Ontario and Ottawa traditionally make tax policy, the two cases reveal that Ontario tax officials incorporated considerable outside expertise from line ministries when designing OIWOP and considering the shift from grants to tax credits for seniors. Perhaps the most important explanation for this different deliberative style is that analysis took place *outside* the budget process. MTE officials were liberated from the press of budget making and the strictures of budget secrecy.

A more subtle finding is that tax collection agreements with Ottawa seriously constrain how policy makers at Queen's Park handle tax expenditures. The Canadian literature has explored tax expenditures usually from Ottawa's vantage point. Like U.S. state governments, Canadian provinces must cope with changes in passive tax expenditures and seek to tailor tax policy to meet their own interests. Tax collection agreements limit Ontario's options, even though federal policy makers seem more liberal than they have been in the past. The federal interest is to strive for uniformity across provinces, protect the base, and maintain the integrity of the tax system. Agreements that grant provinces tax points in lieu of direct expenditures help control costs and force provinces to weigh carefully alternative instruments for achieving specific policy objectives. In addition, when a province uses Ottawa to implement a tax program, the latter receives 1 per cent of the flow of funds as an administrative fee, and so use of the tax policy instrument is not free of overhead. While tax agreements and federal chauvinism are undoubtedly frustrating to provincial tax policy makers, they may contribute to more informed tax expenditure thinking because other options must be explored.

These findings must be put in perspective. The Ontario Services Tax Credit and OIWOP are not representative of all decision making on tax expenditures. A proper sample would have required far more cases. Both cases, however, deal with recent decisions of the government and provide glimpses of a new style of treasury decision making. Both cases indicate the willingness of MTE officials to work with outsiders when reviewing tax options. This flexibility did not come naturally for MTE officials, who became involved in both initiatives only at the behest of the cabinet. Taking part in more complicated and time-consuming consultations was probably quite frustrating at times, but officials seemed satisfied with the results. However, more open consultation within the government does not remove tensions between MTE and line ministries, particularly as MTE will not relinquish its status as guardian and designer of tax policy.

Instruments and Strategies for Reform

This paper has examined review of tax expenditures in the United States, Canada, and Ontario and has considered the link between tax expenditure reform and tax policy making. This section reviews several broad proposals or instruments that hold promise for increasing the visibility and improving the scrutiny of tax expenditures. The list of proposals is based on a review of practices in all jurisdictions dealt with in this study.

This section clusters the instruments into more fundamental strategic orientations towards reform and sets out four such strategies. Each instrument in effect constitutes a category, however, since the extent of reform and the actors involved can vary considerably. For this reason, new review bodies (such as bureaucratic units, legislative committees, or ongoing commissions) are not listed as separate instruments, since they would have to perform a function involving one of the instruments and thus constitute a variation within any given category. However, different reforms are motivated by different theories of influence. The extent to which such theories seem plausible will inform any assessment of the effectiveness of any regime employed by a country to scrutinize tax expenditures. These strategies can be used in isolation or in combination.

Any reform must anticipate conventional politics as well as change. In other words, proposals must not lose sight of politics as usual in Ontario – for example, intermittent, selective, and ongoing review of tax expenditures as part of the budgetary process or tax reform – as well as larger developments in the budgetary process and public service reform. The final section considers how reform proposals are linked to these developments.

Improving Information on Tax Expenditures

The set of reforms touted most often involves improving the information available on tax expenditures, by publishing tax expenditure accounts, budgets, or reports; including tax expenditures along with direct expenditure estimates; and ensuring that data on tax expenditures inform budget consultations. Such reforms presuppose rational decision making: pertinent data – lists and estimates of tax expenditures –will alert and inform policy makers and the public. Increased knowledge of individual and aggregate costs of tax expenditures will modify future decisions about whether to introduce new tax expenditures or adjust old ones.

Creating a tax expenditure account is a staple for reformers. It aims at making tax expenditures more visible by grouping them together in one document and by indicating the revenue loss associated with each provision. There are, however, several variations on the basic idea. The first has to do with the comprehensiveness of the account. It can be a simple list of tax expenditures or can include statutory authority, policy intent, target groups, revenue loss estimates, and/or alternative means for accomplishing the objective. Accounts may focus on certain categories of tax expenditures. A second variation concerns public versus internal circulation. If the former, will it simply be made public, or will it receive mandatory review? If the latter, the Treasury Board, pertinent cabinet policy committees, program review committees, a legislative committee, or perhaps an ongoing tax reform commission might undertake a review.

Once a tax expenditure account has been developed, the information in it can be used in other ways. For example, data could be categorized by functional policy areas, and relevant tax expenditure figures displayed with the estimates in order to convey more accurately the government's involvement in given sectors. This innovation has been adopted by the state of Massachusetts. The figures as well can inform internal program reviews and pre-budget consultations with outside groups.

Improving Evaluation of Tax Expenditure Programs

A second cluster of reforms also seeks to generate information on existing tax expenditures to inform future decision making. However, rather than simply providing lists and estimates of tax expenditures, these reforms attempt to evaluate their effectiveness and perhaps their comparative advantage. These reforms include attaching sunset procedures to tax expenditures, subjecting tax expenditures to formal evaluation, incorporating tax expenditures in program review, and encouraging reviews by the provincial auditor. The underlying logic is that the best way to learn about the merits of tax expenditures is by experience. The reforms are also consistent with conventional notions of accountability. Moreover, they share with proposals for informational reform a presumption that policy makers will listen to them and then use the findings from evaluations.

Sunset provisions seek to reduce the proliferation of tax expenditures by placing a time limit (say five years) on statutory authority. Once the time limit is reached, and legislators fail to reauthorize the measure, the tax expenditure automatically lapses. The hope is that such arrangements will encourage review of tax expenditures in place and that legislators will reauthorize only those that remain relevant to policy. There are various ways in which sunset provisions can be put in place. First, they could apply to new tax expenditures as they are adopted or apply retroactively to all existing tax expenditures. Second, legislators could attach them to certain kinds of tax measures. Third, the legislature could reauthorize an existing tax expenditure but with different kinds of review to determine how well the provision performed. Since legislative hearings no doubt would be held, the committee's staff could attempt its own evaluation; or the government could be mandated to prepare a report outlining why the measure should be retained or not; or perhaps a more independent body such as a tax reform commission could take on this responsibility.

The next proposal seeks to ensure that every tax expenditure receives scrutiny regularly, similar to what some governments have attempted in the area of regulatory reform. Two related dimensions are the regularity and thoroughness of the review. The deeper the review – going beyond examining a tax expenditure on its own terms and considering other possibilities – the more time and resources required, so it makes sense not to review tax expenditures every year (equivalent to producing an annual comprehensive tax expenditure account) and to consider reviewing each program at least once every three or four years. Who should undertake the review? One approach in Ontario is to create the capacity inside the public service: possibilities include a special unit within MTE's Tax Policy Branch, an MTE unit outside the branch, and an inter-ministerial committee. Alternatively, a non–public service capacity could result from mandating a legislative committee to execute the review or from contracting out the responsibility to a neutral external organization (such as the Canadian Tax Foundation), academics, or a tax reform commission. As well, the Treasury Board, a sectoral cabinet policy committee, or a legislative committee might review completed reports.

A somewhat different approach would incorporate tax expenditures as part of program reviews, to be evaluated as one element of a complex of policies in any given sector. Review of their efficacy, therefore, would be liberated from purely a tax or revenue perspective and would be rooted in an overall, corporate view of the government's goals in particular sectors. Since other programs would be reviewed, it would be easier to assess tax expenditures' effectiveness, efficiency, relevance, and ability to target and easier to consider alternatives. Treasury officials or a wider group representing concerned central and line ministries could carry out the review. Although program reviews are clearly an internal exercise, the findings should be accessible to the legislature and the public.

Finally, the office of the provincial auditor could go beyond reviewing collection and disbursement of public monies to auditing revenue forgone. Tax expenditure programs would receive the same scrutiny as direct expenditure programs. The provincial auditor would, from time to time, examine how certain tax expenditures were administered, evaluate who benefited from them, and consider whether these results were consistent with the original policy intent. The auditor might also monitor review procedures and their effectiveness and consider program alternatives, if consistent in terms of value for money, with stated policy objectives, assessments, and recommendations.

Linking Tax Expenditures to the Budgetary Process

A third group of proposals seeks to integrate tax expenditure decisions into the budgetary process. These reforms are, by design, considerably more coercive. They include capping the amount of revenue forgone through tax expenditures and employing "envelopes" to account for tax expenditures.

These reforms presume that decision makers are unable to constrain and discipline their use of tax expenditure instruments or are vulnerable to the pressures of special interest groups. To embrace these reforms, decision makers must admit that such problems exist; only then could they agree to build new procedures into the decision making. These reforms can work only with sophisticated and reliable techniques for accounting for tax expenditures; otherwise, they will not have the confidence of actors inside and outside government.

The first method proposal seeks to control tax expenditures by limiting the total amount of them granted by the province. If total losses from tax expenditures were to exceed this limit, then the government could be forced to sequester direct expenditures as compensation. The limit could be set in terms of absolute or relative aggregates. In the latter case, what might serve as the denominator –provincial revenues, direct expenditures, or some measure of the province's economic growth? Should indicators be based on forecasts or on firmer figures from the past?

A less focused approach would include tax expenditures as part of sectoral allocations, as did PEMS in Ottawa. Where appropriate, their cost would be assigned to particular sectoral resource envelopes. As the relative cost and performance of the tax expenditure altered, there would be incentives for line ministries in the sector to weigh the merits of retaining the tax expenditure as one of its battery of instruments. At the very least, such use of the tax system would reduce direct expenditure allocations proportionately. Line ministries might exert significant leverage over the decision to eliminate or modify a tax expenditure.

Improving the Design Process

The final cluster of reforms relies less on conventional notions of accounting and accountability but seeks to improve the process by which tax expenditures are designed. Possibilities include consulting line ministries when developing tax policy, opening up budgeting to more outside groups, and developing tax policy outside the budget process.

The premiss is that improving the decision-making process would bring to light additional perspectives on tax expenditure decisions and alternative ways to accomplish a given policy objective. Moreover, this approach may well be the most efficient and effective, because it is a "front-end" investment that could forestall serious mistakes.

One method would necessitate representatives from line ministries being present when tax expenditures are conceived or altered. At base, this is a call for a more open budget process. Invitations would be extended to those ministries that might have tax measures impinging on their sectors to assess the merits of the proposals and, perhaps, offer better alternatives. Representatives from the ministries may offer a better sense of how proposed measures might influence the behaviour of individuals, households, or corporations. The treasurer would not relinquish authority for making final decisions about tax policy and broader budget priorities. Analysis of tax measures occurs not just when budgets are put together, and so consultations with ministries could precede preparation of budgets.

The above proposals focus on expanding "in-house" scrutiny of tax expenditures. How can outside scrutiny be increased? Sectoral roundtables with representatives from all sectors could examine tax expenditures with revenue estimates appended. As a variant, a legislative committee could receive submissions, hold hearings on tax expenditures, and then report to the treasurer as part of the work-up to the budget. A different approach would see tax policy developed outside the budget process, perhaps by wide-ranging commissions such as the Fair Tax Commission, task forces with more focused agendas, or a free-standing tax review commission. All would have the capability to conduct research, invite outside groups to review proposals and suggest alternatives, and submit reports for consideration by the government.

The Context for Tax Expenditure Reform

This study is dedicated to identifying ways to change tax policy making so as to make the tax system fairer and more effective. However, tax expenditure thinking reflects broader themes about improving governance. For example, many of the proposals catalogued above could have been cast as attempts to increase public knowledge and awareness and, in turn, to make policy makers more responsive. To the extent that this is true, then we must be aware of other reform initiatives in progress. Most reform proposals have been floating around for some time and therefore were first advanced against the backdrop of traditional policy processes. It may be possible to capitalize on momentum elsewhere, perhaps by limiting the resources that need to be channelled into tax expenditure reform as such.

We saw above that budgets are not the only opportunity for scrutinizing tax expenditures. There are many mechanisms available outside the budget process, such as discussion papers, task forces, royal commissions, and legislative committees. The most current example, of course, is the Fair Tax Commission. Such reform efforts, although they can produce lasting new concepts and ways of approaching tax issues, are usually episodic. If one expects such mechanisms to emerge every few years, then it is important to consider to what extent they will supplant or overlap reforms intended to review tax expenditures. At the very least, we must ask where the "added value" lies.

Recent developments in the organization of budget processes, at least in Ontario, hold promise for some tax expenditure reforms. As has been seen, the traditional budget process was not conducive to the kind of cross-ministerial perspectives that should be brought to bear on the design of tax expenditures. The effort to bring line ministries and various interested parties into the process on a sectoral basis seems a major step in the right direction. If tax expenditures, old or newly proposed, are put on the table, and if discussion is well-informed, then this information can help shape final budget decisions. However, as Doern (this volume) points out, the shackles of budget secrecy are not yet fully broken, and partaking in roundtable discussions is not a substitute for being in the room where the final trade-offs are made.

Finally, there is the larger movement to reform the public service in Canada. Given the increasing resistance to paying higher taxes and ongoing demand for public programs, governments are searching for new ways to be more productive, efficient, flexible, and innovative. The traditional inclination to control the activities of line ministries is giving way somewhat to delegating of authority and establishing of partnerships. A "client orientation" has emerged in delivery of programs, with interest increasing in the implications of multiple programs from different ministries for particular groups of clients. Moreover, since all areas of government have fewer resources, ministries must find ways to cooperate and share resources and to do away with unnecessary duplication and overlap. These trends – increased lateral thinking within the public service, central agencies less inclined to treat line ministries as subservient, and a focus on the accumulated impact of programs – should create a climate far more receptive to tax expenditure thinking and associated reforms than was the case a decade earlier.

A final comment: proper tax expenditure analysis and review require a different way of doing business – namely, staff would be expected to consult more with the line ministries and the public and to produce more documentation. These are not the only management reforms in train; all of these tasks, newor old, must be accomplished with current or considerably reduced resources. Like other ministries and levels of government, central agency officials are short of resources. Ultimately, the most urgent tasks will receive priority, such as drafting the budget and "fire-fighting" for the minister. Any recommendations for reform must take into account these realities.

Recommendations for Reform

This section sets out eight recommendations for improving the scrutiny of tax expenditures in Ontario for consideration by the Fair Tax Commission and the Government of Ontario. Several criteria were employed as guides for selecting among the proposals reviewed in the previous section and are grouped in four categories and listed below as key questions.

Cost. What is the cost attached to a proposal in terms of resources and person-years? Does this proposal imply one-time only, intermittent, annual, or some other form of regular review? Does the proposal require much information?

Target of reform. Are the reforms designed to inform or modify the behaviour of ministers, MTE (now Finance) officials, and line ministries? Or are they also designed to empower legislators, organized interests, and the public?

Effectiveness. Will the reforms lead to more meaningful review of tax expenditures? Will they draw attention to tax expenditures? Will they create a constituency made up of groups not favoured by certain tax expenditures? Will the reforms produce information that has educational value for groups outside the government?

Integration. Do proposals complement or work against each other? How would a proposal fit in with important government decision-making processes – the tax policy process, the budget process, program reviews, and priority setting?

Individual proposals cannot address all the issues and needs implied by these questions. Each idea for reform (some better than others) deals only with certain facets of the difficulties associated with tax expenditures. Thus the reforms identified below constitute a package. The package as a whole, as well as its constituent elements, requires evaluation. The final sub-section discusses the rationale for the choices and the balance struck in the package.

Eight Proposals for Reform

1. *Publish a Tax Expenditure Account.* An account should be published on a regular basis and should include the objectives of tax expenditures, their statutory authority, and revenue estimates. Such an account has been produced for the Fair Tax Commission with the cooperation of the Ministry of Finance. However, as a reform, it should not stand alone. The account should complement *other* measures that would draw attention to tax expenditures and encourage better analysis of the achievement of policy objectives as well as alternative approaches that may be more effective and efficient. In other words, the account should not be comprehensive or attempt a full-scale review of tax expenditures each year. Rather, its value would be symbolic, identifying a major source of pressure on government finances, and it would serve also as an organizing device and reference, listing the full range of tax expenditures and indicating the relative size of provisions.

2. *Promulgate a Total Revenue Loss Estimate.* This is bound to be the most controversial recommendation. To calculate and promulgate such figures would be thought unscientific or even irresponsible by many analysts inside and outside government. However, policy makers have permitted their analysts to focus on tax expenditure budgets as accounting devices and to debate over precise technical definitions. Working on such details has not added much to the public debate and has muffled the impact of tax expenditure accounting. Policy makers have lost one of their most valuable weapons inthe effort to encourage more responsible tax policy and budgeting. The tax expenditure concept had its greatest impact during the 1970s, when crude attempts were made to estimate total revenue drain. While such estimates did not account for interaction effects, when governments and critics announced that 30 per cent, 50 per cent, or more of revenues had been forgone through tax expenditures, they immediately drew the attention of policy makers and the public to the basic problem. It is for this reason that total revenue-loss figures should be calculated be either discounted by an appropriate amount or accompanied by a "revenue recoverable" estimate, and then be promulgated to the public.

3. *Supplement Budget Documents.* Tax expenditures listed in the account should also be listed in the estimates in specific functional categories so as to indicate all the government programs in that policy domain. Legitimate qualms about the accuracy of revenue estimates relative to direct expenditures should simply be noted in the text. The point is to educate legislators, interests, and the public about the extent of government activity in a given policy domain and to give a sense of the relation between indirect and direct outlays.

4. *Include Tax Expenditures in Program Reviews.* Queen's Park started program reviews to find ways to contain and reduce expenditures and, where possible, to rationalize programs. It is illogical that tax expenditures are not part of this process. Not all tax expenditures can be thought of in terms of particular policy domains, but reviews should include those that can be. Because reviews are selective, not all tax expenditures would be examined each year or be tied closely to the government's priorities. Tax officials will have reservations about outside ministries dictating tax policy. However, if they look at reviews as an opportunity to get other ministries to generate useful data about the relative effectiveness of certain tax expenditures, they

will be gaining much more information. Moreover, it is hard to believe that any treasurer would relinquish the prerogative to determine tax policy.

5. *Sponsor Rotating Evaluations of Tax Expenditures.* This recommendation seeks to go beyond the revenue-based analysis associated with the Tax Policy Branch and to obtain an in-depth, interdisciplinary review of tax expenditures. This work would be similar to program evaluation and would attempt to gauge the impact of tax expenditures on the behaviour of individuals, households, and corporations. To ensure its integrity, the evaluation would be co-sponsored with an independent organization such as the Canadian Tax Foundation and would be submitted to peer review by academics. Officials from the Ministry of Finance (formerly MTE) and pertinent line ministries should also be involved, since they would contribute critical data and valuable perspectives. Once completed, evaluations would complement and feed into program reviews and the budget process.

6. *Inform Budget Roundtables.* The tax expenditure account, program reviews, and evaluations should be available to the budget roundtable discussions. The tax expenditure account will give participants some sense of proportion, while selected program reviews and evaluations should inform certain sectoral discussions.

7. *Selectively Introduce Sunset Clauses.* The evidence is mixed on whether or not sunset legislation promotes effective review and control of tax expenditures. U.S. commentary indicates that legislators, under pressure from special interests, often find it more convenient to extend deadlines or reauthorize tax expenditures without subjecting them to serious scrutiny. Recent provincial experience makes one less pessimistic about the possibilities. Perhaps the parliamentary system buffers governments sufficiently from special interests to ensure some review and, if appropriate, disappearance of one or more measures. Application of sunset procedures to all tax legislation would quickly overload the capacity of the executive, the legislature, and external reviews to weigh carefully the merits of particular tax expenditures and would encourage superficial reviews and pro forma decisions. Accordingly, the government should, on an experimental basis, attach sunset clauses only to legislation supporting new tax expenditures (or substantially modifying of an existing tax expenditure) whose potential for effectiveness or revenue loss is in question. A

standing committee of the legislature could be assigned to hold hearings on and review the performance of the measure.

8. *Involve the Provincial Auditor.* The auditor should be encouraged to take an interest in how tax expenditure programs are administered and evaluated. The auditor would not get heavily involved in reviewing tax expenditures per se, but, rather, would serve notice that tax expenditure programs deserve the same scrutiny required of all government programs. At base, the idea is to create tension and give governments the incentive to act on other recommendations.

Discussion and Rationale

The recommendations above seek, where possible, to work within existing processes and capacities. The approach is eclectic; it adopts informational, design, and evaluative strategies to draw attention continually to tax expenditures and to encourage broader analysis of their effectiveness and alternatives. However, instruments associated with the coercive strategy are rejected.

I rejected the options of placing limits on tax expenditures or including them in envelope allocations largely because conversion of the tax expenditure concept into a reliable and credible accounting device has proved problematic. Moreover, strict limits would reduce government's flexibility in choosing among different instruments to accomplish a given policy objective. Such limits would also reinforce the traditional tax policy process by adding an external constraint but would not influence the way in which tax expenditures are evaluated and designed. Although envelopes encourage policy makers to make trade-offs between tax and direct expenditures, federal experience indicates that only sophisticated accounting techniques can maintain the integrity of the system. Until accounting problems associated with tax expenditures are solved, proposals involving limits of any kind are bound to encourage "end-runs" and lead to a variety of accounting games.

These proposals recognize the authority and power of the treasury and avoid trying to establish alternative organizations. Rather, they presume the paramountcy of the Ministry of Finance and its Tax Policy Branch in tax policy and seek to take advantage of the ministry's greater receptivity of late to outside contributions. There should be no need to establish specific processes for reviewing new and old tax expenditures when pre-budget consultations, program reviews, and better internal consultation across ministries are already in train. Even the recommendation of regular external review of tax expenditures presumes that the primary client will be the treasurer and top officials, and it recognizes that the ministry will monopolize critical data and expertise. This strategy will flounder, however, if a treasurer decides to revert to a more traditional posture when developing tax policy. While this is possible, one has to consider the benefits and costs of unilateralism and anticipatory policy making (think of the 1981 federal tax reform budget!) to see that treasurers may not be anxious to turn back the clock.

One important criticism of this approach is that it plays down the role of the legislature. Legislative review of the tax expenditure account and other analyses were not recommended because the government has little incentive to take such reviews seriously. A related problem is that legislative committees typically do not have much analytical capacity, and it is difficult to see how this problem could be remedied in a cost-effective manner vis-à-vis tax policy. Generally, committees function better as a forum, and there is no reason why they could not be allowed to review the studies produced by the ministry or outside actors at the behest of the treasurer. Some have argued that the legislature should get more resources.[156] But to increase the capacity of legislative committees involves a larger set of issues and institutional reform well beyond the scope of this study. Moreover, the legislature is already active in pre-budget process consultations, and, if the recommendation to engage the provincial auditor is adopted, so too will be the Public Accounts Committee.

The idea of regular comprehensive reviews of tax expenditures was rejected because it would require vast resources, the results would probably not be used in any given year, and the system might become inured to the reviews. This study recommends production of an annual tax expenditure account because evidence from other jurisdictions has indicated that this can be a relatively inexpensive endeavour, a ready reference tool, and a means of giving staff a broader perspective of the tax system. Moreover, a tax expenditure account and a total revenue-loss figure will function as useful, but relatively cheap symbols that will dovetail with politics and processes that usually entertain tax reform intermittently and selectively.

However, we must put these recommendations in context. Some would argue that, in the end, it does not matter what kind of institutional and procedural reforms are adopted, the crucial element of the recipe is political resolve to turn attention to systematic reviewing of tax expenditures. In other words, although the reforms should improve the scrutiny of tax expenditures in Ontario and provide support for policy makers and interests who want intelligent decisions, none of the recommendations can substitute for political will.

Conclusion

In order to develop a set of recommendations to improve the scrutiny of tax expenditures in Ontario, this study examined how tax expenditures are currently examined in the province and investigated the experience of other jurisdictions in and outside Canada. The research and analysis were driven by two premises. First, reform proposals must anticipate the political realities of tax and budgetary policy making, since reforms that do not mesh well with these larger processes are not likely to have much impact. Second, advocates of reform must have realistic views about the likely effect that changes to the tax expenditure process will have on tax reform.

The study began by introducing the tax expenditure concept. It also ventilated the concerns that many reformers have had about tax expenditures – that they corrode the progressivity and simplicity of the tax system, do not receive sufficient scrutiny, since they are designed in closed processes; and need to be weighed against other policy instruments. Embracing the above concerns, tax expenditure thinking goes further but also seeks to remedy the problems created by tax authorities who, fearing to lose control, are reluctant to allow greater scrutiny of tax expenditures and more input into their design. The tax expenditure concept was diffused rapidly during the 1970s and early 1980s. However, as a technical and accounting tool, it has had problems. Has diffusion of the concept, whether comprehensive or selective, led also to tax reform? Highly fragmentary evidence at the international level suggests that while significant tax reform, consistent with tax expenditure thinking, did occur during the 1980s, it is difficult, because of the many other factors at work, to attribute the changes primarily to the arrival of the concept just a few years earlier.

The U.S. experience is instructive because the tax expenditure concept emerged out of the federal Treasury department and was institutionalized in the federal budgetary process during the 1970s. Moreover, close to half the states have engaged in some form of tax expenditure reporting, although no more than 20 produce accounts regularly. Experiences of state and federal governments attempting to change processes provide our first glimpses of the politics of tax expenditure reform. We saw how tax committees avoided relinquishing responsibility to review tax expenditures regularly and prevented direct linkages to the budgetary process. Despite the major federal tax reform of 1986, which seemed consistent with the precepts of tax expenditure thinking, reporting of tax expenditures did not figure prominently in the debate, but a single study identifying key beneficiaries of tax expenditures triggered considerable indignation. Many observers argue that tax expenditure accounts and thinking have influenced tax policy making indirectly, by shaping perceptions rather than by feeding directly into the deliberations of tax reformers.

The Canadian government's attempts to improve the scrutiny of tax expenditures can help us anticipate the politics of tax expenditure reform in a parliamentary system. David Good's (1980) study demonstrated how traditional tax policy and budgetary processes are not conducive to the kind of analysis advocated by tax expenditure reformers. We examined the emergence of tax expenditure accounts and the PEMS budget system during the late 1970s; the latter was lauded in international literature for accounting for tax expenditures explicitly in expenditure allocations. We noted the mixed records of successive governments in designing tax policy and launching reforms consistent with tax expenditure thinking. Like the U.S. example, there is little evidence to suggest that tax expenditure thinking had a direct influence on these developments, although the concepts were no doubt employed by many policy analysts. Finally, the attitude of tax officials to tax expenditure thinking was highlighted by the early resistance of officials in the Department of Finance to the auditor general's recommendations to review tax expenditure programs systematically. Moreover, not long after creating a dedicated unit for this purpose, the department disbanded the unit, much to the chagrin of the Public Accounts Committee, as a cost-saving measure.

The next section provided a brief survey of provincial experience in monitoring tax expenditures; like state counterparts, several provinces began reviewing tax expenditures in a systematic fashion – British Columbia and Saskatchewan during the early 1980s and Manitoba during mid-decade. Ontario produced tax expenditure accounts in 1986, 1988, and 1989 and found other ways to publicize selected tax expenditures late in the decade. Each of these provinces produced moderately comprehensive accounts, although only Saskatchewan did so regularly. That provinces with considerably less tax-analytical capacity than Ontario have managed to produce accounts suggests that the problem is less one of capacity and more one of political and bureaucratic will. That Ontario, Manitoba, and British Columbia failed to produce accounts consistently demonstrates that such reforms have limited constituencies. Other interesting findings emerged from the survey of provincial practices. First, Nova Scotia and British Columbia have experimented with sunset legislation on tax expenditures. Second, British Columbia (during the early 1980s) and the provincial auditor of Ontario in (1987) have advocated that governments provide total revenue-loss figures for tax expenditures, while recognizing that these figures will be overstated because of interactions.

While Ontario has not been a leader in tax expenditure analysis, it does appear to be in the forefront in opening up budget deliberations and including more ministries in tax policy development. Two rounds of program review as well as two case studies on the handling of particular tax expenditure initiatives during the early 1990s indicate that the Ministry of Treasury and Economics (MTE), at the behest of a new NDP government, expanded its deliberations to include officials from other ministries. This approach was quite time-consuming and frustrating when compared to traditional tax policy making, since it required tax policy officials in MTE to develop different skills. There seems to be a sense, however, that a more open deliberative process has resulted in policy more acceptable to the government, and neither the treasurer nor his officials relinquished authority for developing tax policy.

The final sections were devoted to identifying the range of reform proposals and to recommending a workable package of reforms. I rejected reforms associated with coercion – placing limits on tax expenditures and introducing budget "envelopes," because most experts have found the tax expenditure concept wanting as an accounting device. Some reforms, such as publication of a tax expenditure account and an aggregate revenue-loss figure, are intended to increase the profile of tax expenditures and to improve the flow of information; others simply seek to ensure that the data appear in different venues, such as the main estimates and the sectoral roundtable discussions established for budget consultations. While rejecting wholesale scrutiny of all tax expenditure programs, I recommended reviews outside the budget process and that governments tie tax expenditures more closely to their priorities by including them in program reviews, funding independent evaluations of them, and selectively applying sunset legislation. Finally, the provincial auditor would be given the mandate to monitor the quality of review of tax expenditures.

These reform proposals are not expensive and are appropriate for decisions made intermittently and often diffusely. Rather than trying to create a parallel process and new institutions for reviewing tax expenditures – ones that will probably be eclipsed or ignored by budgetary and program review processes – the recommendations attempt to tap into and inform those processes. While the proposed reforms are not likely to lead to watershed tax reforms, they will educate policy makers and the public about the existence of tax expenditures and encourage them to explore the effectiveness of such programs and perhaps to consider whether policy objectives could be accomplished more efficiently and more effectively with alternative instruments. These reforms will not lead to a consensus as to what constitutes "good" or "bad" tax expenditures, but it is hoped that they will be attractive to governments of any ideological persuasion concerned not only about the integrity and effectiveness of the tax system but also about the relation of tax policy to government intervention in every policy domain.

Notes

1 I would like to acknowledge the helpful comments of Allan M. Maslove and an anonymous reviewer that led to several improvements in this paper. I especially want to thank officials not only at Queen's Park but also in the Canadian and U.S. governments, several provincial, territorial, and state governments, and at the OECD for responding to requests for confidential personal or telephone interviews and for sending documents. Finally, I would like to thank Jeff Goodyear for his research assistance.

2 See Organisation for Economic Cooperation and Development (OECD) (1984, 60).

3 See also McDaniel and Surrey (1985, 4).

4 See OECD (1984, 7).

5 One can use simple accounting estimates for either revenue forgone or revenue gain or employ more sophisticated techniques that model the response of taxpayers to tax policy changes and interactions with other parts of the tax code.

6 OECD (1984, 19).

7 Ibid. (12).

8 Peters (1991, chap. 9) on "Tax Reform."

9 Ibid. (273–76).

10 Ibid. (276–82).

11 Surrey (1973).

12 See Benker (1986, 404) and Hebert (1984, 42).

13 See Hebert (1984, 42).

14 The tax, authorization, and appropriations committees in both chambers developed policy largely in isolation from each other. The only coherence was, ironically, provided by the president's budget. See Ippolito (1978).

15 The seniority system assigned leadership to older, more conservative representatives, who, having a virtual monopoly on procedural tools, could dictate policy development. During the early 1970s, several procedural changes were made by the Democratic caucus of the House of Representatives, such as increasing the number of subcommittees and requiring all chair appointments to receive caucus approval rather than simply being selected by the Democratic leadership. These reforms altered not only the politics of the Democratic-controlled House but also the equilibrium between the House and the Senate.

16 The first OMB account appeared in fiscal year 1976.

17 For these figures, see Benker (1986, 404). For similar figures on Michigan, see Michigan, House Fiscal Agency (1990, 5).

18 However, the reports often did not emerge until several years later. See Benker (1986, 407–8).

19 A survey conducted in 1984 by the U.S. Advisory Commission on Intergovernmental Relations indicated that 17 states were producing comprehensive or partial tax expenditure reports (Benker 1986). Subsequent surveys confirm these early figures but may understate the number of states involved. A survey sponsored by the National Conference of State Legislators (NCSL) in October 1984 reported that 19 states had engaged in some form of tax expenditure reporting – about twice as many as five years earlier (Gold and Nesbary 1988). In 1987, New York state's Legislative Commission on Public-Private Cooperation (LCPP) reviewed 21 reports produced by executive and legislative agencies in 19 states (Edwards 1988). More recently, Michigan's House Fiscal Agency (1990) reported that 17 states required annual tax expenditure reports, and Harris and Hicks (1992) observe that 21 periodically issue reports. However, the latter study focused on ten states that had issued at least three reports covering major taxes.

While these studies add credence to the first, suggesting that only two more states have systematically addressed tax expenditures, closer review indicates that each study understates the total number. For example, the NCSL study does not count four states mentioned in the first, refers to six additional states (Alabama, Arkansas, Florida, Indiana, Kentucky, and Texas), and notes that, at the time of writing, two more states

(Illinois and New York) were proposing some form of reporting. My calculations suggest that at least 25 states have investigated and/or adopted tax expenditure accounting.

20 See Gold and Nesbary (1988, 885).

21 See Benker (1986, 407).

22 Ibid. (409) reported that only Missouri and South Carolina did so, while Gold and Nesbary (1988, 885) mentioned that four legislatures did – California, Indiana, Kentucky, and Missouri.

23 Benker (1986, 413).

24 Confidential telephone interview.

25 Confidential telephone interviews.

26 See Michigan, House Fiscal Agency (1990, 25).

27 See Gold and Nesbary (1988, 888).

28 As a result, the legislature began to explore alternative approaches to handling tax expenditures. In late 1983, the State Assembly Committee on Revenue and Taxation held hearings on a bill that would require more stringent procedures. See Lindquist (1983).

29 Benker (1986, 415).

30 See California, Office of the Legislative Analyst (1984, 135).

31 It was at this time that the governor complained that such reports were costly and did not influence policy making and recommended that the account should be either circumscribed or eliminated. See Gold and Nesbary (1988, 887).

32 For more details, see California, Legislative Analyst's Office (1991a, 113–22).

33 Benker (1986, 415).

34 See ibid. (415). In 1990, Michigan's House Fiscal Agency issued a detailed report on tax expenditures and offered an extensive set of recommendations for improving tax expenditure reviews. A legislative task force, with representation from the tax and fiscal (budget) committees, reviewed the report and responded with its own recommendations.

35 Salamone (1988, 28).

36 Benker (1986, 415).

37 From Alice Rivlin's testimony to the House Rule Committee in 1981. See Hebert (1984, 43).

38 United States, Congressional Budget Office (1988, 7).

39 Ibid. (8).

40 Richardson (1988, 26).

41 From Rivlin in Hebert (1984, 42).

42 White and Wildavsky (1989, 431).

43 For one perspective, see Wildavsky (1980).

44 To sequester is to impose an across-the-board reduction, whereas an impoundment is a reduction of authorized funding for particular programs.

45 Other measures included imposing sequester orders if the president and Congress became deadlocked and moving onto an accelerated budget timetable. See White and Wildavsky (1989, 516).

46 Ibid. (458).

47 Neubig (1988, 248).

48 See Birnbaum and Murray (1987) and White and Wildavsky (1989, chap. 20), "Counterpoint: The Improbable Triumph of Tax Reform."

49 White and Wildavsky (1989, 481).

50 Hildred and Pinto (1990).

51 This was a key obstacle early in the effort to reform the tax code; the agreement by Rostenkowski and others to retain the provision was pivotal in securing support for other elements of the package. See Birnbaum and Murray (1987, 128–30).

52 See, for example, Birnbaum and Murray (1987) and White and Wildavsky (1989).

53 Gold and Nesbary (1988, 887) drew on comments from California's Department of Finance to encapsulate the experience of the states: "Even the sunsetting recommendation ... has proved to be ineffective since a tax expenditure once enacted is easily reenacted upon its expiration. Special interest groups have been too effective in maintaining their special privileges to achieve any significant reform."

54 Birnbaum and Murray (1987, 12–13).

55 Michigan, House Fiscal Agency (1990, 25).

56 Neubig (1988, 240).

57 Richardson (1988, 27).

58 Confidential telephone interview.

59 This does not mean, however, that these states do not take tax expenditures seriously; some may have decided not to rely on formal review mechanisms.

60 Indeed, Gold and Nesbary (1988, 888) think it more important to ensure that policy makers have available an adequate number of well-trained staff: "The preparation of a tax expenditure budget makes sense as part of a well-balanced continuing policy of fiscal oversight, but it is no substitute for adequate financial support of Revenue Department and legislative tax research staffs."

61 See Richardson (1988, 25); Gold and Nesbary (1988, 885 and 888); Benker (1986, 415); and OECD (1984). The author was asked to provide testimony on PEMS and tax expenditures to the California legislature in the early 1980s; see Lindquist (1983).

62 See Drache (1978); d'Aquino, Doern, and Blair (1979); Good (1980); Hartle (1982); Canada (1982); Lindquist (1985); Canada (1985a); Maslove, Prince, and Doern (1986); Savoie (1990); and Doern, Maslove, and Prince (1988); and for citations of all the studies by the Canadian Tax Foundation on this subject, see Canadian Tax Foundation Committee on the Budget Process (1986).

63 Good's study (1980) did generate some controversy. See Doern and Phidd (1983, 300–5) for pertinent citations and a brief review of the debate.

64 Drache (1978, 11).

65 Savoie (1990, 92–93).

66 Savoie states that these arrangements lowered EPF outlays from 10.2 per cent to 7.1 per cent in 1977–78 and the cost of childcare tax credits from a projected $2.1 billion outlay to $650 million. See Savoie (1990, 162).

67 See comments of "01" opposite Hartle (1982, 15); and OECD (1984, 36).

68 Doug Hartle asserted that the Department of Finance sought to ward off further assaults on the Treasury, although an observer argues that the research had recently been completed and that the time – presumably the change of government, the shift to a new cabinet and budgetary decision-making system, and a tight economy – was right. See Hartle (1982, 15).

69 See Savoie (1990, 93–94) and OECD (1984, 37).

70 On this point, see French (1980); Van Loon (1984); and Savoie (1990).

71 Poddar (1988, 265).

72 Gillespie (1991, 199).

73 Lindquist (1985, 14).

74 See Committee on the Budget Process (1982) and Canada, Department of Finance (1982).

75 Lindquist (1985).

76 These modifications were made in December 1981, June 1982, and October 1982, respectively. See Gillespie (1991, 202).

77 On this episode, see the case study on reform of the tax policy process in Lindquist (1989, passim).

78 In the ultimate "end-run" a spending minister would persuade cabinet colleagues that a proposal was a government initiative, and therefore should be funded out of the policy reserve and not the pertinent envelope.

79 See Savoie (1990, 323); and Doern (1989).

80 On the corrosion of PEMS, see Lindquist (1991).

81 For details on its genesis and the impact of the program review, see Wilson (1988); Hartle (1988, chap. 10); and Savoie (1990, 132–42).

82 Canada (1985a).

83 Savoie (1990, 136).

84 Wilson (1988, 37).

85 Savoie (1990, 136).

86 Doern (1989).

87 Another possible twist was to treat tax credits as taxable income, so that individuals with higher incomes would pay back some or all of the credit, thereby preserving the universality of a program for symbolic reasons while targeting its benefits.

88 See Doern (1989, 91–92). The Social Policy Reform Group (SPRG) was a coalition of social advocacy and research organizations that had mobilized to assert collective pressure on the newly elected Conservative government through consensus positions. See Social Policy Reform Group (1987).

89 Gillespie (1991, 205).

90 Those tax expenditures included the following: decreasing the dividend tax credit, capital cost allowances, and the lifetime capital gains exemption; tightening up of investment tax credits; providing write-offs on Multiple Unit Residential Buildings (MURBs), films, earned depletion, and other business and professional expenses; delaying increase of RRSP contribution limits; and eliminating the investment deduction and the standard employment deduction. See ibid. (205 and 322 n. 69).

91 The Federal Sales Tax Review Committee appointed by Allan MacEachen recommended dropping of the wholesale sales tax proposal and that the Department of Finance seriously consider a value-added tax similar to that of many European countries. See ibid. (220–21).

92 Savoie (1990, 94).

93 Doern (1989).

94 McQuaig (1987).

95 On this episode, see ibid., particularly chap. 9, "Tax Credits for Sale."

96 Elkin (1989).

97 See Canada, Public Accounts Committee (PAC) (1991b).

98 Savoie (1990, 94).

99 The papers and commentary are contained in Bruce (1988).

100 Gorbet (1991a).

101 Bennett (1991).

102 Gauthier (1991a).

103 See Gorbet's testimony in PAC (1991a).

104 PAC (1991b, 7).

105 Gauthier (1991b).

106 See Gauthier (1992); see also Gorbet (1992).

107 PAC (1992).
108 Welsh (1992).
109 PAC (1992).
110 British Columbia, Ministry of Finance (1980a, 1981, 1982).
111 Ibid. (1980b).
112 Confidential interview.
113 British Columbia, Ministry of Finance (1981, 30).
114 Ibid. (43).
115 Confidential interview.
116 Saskatchewan (1981, 1990, 1992a).
117 Confidential interview.
118 Confidential interview.
119 See Saskatchewan (1992b, 90–93).
120 Manitoba (1986; 1987; 1988).
121 Confidential interview.
122 Confidential interview.
123 See Ontario, Ministry of Treasury, and Economics (1991a, b).
124 Ontario (1983, 10).
125 Ibid. (14).
126 Ontario, Ministry of Treasury and Economics (MTE) (1985).
127 MTE (1986).
128 Ontario, Office of the Provincial Auditor (1987, 18).
129 Ibid.
130 Confidential interviews.
131 MTE (1988b, 1989, 1990, 1991b, 1992); Ontario, Ministry of Finance (1993).
132 Confidential interviews.
133 Confidential interview.
134 Quebec, Ministères des Finances et Conseil du trésor (1993, 97–114).
135 Ibid. (chap. 6).
136 Lindquist (1985).
137 Prince (1989, 114).
138 See Doern (1993).
139 MTE (1985).
140 This response to the process bears a striking similarity to a prominent explanation for the failure of the federal budget of November 1981.
141 Daigneault (1993).
142 Confidential interview.
143 Ontario, Department of Treasury and Economics (1971) and MTE (1969, 56).
144 MTE (1972, 12–13 and 77–99).
145 Ibid. (93).

146 Ontario, Ministry of Treasury, Economics, and Intergovernmental Affairs (1974, 3–4).
147 Ontario (1978).
148 However, the province did place restrictions on the property tax credit. For example, individuals living in properties exempt from property taxation could no longer claim the credit, and the province would not incorporate local user fees for improvements into its definition of property tax.
149 This option was rejected because most of the tax revenues would have gone to Ottawa.
150 This option was rejected because of too long a period before receipt of benefits.
151 See MTE (1992, 18).
152 The Worker Ownership Development Foundation had done work for two ministries – Labour, and Industry, Trade and Technology – and had also dealt with two others – Financial Institutions, and Consumer and Corporate Relations – regarding regulations governing cooperatives.
153 See MTE (1991a).
154 See ibid. (23).
155 By late summer, one MTE official reported that preliminary data obtained from Revenue Canada indicated that about 10,000 individuals had invested $28 million – roughly $2800 per person on average. So the program was well on target.
156 This argument has been made by an anonymous reviewer of this study.

Bibliography

Alberta. Alberta Legislature. 1985. *Report of the Auditor General for the Year ended March 31, 1985*
– 1986. *Annual Report of the Auditor General 1985–86*
– 1987. *Annual Report of the Auditor General 1986–87*
– 1988. *Annual Report of the Auditor General 1987–88*
Alberta. Alberta Treasury. 1981. *1981 Budget Address*. Alberta: Queen's Printer for Alberta, April
– 1990. *1990 Budget Address*. Alberta: Queen's Printer for Alberta, March
Benker, K.M. 1986. "Tax Expenditure Reporting: Closing the Loophole in State Budget Oversight." *National Tax Journal*, 39 (4): 403–17
Bennett, I.E. 1991. "Tax Evaluation: Re-Organization." Memo to Tax Policy Branch staff in the (federal) Department of Finance, 15 July
Bergeron, M. 1983. "Some Misunderstandings about Tax Expenditures." *Canadian Public Policy*, 9 (1): 140–43

Bird, R.M., and J.M. Mintz, eds. 1992. *Taxation to 2000 and Beyond*. Canadian Tax Paper No. 93. Toronto: Canadian Tax Foundation

Birnbaum, J.H., and A.S. Murray. 1987. *Showdown at Gucci Gulch: Lawmakers, Lobbyists, and the Unlikely Triumph of Tax Reform*. New York: Random House

Block, S.M., and Allan M. Maslove. Forthcoming. "Ontario Tax Expenditures." In *Taxes as Instruments of Public Policy*, ed. Allan M. Maslove. Fair Tax Commission, Research Studies. Toronto: University of Toronto Press

British Columbia. Ministry of Finance. 1980a. *Medium-Term Economic Outlook and Fiscal Analysis*. British Columbia: Ministry of Finance

– 1980b. *The Budget, 1980: Budget Papers, Presented ... March 11, 1980*. British Columbia: Ministry of Finance

– 1981. *Background Papers to the 1981 Budget*. British Columbia: Ministry of Finance

– 1982. *Background Papers to the 1982 Budget*. British Columbia: Ministry of Finance

Brooks, N., ed. 1988. *The Quest for Tax Reform*. Toronto: Carswell

Bruce, N., ed. 1988. *Tax Expenditures and Government Policy*. Kingston, Ont.: John Deutsch Institute for the Study of Economic Policy

California. Legislative Analyst's Office (LAO). 1991a. *Analysis of the 1991–92 Tax Expenditure Budget: Overview and Detailed Compendium of Individual Tax Expenditure Programs*. May

– 1991b. *The 1991–92 Budget: Perspectives and Issues*. Sacramento

California. Office of the Legislative Analyst. 1984. *The 1984–85 Budget: Perspectives and Issues*. Sacramento

Canada. Department of Finance. 1980. *Tax Expenditure Account*. Ottawa: Supply and Services Canada, December

– 1982. *The Budget Process: A Paper on Budget Secrecy and Proposals for Broader Constitution*. Ottawa: Supply and Services Canada, April

– 1985a. *Account of the Cost of Selective Tax Expenditures*. Ottawa: Supply and Services Canada

– 1985b. *The Budget Process: Proposals for Improvement*. Ottawa: Supply and Services Canada, May

– 1992. *Government of Canada Personal Income Tax Expenditures*. Ottawa: Supply and Services Canada, December

Canada. Office of the Auditor General. 1986. *Federal Government Reporting Study*. A Joint Study by the Office of the Auditor General of Canada and the United States General Accounting Office. Ottawa: Office of the Auditor General

– Canada Public Accounts Committee (PAC). House of Commons. 1991a. Minutes of Proceedings and Evidence of the Standing Committee on Public Accounts. Issue No. 6, 3 and 8 October 1991

- 1991b. Minutes of Proceedings and Evidence of the Standing Committee on Public Accounts. *Second Report to the House*, 4–9. Issue No. 9, 5 November
- 1992. Minutes of Proceedings and Evidence of the Standing Committee on Public Accounts. *Seventh Report to the House*, 3–4. Issue No. 24, 30 April

Canada. Royal Commission on Taxation (Carter Commission). 1966. Report. 6 vols. Tabled in Parliament 1966

Canadian Tax Foundation Committee on the Budget Process. 1986. "The Canadian Budget Process." *Canadian Tax Journal*, 34 (5): 989–1094

Committee on the Budget Process. 1982. "On Opening up the Budget Process: A Report to the Honourable Allan J. MacEachen, Minister of Finance, from a Committee Formed under the Auspices of the Canadian Tax Foundation." *Canadian Tax Journal*, 30: 167

Daigneault, Jean. 1993. "Putting aside Budget Secrecy: Improving the Budget Consultation Process by Tapping into Policy Communities." *Policy Options*, 14 (5): 21–24

d'Aquino, T., G.B. Doern, and C. Blair. 1979. *Parliamentary Government in Canada: A Critical Assessment and Suggestions for Change*. Ottawa: Intercounsel Limited

Doern, G.B. 1988. "Tax Expenditure Decisions and the Budgetary Decision Process." In *Tax Expenditures and Government Policy*, ed. N. Bruce, 105–22. Kingston, Ont.: John Deutsch Institute for the Study of Economic Policy
- 1989. "Tax Expenditures and Tory Times: More or Less Policy Discretion?" In *How Ottawa Spends, 1989–90: The Buck Stops Where?*, ed. K.A. Graham, 75–105. Ottawa: Carleton University Press
- 1993. "Fairness, Budget Secrecy, and Pre-Budget Consultation in Ontario, 1985-1992." In *Taxing and Spending: Issues of Process*, ed. Allan M. Maslove. Fair Tax Commission, Research Studies. Toronto: University of Toronto Press

Doern, G.B., A.M. Maslove, and M.J. Prince. 1988. *Public Budgeting in Canada: Politics, Economics, and Management*. Ottawa: Carleton University Press

Doern, G.B., and R.W. Phidd. 1983. *Canadian Public Policy*. Toronto: Methuen

Drache, A.B.C. 1978. "Income Tax Policy Formulation in Canada, 1972–76." *Osgoode Hall Law Journal*, 16 (1): 1–17

Drummond, R.J. 1983. "Ontario Revenue Budgets 1960–80." *Journal of Canadian Studies*, 18 (1): 79–91

Edwards, K.K. 1988. "Reporting for Tax Expenditures and Tax Abatement." *Government Finance Review*, 4 (4): 13–17

Elkin, B. 1989. "Auditing Tax Expenditures, or Spending through the Tax System." *International Journal of Government Auditing*, 16 (1): 7–9 and 16

French, R.D. 1980. *How Ottawa Decides: Planning and Industrial Policy Making 1968–1984*. Toronto: Lorimer

Gauthier, J.R. 1991a. Correspondence to F.W. Gorbet, Deputy Minister of Finance, 20 August
– 1991b. Correspondence to F.W. Gorbet, Deputy Minister of Finance, 24 October
– 1992. Correspondence to F.W. Gorbet, Deputy Minister of Finance, 29 January
Gillespie, W.I. 1991. *Tax, Borrow and Spend: Financing Federal Spending in Canada, 1867–1990*. Ottawa: Carleton University Press
Gold, S.D., and D. Nesbary. 1988. "State Tax Expenditure Review Mechanisms." *Tax Notes*, 30: 883–91
Good, D.A., ed. 1980. "The Tax Process and Federal Housing Policy." In *The Politics of Anticipation: Making Canadian Federal Tax Policy*, 163–82. Ottawa: School of Public Administration, Carleton University
Gorbet, F.W. 1991a. Correspondence to J.R. Gauthier, MP, 16 September
– 1991b. Correspondence to J.R. Gauthier, MP, 4 December
– 1992. Correspondence to J.R. Gauthier, MP, 10 February
Harris, J.E., and S.A. Hicks. 1992. "Tax Expenditure Reporting: The Utilization of an Innovation." *Public Budgeting and Finance*, 12 (3): 32–49
Hartle, D.G. 1982. *The Revenue Budget Process of the Government of Canada: Description, Appraisal, and Proposals*. Toronto: Canadian Tax Foundation
– 1988. *The Expenditure Budget Process of the Government of Canada: A Public Choice–Rent-Seeking Perspective*. Toronto: Canadian Tax Foundation
Hebert, F.T. 1984. "Congressional Budgeting, 1977–1983: Continuity and Change." In *Congressional Budgeting: Politics, Process, and Power*, ed. W.T. Wander, F.T. Hebert, and G.W. Copeland, 31–48. Baltimore, Md.: Johns Hopkins University Press
Heidenheimer, A.J., H. Heclo, and C.T. Adams. 1990. *Comparative Public Policy: The Politics of Social Choice in America, Europe, and Japan*. 3rd ed. New York: St Martin's Press
Hildred, W.M., and J.V. Pinto. 1990. "Impact of the 1986 Federal Tax Reform on the Passive Tax Expenditures of States." *Journal of Economic Issues*, 24 (1): 225–38
Hughes, J.W., and J. Motekat. 1988. "Tax Expenditures for Local Governments." *Public Budgeting and Finance*, 8 (4): 68–73
Ippolito, D. 1978. *The Budget and National Politics*. San Francisco: Freeman
Lindquist, E. 1983. "The Policy and Expenditure Management System and Tax Expenditures: Perspectives on AB1894 from Canada." Brief prepared for the California Assembly Committee on Revenue and Taxation, 16 November
– 1985. "Further Lessons: The Annual Budget Process in Ontario." In *Consultation and Budget Secrecy*, 73–85. Ottawa: Conference Board of Canada

- 1989. "Behind the Myth of Think Tanks: The Organization and Relevance of Canadian Policy Institutes." Doctoral dissertation, Graduate School of Public Policy, University of California, Berkeley
- 1991. "The Cabinet Decision-making System: A Process without a Name." In *Politics: Canada*, ed. P.W. Fox and G. White, 390–95. Toronto: McGraw-Hill Ryerson

McDaniel, P.R. 1988. "The Impact of the Tax Expenditure Concept on Tax Reform." In *The Quest for Tax Reform*, ed. N. Brooks, 387–96. Toronto: Carswell

McDaniel, P.R., and S.S. Surrey, eds. 1985. *International Aspects of Tax Expenditures: A Comparative Study.* Deventer, The Netherlands: Kluwer

McLoughlin, K., and S.B. Proudfoot. 1981. "Giving by Not Taking: A Primer on Tax Expenditures." *Canadian Public Policy,* 7 (2): 328–37

McQuaig, L. 1987. *Behind Closed Doors: How the Rich Won Control of Canada's Tax System.* Markham: Viking Books

Manitoba. 1986. *The 1986 Manitoba Budget Address, Presented ... May 22, 1986.* Winnipeg
- 1987. *The 1987 Manitoba Budget Address, Presented ... March 16, 1987.* Winnipeg
- 1988. *The 1988 Manitoba Budget Address, Presented ... February 26, 1988.* Winnipeg

Maslove, A.M. 1979. "The Other Side of Public Spending: Tax Expenditures in Canada." In *The Public Evaluation of Government Spending*, ed. G.B. Doern and A.M. Maslove, 149–68. Montreal: Institute for Research on Public Policy
- ed. 1989. *Budgeting in the Provinces: Leadership and the Premiers.* Toronto: Institute of Public Administration of Canada

Maslove, A.M., and H.I. Eicher. 1987. "Reforming Taxes: Where to Go and How to Get There." In *How Ottawa Spends, 1987–88: Restraining the State,* ed. M.J. Prince, 176–210. Toronto: Methuen

Maslove, A.M., M.J. Prince, and G.B. Doern. 1986. *Federal and Provincial Budgeting.* Study No. 41 of the Royal Commission on the Economic Union and Development Prospects for Canada. Toronto: University of Toronto Press

Meyers, A.E. 1989. *Evolution of United States Budgeting: Changing Fiscal and Financial Concepts.* New York: Greenwood Press

Michigan. House of Representatives. House Fiscal Agency. 1990. *Silent Spending: Tax Expenditures and the Competition for Public Dollars.* Lansing, Mich., May
- Task Force on Tax Expenditures and the Budget. 1991. *Report.* Michigan, February

National Council of Welfare. 1976. *The Hidden Welfare System.* Ottawa: Health and Welfare Canada

National Tax Association – Tax Institute of America. 1988. *Proceedings of the 81st Annual Conference*, Second Concurrent Conference Session, "Tax Expenditure Reporting and Measurements: State and Federal Experience," Columbus, Ohio

– 1979. *The Hidden Welfare System Revisited*. Ottawa: Health and Welfare Canada

Neubig, T.S. 1988. "The Current Role of the Tax Expenditure Budget in U.S. Policymaking." In *Tax Expenditures and Government Policy*, ed. N. Bruce, 239–58. Kingston, Ont.: Queen's University

New York State. Legislative Commission on Public-Private Cooperation (LCPP). 1987. *Tax Expenditure Reporting: An Effective Way to Monitor Back-Door Spending*. Albany, November

Ontario. 1978. "Budget Paper B: Relieving Property Tax Burden on Senior Citizens." *1978 Ontario Budget*. Toronto: Queen's Printer for Ontario, March

Ontario. Department of Treasury and Economics. 1971. *1971 Budget – Ontario, Presented ... April 26 1971*. Toronto: Queen's Printer for Ontario

Ontario. Ministry of Finance. 1993. *1993 Ontario Budget, Presented ... May 19 1993*. Toronto: Queen's Printer for Ontario

Ontario. Ministry of Revenue. 1991a. *Tax Preference Papers*. Vol. 1, May

– 1991b. *Tax Preference Papers*. Vol. 2, July

Ontario. Ministry of Treasury and Economics (MTE). 1969. *1969 Ontario Budget, 1969*. Toronto: Queen's Printer for Ontario

– 1971. "Preliminary Outline of a System of Property and Sales Tax Credits for Ontario Taxpayers." Paper drafted by the Taxation and Fiscal Policy Branch and presented to the meeting of Ministers of Finance, Ottawa, 1–2 November

– 1972. *1972 Ontario Budget: Ontario's Property Tax Credit Plan*. Toronto: Queen's Printer for Ontario

– 1983. *1983 Ontario Budget Paper: "The Structure of Provincial Revenues."* Toronto: Queen's Printer for Ontario

– 1985. *Reforming the Budget Process: A Discussion Paper*

– 1986. *Ontario's Tax Expenditures*. May

– 1988a. *Economic Outlook and Fiscal Review: Ontario 1988*. December

– 1988b. *1988 Ontario Budget*. 20 April 1988

– 1989a. *Economic Outlook and Fiscal Review: Ontario 1989*. November

– 1989b. *1989 Ontario Budget, Presented ... May 17 1989*. Toronto: Queen's Printer for Ontario

– 1990. *1990 Ontario Budget, Presented ... April 24 1990*. Toronto: Queen's Printer for Ontario

– 1991a. *Ontario Investment and Worker Ownership Program: A Proposal for Discussion.* August. Mimeo
– 1991b. *1991 Ontario Budget,* 29 April. Toronto: Queen's Printer for Ontario
– 1992. *1992 Ontario Budget: Meeting Ontario's Priorities, Presented ... April 30 1992.* Toronto: Queen's Printer for Ontario
Ontario. Ministry of Treasury, Economics, and Intergovernmental Affairs. 1974. *1974 Ontario Budget, Presented ... April 9 1974.* Toronto: Queen's Printer for Ontario
– 1977. *Reduction of Tax Burdens through Tax Credits: Ontario's Experience.* Ontario Tax Studies No. 14
Ontario. Office of the Provincial Auditor. 1987. "Comments on Government-Wide Matters and Special Reviews." In *Annual Report of the Provincial Auditor of Ontario for the Year ended March 31, 1987,* chap. 3. Toronto: Queen's Printer for Ontario
Organisation for Economic Cooperation and Development (OECD). 1984. *Tax Expenditures: A Review of the Issues and Country Practice.* Paris: OECD
Peters, B.G. 1991. *The Politics of Taxation: A Comparative Perspective.* Oxford: Basil Blackwell
Poddar, S. 1988. "Integration of Tax Expenditures into the Expenditure Management System: The Canadian Experience." In *Tax Expenditures and Government Policy,* ed. N. Bruce, 259–68. Kingston, Ont.: John Deutsch Institute for the Study of Economic Policy
Pomp, R. 1988. "Discussion: State Tax Expenditure – and Beyond." In National Tax Association (1988), 33–36
Prince, M.J. 1989. "The Bland Stops Here: Ontario Budgeting in the Davis Era, 1971–1985." In *Budgeting in the Provinces: Leadership and the Premiers,* ed. A.M. Maslove, 87–119. Toronto: Institute of Public Administration of Canada
Quebec. Ministères des Finances et Conseil du trésor. 1993. *Québec's Public Finances: Living within Our Means.* Quebec
Richardson, P. 1988. "Tax Expenditures and Tax Reform: The Federal Experience." In National Tax Association (1988), 23–28
Salamone, D. 1988. "Minnesota's Experience with Tax Expenditure Reporting." In National Tax Association (1988), 28–33
Saskatchewan. 1981. *Budget Speech.* March
– 1990. *Budget Address.* March
– 1992a. *Budget Address.* May
– 1992b. Financial Management Review Commission. *Report.* Regina
– 1992c. *Saskatchewan Financial Management Review Commission. Report.* Regina

– 1993. *Budget Address.* March

Savoie, D.S. 1990. *The Politics of Public Spending in Canada.* Toronto: University of Toronto Press

Smith, R.S. 1979. *Tax Expenditures: An Examination of Tax Incentives and Tax Preferences in the Canadian Federal Income Tax System.* Toronto: Canadian Tax Foundation

Social Policy Reform Group (SPRG). 1987. "Response to the White Paper on Tax Reform." Mimeo

Surrey, S.S. 1973. *Pathways to Tax Reform: The Concept of Tax Expenditures.* Cambridge, Mass.: Harvard University Press

Surrey, S.S., and P.R. McDaniel. 1985. *Tax Expenditures.* Cambridge, Mass.: Harvard University Press

United States. Congressional Budget Office (CBO). 1988. *The Effects of Tax Reform on Tax Expenditures.* March

Van Loon, R. 1984. "Planning in the Eighties." In *How Ottawa Decides: Planning and Industrial Policy Making 1968–1984*, 2nd ed., ed. R.D. French, chap. 9. Toronto: Lorimer

Welsh, L. 1992. "Tax Breaks Cost Canada Billions: Finance Department Study Lists Losses," *Globe and Mail* (Toronto). 24 December 1992

White, J., and A. Wildavsky. 1989. *The Deficit and the Public Interest: The Search for Responsible Budgeting in the 1980s.* Berkeley: University of California Press

Wildavsky, A.B. 1980. *How to Limit Spending.* Berkeley: University of California Press

– 1986. "Keeping Kosher: The Epistemology of Tax Expenditures." *Journal of Public Policy,* 5 (3): 413–31

Wilson, V.S. 1988. "What Legacy? The Nielsen Task Force Program Review." In *How Ottawa Spends, 1988/89: The Conservatives Heading into the Stretch*, ed. K.A. Graham, 23–47. Ottawa: Carleton University Press

Witte, J. 1985. *The Politics and Development of the Federal Income Tax.* Madison: University of Wisconsin Press

Woodside, K. 1983. "The Political Economy of Policy Instruments: Tax Expenditures and Subsidies in Canada." In *The Politics of Canadian Public Policy,* ed. M.M. Atkinson and M.A. Chandler, 173–97. Toronto: University of Toronto Press

3 Earmarked Taxes in Ontario: Solution or Problem?

WAYNE R. THIRSK and RICHARD M. BIRD

Introduction and Summary

Earmarking is among the most ancient of recorded fiscal practices: "Governments from the earliest times administered taxing and spending by earmarking: revenue from each tax went into a specific independent fund; in turn, fund balances defrayed predetermined classes of expenditure."[1] Such earmarking was extensively employed to simplify and control financial administration in ancient Athens and Rome, as well as in various parts of Europe in medieval times and later.

Earmarking remains common today in many developing countries, especially in Latin America, in part so that governments can provide more stable funding over time to their favoured activities in the face of endemic economic, political, and budgetary instability.[2] It is also common in U.S. states, as noted below. In practice, however, whether in ancient Rome or modern-day Ecuador or Indiana, the results of widespread earmarking seem seldom to have been beneficial, both because of the difficulty of controlling many separate funds and the inappropriateness of many of the linkages established between revenues and expenditures.

For this reason, earmarking has long been out of favour. The conventional wisdom is that "from the point of view of desirable budgeting practice, little justification can be made for earmarking receipts for special purposes that set these specially financed activities apart from normal budgetary procedures."[3] Nowhere has this dislike for earmarking been stronger than in countries such as Canada that follow the "British" budgetary practice, under which, in principle, all taxes flow into, and all expenditures are made out of, a single, consolidated revenue fund.

Recently, however, the fiscal pendulum seems to have swung in favour of earmarking, as politicians have begun to view it as one way of reducing taxpayers' resistance ot higher taxes and as taxpayers have pressed for greater accountability with respect to how their tax dollars are spent. There has thus been considerable revival of interest in earmarking, not least in Canada. Both the Royal Commission on National Passenger Transportation and the federal Government and Competitiveness Project have, for example, recently commissioned survey papers on the subject.[4] The proximate origin of this recent interest is, no doubt, the current desperate state of fiscal affairs at all levels of government. Not only is there no money in the coffers for any new expenditure initiatives, but taxpayers are increasingly resistant to even the modest increases in taxation that may be needed simply to maintain the present level of government activities. In these circumstances, linking taxes with activities thought to be favoured by taxpayers undoubtedly seems to some an attractive way out of the fiscal dilemma.

In addition to such possibly transitory fiscal expediency, this ancient and often discredited device has acquired a new aura of theoretical respectability. Beginning with a seminal 1963 paper by James Buchanan, there has been a small but steady stream of literature making a strong case for earmarking – not as a "second-best" way of dealing with a transitory fiscal squeeze but rather as, in principle, the best operational way of dealing with the fundamental normative problem of public economics: how to provide people with what they really want.[5] To quote Richard Musgrave (1938), the doyen of modern public finance, "The principle of earmarking applies in its full sense of linking tax and expenditure determination for each program."[6]

The present paper considers the potential role of earmarked revenues in Ontario and is divided into four sections. In the first section, "earmarking" is first defined more precisely. Not only does this task require careful consideration of the relationship between three distinct concepts – earmarking, benefit taxation, and user charges – but there are also many variant forms in both theory and practice.

The present use of earmarking at both the provincial and the local level in Ontario is then reviewed in the second section, with briefer reference being made to experience elsewhere in Canada and the United States. Two conclusions emerge. First, while there is much less use of earmarking in Ontario than in many other jurisdictions, there is some evidence that it has been increasing in importance in recent years. Second, almost all so-called earmarking in Ontario is "notional" – revenues flow into the general fund and suffice to finance only part of the expenditure in question.

The third section reviews briefly arguments for and against earmarking in terms of its effects on budgetary processes, the size of government, and taxpayers' attitudes. Both the theoretical literature and the surprisingly sparse empirical evidence are considered. Our conclusion is that there is indeed a case for earmarking, probably for more of it than currently exists in Ontario, but that both the rationale for, and the effects of, such earmarking are rather different than may at first be thought.

Finally, the potential for earmarking in Ontario is considered briefly in the fourth section. While there is, of course, much to be said in favour of both "green taxes" and "green expenditures," the case for earmarking environmental taxes and fees to environmental outlays is weak. More can be said for earmarking some "tourist taxes" to tourist promotion and perhaps also some payroll taxes (or at least tax credits) to worker training, but even these links are far from unarguable. In the end, both more earmarking and better methods of doing so seem warranted in the traditional area of user charges, including road finance. All things considered, introducing earmarking that goes much beyond these areas does not seem economically advisable – although it may, of course, prove politically expedient as taxpayers' resistance increases.

What Is Earmarking?

The Broad Concept

Earmarking in the broadest sense occurs whenever revenues are raised from a specific source and dedicated to financing a particular set of expenditures. For example, property tax revenues may be said to be earmarked to finance local and school expenditures; local revenues in general, to local expenditures; and revenues raised by public enterprises, as a rule, to expenditures undertaken by those enterprises. An especially important example in many countries, including Canada, is financing of social insurance systems through payroll taxes. Another form often found in practice (though seldom in Canada) is dedication of a fixed proportion of some particular tax or of all tax revenues to some specified purpose, such as intergovernmental transfers or education.

All theses practices establish a budgetary process different from "general fund" financing. Under the latter, in principle, all government revenues flow into one big pot, and all government expenditures are ladled out of this pot. Decisions regarding allocation of taxation and of expenditure are made completely separately. There is no link between revenues generated by any particular tax and the level of expenditure on any particular activity.

Under general fund financing, if a government wishes to increase spending on any activity, it has three choices: it can raise taxes, issue debt, or cut other expenditure. While there may occasionally be public debate on how expenditures will be financed, governments are not bound by such discussions and citizens have no way of knowing which of these options will be chosen in the end. For example, would expansion of subsidized day care imply fewer health care services, larger public debt, less foreign aid, higher income taxes, higher sales taxes, some combination of all of these outcomes, or possibly none of them? No one can know, but clearly how people feel about day care is likely to depend, in part, on how they think that the program will be financed. Rational choice by voters is thus difficult under general fund financing because of the lack of information concerning the true costs of choosing a particular level of spending on any particular activity. Each expenditure proposal is, in effect, examined independent of how it can be financed, and tax decisions reflect previous, unrelated expenditure decisions.[7]

Under strict earmarking, however, the sequence of tax and expenditure decisions is in effect reversed: tax collections drive subsequent expenditure levels. Since taxpayers are aware that when certain tax payments are extracted from them the funds will be used to pay for certain kinds of expenditures, they may be expected to support earmarked taxes if they support expansion in the supply of government services for which the taxes are earmarked. Under this system, taxpayers in principle have the information needed to make rational expenditure decisions because they know exactly how their tax dollars will be spent. How this ideal might work out in practice, however, obviously depends on many factors, including the precise structure of the earmarking program.

User Charges and Benefit Taxes

Earmarking is related to, but not identical to, two other important concepts – user charges and benefit taxes. In principle, for example, the variable costs of providing road services should be recovered by imposing charges on road users.[8] Indeed, when feasible, a separate "road fund" could be established and run essentially like any other public enterprise, as Switzerland, for instance, is increasingly trying to do.[9] As a rule, however, the cost of charging makes the direct imposition of road user charges impractical.[10]

If so, the next best method of paying for road services may be to levy a tax on motor fuels and to earmark the proceeds for construction and improvement of roads and highways. Such an earmarked fuel tax – often called a benefit tax because those who pay it are presumed to benefit as a group from the services that it finances – is, in effect, a crude proxy for a price (user charge) that charges road users the marginal costs of providing road services. At least three types of "charge" revenue exist almost everywhere: service fees, public prices, and specific benefit charges.

Service fees are licence fees (marriage, business, dog, and vehicle) and various small charges levied by governments essentially for performing specific services –registering this or providing a copy of that – for identifiable individuals. In effect, such fees constitute cost reimbursement from the private to the public sector. Some budgetary systems "net out" such cost recoveries and show only expenditures net of recoveries. Charging people for something that they are required by law to do may not always be sensible (for example, if the benefit of registration is general and the cost is specific), but, on the whole, there is seldom much harm, or much revenue, in thus recovering the cost of providing the service in question.

Public prices are revenues received by governments from sale of private goods and services (other than the cost reimbursement just described). All sales of publicly provided private services to identifiable private individuals, whether public utility charges or admission charges to recreation facilities, fall under this general heading. In principle, such prices should be set at the competitive private level, with no tax or subsidy element included, except when doing so is the most efficient way of achieving public policy goals. Even then, it is best if the tax-subsidy element is accounted for separately.

Specific benefit taxes are distinct from service fees and public prices because they do not arise from provision or sale of a specific good or service to an identifiable private individual. Unlike prices, which are voluntarily paid – though like fees, which are paid for services that may be required by law – taxes represent compulsory contributions to public revenues. Nonetheless, specific benefit taxes are related in some way to benefits received by the taxpayer. In contrast to such general benefit taxes (such as fuel taxes levied on road users as a class, or local taxes in general viewed as a price paid for local collective goods), specific benefit taxes relate to the actual benefits supposedly received by certain taxpayers. Examples abound in local finance – special assessments, land-value increment taxes, improvement taxes, front footage levies, supplementary property taxes related to provision of sewers or streetlighting, development exactions and charges, delineation levies, and so on.

Much of what the public sector does in Canada, as in most countries, is in effect to provide private services to specifically identifiable individuals or (as in the case of road users) groups. In principle, whenever it is feasible to apply user charges for publicly provided private services such as garbage collection, unless there is some strong public policy reason to the contrary (such as the desire to effect redistribution in kind), consumers should be charged a price in line with the marginal costs of supply. Moreover, the proceeds from these user charges should be earmarked to pay for the costs of provision. If the publicly provided service confers external benefits on non-users – as, for example, in the case of an immunization program – user charges less than marginal costs are warranted, with any shortfall between total costs and the amount of earmarked user charges being covered out of general revenues. But prices should still be charged, and the proceeds earmarked, in such cases, as discussed further in the third section.

Imposing user charges on consumes of publicly provided private services is perhaps the most obvious and important form of earmarking, whether it is done directly by a government department or indirectly through the agency of a public enterprise. In practice, however, less use is made of such charges by the public sector than seems warranted, partly because user charges are often thought to produce adverse distributional effects. If a service previously provided free of charge to everyone will now extract the same payment from everyone who uses it, how can user charges not hurt low-income households? It seems equally obvious to many that user charges (and earmarked taxes, more generally) will increase public revenues.

Both of these arguments, however, are likely to be wrong, because they both ignore the key features of the counterfactual situation. Figure 1 conveys the essence of the argument.[11] The demand curve D–D measures the amount of the public service that would be purchased

Figure 1
Efficiency and Equity Effects of Failure to Charge User Fees

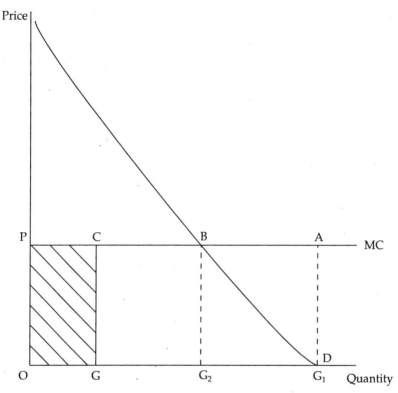

at different prices (P), or user charges. The publicly provided service in question (such as water) is assumed to have the characteristics of a private good, and the marginal cost of supply (MC) is positive and, for simplicity, is assumed to be constant.[12]

If no user charge were assessed, consumers would demand the quantity OG_1 and politicians would face strong political pressures to supply the amount demanded. The cost of supplying this quantity of the public service would be equal to the rectangular area $OPAG_1$, which also measures the amount of revenue that would have to be raised from general fund financing. Who benefits from this zero price policy? While the subject has been little studied, there is no evidence that lower-income households benefit disproportionately from consumption of free, or low-cost, public services.[13] Flat-rate water charges, for example, may favour households with children (who may or may not be poor), but they also favour those with large lawns to water and multiple vehicles to wash. Similarly, low storage and landing fees at local airports and docks benefit the few households that own private airplanes and yachts.

If a user charge of OP were introduced in these circumstances, sufficient to cover marginal costs (thus ensuring that the value placed by users on the resources used to produce the public service is at least equal to the value that would be realized by using these resources for some other purpose), demand would be rationed to OG_2, the area of $OPBG_2$ would be collected in earmarked user charges, and tax revenue in the amount $OPAG_1$ would be saved (and, the argument assumes, perhaps unreasonably, returned to taxpayers). The resulting improvement in economic efficiency is shown in the figure as the triangular area BAD. In this case, introducing earmarked user charges does not raise extra revenue but rather, by rationing demand for public services, reduces the size of the public sector. Moreover, if properly designed and applied, user charges coupled with the resulting reductions in general taxes (or, if considered desirable, increases in direct transfers) can improve both efficiency and equity.

Similar arguments may be made with respect to benefit taxation more generally, such as the road user taxes mentioned above. Both user charges and specific benefit taxes, if designed properly and applied where the public sector provides essentially "private" services, may be acceptable in terms of both efficiency and equity. When earmarked to the services for which they are charged, as they should be,[14] user charges and specific benefit taxes provide unique information to governments about the level and nature of the services that citizens wish them to provide. The strongest case for earmarking is thus with respect to user charges and specific benefit taxes – that is, when it makes sense to introduce market forces directly into determination of public expenditures and revenues. Obviously, there is much that the public sector does – notably, redistribution and provision of such "pure" public goods as national defence – where this approach is not appropriate. Equally obviously, however, there is also much that is done, particularly by local government, where it is appropriate.

A Taxonomy of Earmarking

The strongest case for earmarking can thus be made when there is a strong "benefit" link between the tax (or charge) levied and the expenditure financed. In practice, however, not all benefit taxes or user charges are earmarked. In fact, in Canada such revenues as a rule simply flow into the general pool of funds, to be used for various government purposes. Similarly, not all earmarked revenues flow to activities that contribute directly to the welfare of those who pay them. The link between GST revenues and the Debt Servicing and Reduction Account recently established by the federal government, for example, clearly has no benefit rationale.[15]

Quite apart from any logical connection between the source and the use of earmarked revenues, earmarking may vary (see Table 1) in the degree of specificity of taxes and expenditures involved (column 1) and in the strength and nature of the linkage between them (column 2).[16]

The list in Table 1 refers only to the earmarking of specific revenue sources. As noted above, it is not difficult to find instances of more general earmarking, whether of expenditures or of revenues. Such general earmarking is common in some developing countries. For example, Columbia has a constitutional requirement directing at least 20 per cent of the central government's current expenditures to education – "expenditure earmarking" – and at least 15 per cent of its current revenues to transfers to subnational governments for health and education.[17]

On the whole, however, such instances of earmarking of general revenue stretch the meaning of earmarking beyond both normal discourse and what can usefully be discussed in this paper. The taxonomy here distinguishes instances of earmarking in which a specific tax (or charge) is used to finance some specific or broad expenditure area and cases in which the connection between expenditures and revenues is "tight" (the amount of expenditure on the activity in question depends closely on the yield of the earmarked tax) or "loose" (see column 2). In addition, there may, or may not, be a "benefit" rationale for the revenue-expenditure linkage (see column 3).

There are thus *eight* possible ways in which specific taxes or fees may be earmarked, as shown in Table 1, depending on the specificity of the expenditure designation, the tightness of the revenue-expenditure link (when the connection is tight, it is sometimes called strong earmarking), and the existence or not of a benefit rationale for the link (when there is such a rationale, it is sometimes called rational earmarking).

Type A in Table 1 is clearly the strongest and most rational form of

TABLE 1
Varieties of Earmarking

Variety	1 Expenditure	2 Linkage	3 Rationale	4 Example
A	Specific	Tight	Benefit	Public enterprise
B	Specific	Loose	Benefit	Gasoline tax
C	Broad	Tight	Benefit	Social insurance
D	Broad	Loose	Benefit	Tobacco taxes
E	Specific	Tight	None	"Green" taxes
F	Specific	Loose	None	Payroll tax
G	Broad	Tight	None	Revenue sharing
H	Broad	Loose	None	Lottery proceeds

earmarking. The expenditure use is clearly specified and linked tightly to a revenue derived from those who benefit from the expenditures. An example might be a self-financing public enterprise in which revenues from a particular source (for example, the sale of electricity) and only those revenues can be used to finance operation and expansion of the activity in question.[18] In contrast, type B earmarking may be equally specific in terms of what is earmarked for what purpose – gasoline taxes for highway expenditures, for instance – but fluctuations in revenues do not necessarily affect expenditures. Expenditures do not invariably increase if revenue rises, nor decrease if it falls. Of course, when the earmarked tax contributes only a small proportion of the total expenditure on the activity, earmarking may, in any case, have no effect at the margin.[19]

Type C is similar to type A, but the expenditure area is less narrowly defined. An example might be a social insurance system that finances various sorts of payments for contributors only – pensions, maternity benefits, sick pay, and so on – in which the amount spent on the area in total, but not on any one benefit in particular, is related to revenues received. Similarly, type D is analogous to type B, with a conceivable "benefit" connection (in the sense that smokers both pay tobacco taxes and may benefit disproportionately from health care outlays),[20] but the connection between taxes collected and expenditures made in the broad area for which the revenues are earmarked is quite loose.

The remaining varieties of earmarking do not have even this vestige of a benefit rationale. For example, revenues from an environmental levy might be directed to some general expenditure area such as the environment, with the total amount of expenditure being determined strictly by the amount of such earmarked revenues (type

E). But there is no necessary or logical connection between those who pay the tax and those who benefit from the expenditure. Alternatively, the connection between revenue source (such as a payroll tax) and general expenditure area financed (such as health) might be both loose and unrelated to any conceivable benefit rationale (type F).

The last two varieties of earmarking are even more remote from any conceivable benefit rationale. An example of type G (in which the yield of a non-benefit tax determines strictly the amount spent on a particular outlay) might be allocating a fixed share of income (or other) tax revenues to finance transfers to local governments.[21] An example of type H, in which the expenditure area is equally broad but the amount spent is connected only loosely with the amount collected, might be the common earmarking of lottery proceeds to such worthy causes as culture, recreation, and health.

Of course, many additional variables also need to be taken into account in assessing any particular existing or proposed type of earmarking. Who receives the earmarked revenues? They may, for example, be collected by the government, or they may flow directly to the benefiting institution (as is usually the case with enterprise revenues). What is the relevant time period? Is the earmarking for a definite or an indefinite period? Is the rate of the earmarked tax fixed or subject to change? Must earmarked revenues be spent in the period in which they are received?

Within the house of earmarking, there are thus many, and diverse, rooms. Generalizations as to the virtues, or vices, of earmarking are singularly useless unless the term is defined precisely vis-à-vis the various characteristics discussed above.

Operational Definitions

When we move from the conceptual to the operational, it is useful to define three approaches to earmarking – pure, notional, and effective – each with quite different fiscal implications.

Pure earmarking assigns certain tax (or charge) revenues to a special fund, which becomes the sole, or at least the primary, source of funding for a set of particular expenditures. There may or may not be a benefit rationale. Since by the terms used in Table 1 the link is "tight," a larger amount in the special fund soon generates greater expenditures in the earmarked area, more or less on a dollar-for-dollar basis.

With this system, the taxpayer-voter in effect decides on the marginal expenditure. Provided that there is some logical (benefit) connection between source of funds and services purchased – and there is no overriding distributive or other reason to sever this connection – such strong earmarking, by introducing the logic of the market into the budgetary process, potentially offers a most desirable method of financing publicly provided private activities.

Notional earmarking designates certain types of taxes (or charges) to help pay for particular government services, but the revenues from these taxes flow into a general (or consolidated revenue) fund and finance only a portion of the service in question. At best, however, there is only an extremely loose connection between the growth of earmarked revenues and higher government spending in the designated area. Nor does the government need to forge a close link between the amount of earmarked revenues and the volume of services to which they are nominally tied. Moreover, there is seldom any benefit rationale. The amount of earmarked revenues may thus rise or fall while the level of associated services remains the same. In contrast to pure earmarking, decisions about marginal expenditures remain firmly in the hands of budgetary authorities.

Effective earmarking is a hybrid of these two approaches. As in notional earmarking, revenue from earmarked sources flows into the general fund. However, there is some more or less binding provision for (or commitment to) "equivalent funding" of specific services, so that there is some (less than perfect) correlation between amounts of earmarked revenues and amounts spent on designated activities. As discussed below, there is some weak evidence of such effective earmarking for certain environmental charges in Ontario. Nonetheless, despite a possible association between greater environmental spending and collection of more revenue from taxes linked to use of the environment, this relationship is not automatic (as it would be in pure earmarking) or particularly rational (as it would be in earmarked benefit taxes).

Moreover, it is not easy to determine empirically whether effective earmarking actually increases expenditures in any given area. Effectiveness in this sense may be promoted by defining the designated expenditure area more narrowly – for example, "improving public transportation facilities for elderly patrons" (Project LIFT) rather than "care of the elderly." But there is no way to be sure that funds spent from an earmarked source on even the most carefully defined program are new funds rather than simply substitutes for general budget funds that would have been spent on this program in any case. As noted below, despite the worldwide popularity of

Figure 2
Alternative Budgeting Processes

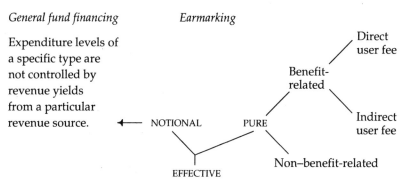

General fund financing   *Earmarking*

Expenditure levels of a specific type are not controlled by revenue yields from a particular revenue source.

earmarking, there is, in fact, very limited evidence of its efficacy either in increasing spending on designated projects or in increasing total revenues.

In any case, when there is a pure or an effective method, an earmarked tax may constitute an indirect form of user charge if there is a clear benefit link – as there is, for instance, when the tax base is complementary in consumption with use of the public services financed by the earmarked tax. Taxing a complement (such as fuel use) to a public service (such as provision of roads) in effect substitutes for a direct charge on use of the public service. In addition, as already observed, when direct user charges are imposed for publicly supplied private services, their proceeds should usually also be earmarked to finance the expenditures giving rise to the benefits for which citizens are charged. Notional earmarking, in contrast, seldom has any persuasive benefit rationale.

Figure 2 presents a chart to clarify and summarize the conceptual distinctions drawn so far. It shows that the notional type of earmarking cannot be usefully distinguished from general fund financing, that the pure version may be either benefit-related or not, that the benefit-related pure variety may invoke either direct or indirect user fees, and that the effective version contains elements of both the pure and the notional variants. What the chart fails to reveal is whether earmarking, or its alternative of general fund financing, yields more efficient expenditure decisions. We grapple with this issue in the remainder of the paper. But, first, we examine earmarking practices in Canada and the United States.

Experience with Earmarking

Ontario Provincial Experience

In terms of the three concepts of earmarking just defined, there appears to be no pure earmarking in Ontario at the provincial level, and only limited (and recent) pure earmarking takes place at the local level. This gap is least surprising at Queen's Park, where about two-thirds of total spending is supposed to be redistributive and there is clearly no economic case for financing it from benefit-related taxes. Nor, given the unpopularity of welfare spending, is there a strong political case for earmarking. Nonetheless, as Krashinsky (1981) demonstrates convincingly, there is still a potentially important albeit limited, role for properly designed user charges in many social services in Ontario, including day care, institutional care and outreach programs for the aged, visiting homemakers and nurses, vocational rehabilitation, and transportation for the physically disabled.[22]

Although a strong political case might be made for earmarking with respect to much more of health care expenditure, the Canada Health Act effectively prohibits direct user fees and other benefit-related charges. In social services, however, there may be an important role in principle for user-charge financing in the health services. Although, as Bird (1976) claims, the argument for any sort of "full-cost" charges for health services to individuals is weak, there is good reason to introduce more rational pricing both within health care (for example, in hospitals) – indeed, Ontario recently took some steps in this direction – and, as noted below, to a limited extent for health-care consumers.

In primary and secondary education, Ontario has a long-standing commitment to maintain universal access and avoid imposition of significant user fees. Even for postsecondary education – where the case for such heavy subsidization is particularly suspect in terms of both equity and efficiency (Stager 1989) – tuition fees currently cover only about 15 per cent of the system's operating costs. University administrations have been pressing for the right to assess higher fees in a bid to obtain extra funding, but the province has resisted those overtures – misguidedly, on both efficiency and equity grounds.

In sharp contrast to the U.S. situation, there is also no earmarking of road user charges to road finance in Ontario or, for that matter, in any other Canadian province. Politicians, truckers, and the Canadian Automobile Association may often talk (and put up signs) as though there is a link between, say, fuel taxes and road expenditures, but legally there is not. As many studies of highway finance have demonstrated, however, although an economically correct (not to mention politically acceptable) system of road pricing is by no means easy to establish, there *is* a strong, indeed overwhelming, economic case for earmarking in this area.[23] Despite the strong logic of earmarked-benefit finance for transport in general, Ontario's only examples are transport services provided by separately funded public enterprises, such as the Government of Ontario (GO) commuter railway system and the Toronto Transit Commission (TTC), with its buses, streetcars, subway, and light rail transit.

Notional earmarking, in contrast, has been gaining ground in the province in recent years. A number of new taxes and tax increases have been justified as helping finance greater expenditure on health, the environment, and transportation infrastructure. In 1990, for example, the province abandoned flat-rate premiums for the Ontario Hospital Insurance Plan (OHIP) and introduced an Employer Health Tax (EHT) on payrolls. This tax is applied at graduated rates ranging from 0.98 to 1.95 per cent, depending on the size of the employer's payroll. Of the approximately $14 billion spent on insured health care services in fiscal year 1989–90, $2.6 billion was covered by proceeds from this new tax. Since the amount earmarked is substantially less than that spent on the designated function, earmarking has no effect at the margin.[24]

The next proceeds from the provincial lottery are also earmarked loosely to physical fitness, sports, and cultural and recreational activities and facilities. Any unallocated funds are designated to assist operation of hospitals. As with other notionally earmarked taxes, lottery proceeds are deposited initially into the consolidated revenue fund, and "equivalent funding" is supposed to be made available for designated purposes.

Beginning in the late 1980s, Queen's Park unveiled a series of environmental initiatives featuring new "green" taxes intended to help pay for more spending to maintain and upgrade the environment. In 1988, excise taxes on consumption of leaded gasoline increased significantly. In 1989, a tire tax ($5 per tire on new purchases) was introduced, along with a so-called fuel conservation ("gas guzzler") tax on the purchase price of new vehicles, according to their relative fuel inefficiency – as much as $7000 on a vehicle that consumes more than 18 litres of fuel for every 100 kilometres.[25] Simultaneously, a dispenser disposal tax of 5 cents (now 10 cents) per container was

TABLE 2
Notional Earmarking in Ontario, 1990–91

Tax	Collections ($million)
Employer Health Tax (EHT)	2,662
Gasoline Tax	1,424
Fuel Conservation Tax	340
Commercial Concentration Tax (CCT)	102
Tire Tax (estimate)	40
Vehicle/Driver Registration Fees	665
OHIP Premiums	4
Subtotal	5,237
(Total budget expenditures)	(43,429)

NOTE: Revenues from the tire tax are estimated based on information obtained from the Ontario Treasury; this tax is collected as part of the general provincial sales tax.
SOURCE: Ontario, Ministry of Treasury and Economics (1992, Table C-2, p. 60).

imposed on non-returnable or non-recyclable vessels for liquor, wine, or beer.

Most recently, as part of its response to the growing transportation needs of the Greater Toronto Area (GTA), the province adopted a commercial concentration tax (CCT) to help defray the cost of new transportation infrastructure in the Toronto region. The CCT is levied annually at a rate of $1 per square foot (0.0929 square metres) on commercial property and associated parking located within the GTA. All commercial parking lots and garages in this area are also subject to the tax. Industrial property, racetracks, and trucking depots are exempted. As a related measure, passenger vehicle registration fees were raised differentially for vehicle owners residing in the GTA.

Table 2 indicates how important such notional earmarking has become in the Ontario revenue structure. In 1990–91, total collections from the EHT (and the remnants of the old OHIP premium), fuel, tire, and fuel conservation taxes, and the two infrastructure taxes for residents of the GTA amounted to $5.237 billion, or approximately 12 per cent of total budgeted provincial expenditures.[26]

Has this notional earmarking been "effective" – is there a discernible correlation between the earmarked revenues and the designated expenditure? It seems most unlikely that the health tax, by far the most notable instance of notional earmarking, has stimulated greater

TABLE 3
Provincial Expenditures on Waste Management, Ontario, 1987–91

Fiscal year	Waste management spending ($million)	Capital grants for waste treatment ($million)	Waste management as proportion of environmental services (%)
1987	13.4	4.8	22.7
1988	16.8	4.3	24.6
1989	26.7	12.5	35.3
1990	43.5	21.0	43.8
1991	66.0	35.6	53.8

SOURCES: Ontario, *Public Accounts*, various years.

expenditures on health, since this tax both replaced another notionally earmarked revenue source (the OHIP premium) and provides
only a fraction of the funds flowing to the health sector.

The decision to improve the GTA's transportation facilities appears
to have preceded the decision to impose the two new GTA-related
taxes, although approval of this expenditure may have taken place
with the knowledge that some revenue would be forthcoming from
the new taxes to help finance it. On the whole, however, it *seems*
unlikely that earmarking of these taxes significantly affected expenditure decisions. In contracts, although data are inadequate, there may
have been some effective earmarking in the environmental taxes.
Since introduction of these taxes in 1989, Ontario's spending on waste
management has increased fourfold in absolute terms and has more
than doubled as a share of total expenditures on environmental services (see Table 3). Although there is no formal link between these
expenditures and the yield from the environmental levies, expansion
of expenditure in this case may well have been approved in the
knowledge that extra revenues from the new taxes would be available to finance it. As discussed below, however, it is difficult to ascer-
tain the effects of earmarking on either the level or the composition of
expenditures, and the Ontario evidence is certainly too weak to draw
any clear conclusions on this matter at the provincial level.

Ontario: Municipal Experience

Matters are little different at the municipal level in Ontario, where, except for the recently introduced development charges, there appear to be no significant instances of pure earmarking. Nor is Ontario unique in this respect. Pure earmarking by municipalities in other provinces is also virtually non-existent.

The main revenue sources of municipalities are property taxes (residential and non-residential), conditional and unconditional grants from Queen's Park, and user charges. In contrast to the provincial level, however, all these revenues are to some extent notionally earmarked. When homeowners receive their property tax assessments, for example, they can see immediately what portion is allocated to paying for education in their jurisdiction. On the surface, this may look like pure earmarking – a defined revenue source has been set aside to pay for a specific expenditure. However, there is, at best, only a weak connection between the amount of tax paid and the amount of benefit enjoyed. Moreover, the amount of educational services provided is decided largely at the provincial rather than the local level, and the property tax "mill rate" is struck only after completion of negotiations between local school boards and teachers' federations. Essentially, as with general fund financing, expenditure decisions govern allocation of taxes, rather than vice versa.

The many provincial conditional grants to municipalities are also, of course, nominally earmarked for specific purposes. Such expenditure earmarking is not considered in this study, however, in part because it is not financed from any specific revenue sources. Moreover, given municipalities' opportunities for expenditure substitution (essentially the "fungibility issue" discussed below), such grants are, in any case, far removed from pure earmarking.

Although user charges are common at the local level and, in principle, offer the greatest scope for earmarking, in practice they are rarely funnelled into a separate fund and are usually supplemented by contributions from general revenues. Except for electricity – a special case – user charges in Ontario's municipalities commonly recover at least some of the cost of providing water, sewage treatment (often supplied by regional governments), municipal transit, parking, waste disposal, and a variety of recreational services such as swimming pools, arenas, and golf courses. Over time, such charges have become an increasingly important source of finance for municipalities. Revenue from privileges, permits, and licences and from the sale of goods and services constituted less than 6 per cent of total Ontario municipal revenue in 1975, compared to nearly 13 per cent in 1991 (see Table 4, below). As a percentage of own-source revenue, they accounted for 10 per cent in 1965, and 22 per cent in 1991.[27]

The situation in the region and city of Waterloo is probably broadly representative of experience in the province, where regional tiers of government have been established. User charges levied by the region for provision of water, waste water treatment, and waste management and disposal made up 28 per cent of current revenues in 1991. These revenues were sufficient to cover the cost of these services. In contrast, other regional user charges were minor in magnitude, flowed into general revenues, and were simply subtracted from the amount of total expenditures financed by the regional levy on real property, which is collected by the lower-tier municipalities.

The region of Waterloo sets aside annual contributions to several capital reserve funds – a type of "expenditure earmarking." This practice is in effect part of an intertemporal budgeting strategy that allows for slow, but steady accumulation of funds to pay for anticipated bulges in capital spending at a future date.[28] Between 1988 and 1990, the regional levy grew annually by 2 per cent over the previous year's collections to finance contributions to the capital reserve fund. In 1991, however, the region did not increase its contribution rate because of rising welfare costs and the desire of the regional council to keep the mill rate increase under 10 per cent.

The revenue structure of the city of Waterloo in 1991 is depicted in Table 4. Most revenue comes from the property tax, which accounted for almost three-quarters of the total in 1991. Provincial grants accounted for only 3 per cent, and user charges, almost 17 per cent – not far below the provincial average. Most charge revenue is attributable to water billings and the associated sewer surcharge. Nearly two-thirds of the total revenue raised by the city is transferred to either the region or to local school boards. After deducting these payments, 11 per cent of net municipal revenue came from user charges.

None of these user charges, however, is accounted for separately. All flow into the general revenue account. As at the regional level, only water and sewer charges cover costs of these services and, in this sense, approximate earmarking. Indeed, Ontario municipalities are discouraged from directing collections from water sales into general revenue unless they use these revenues to retire debt issued to pay for water and sewage projects.

The only really pure earmarking at the municipal level appears to occur with the recently enacted development charges. Like earlier lot levies, development charges are perhaps best interpreted as an

TABLE 4
Structure of Revenues, City of Waterloo, 1991

Revenue source	Amount ($)
Property taxes	
Residential and Farm	55,900,924
Commercial-industrial and business	37,314,629
Taxation from other governments (grants-in-lieu)	2,417,701
Grants from	
Province of Ontario	4,275,315
Federal government	–
Other municipalities	987,511
Other	
Investment income	2,588,006
Land sales	–
Other	1,744, 558
User fees	19,844,267
Water billings	6,822,733
Sewer surcharge	6,934,817
Recreational and cultural services fees	1,287,169
Environmental services fees	1,581,198
Transportation services fees	1,426,777
Miscellaneous	1,791,533
Total revenue	125,072,911
(less amounts collected on behalf of the region and	
school boards)	(82,444,275)
Net municipal revenue	42,628,636
Own-source revenue	119,929,699

SOURCE: Corporation of the City of Waterloo, *Treasurer's and Auditors' Report for the Year ended 1991.*

attempt to implement the benefit principle of taxation by requiring residents of new developments to pay for extending municipal services to these locations.

Under Ontario's Development Charges Act of 1989, municipalities must draw up a ten-year plan for the municipal services that will be provided to new developments. Service levels are to be no higher than those provided to current residents. The capital costs net of provincial grants, of providing services to both residential and non-residential occupants are calculated for this ten-year planning period. Separate calculations are made for water, sewage, transportation, and general services, and costs per household are differentiated according to type of residential dwelling (single and semi-detached, townhouses, and multiple units). Costs attributable to non-residential development are assessed for each type of service, by area. As lots are sold and development charges collected, the funds are deposited into the appropriate capital fund and used to pay for past or future capital costs of the development. These funds may not be allocated to any other purpose, and they cannot be supplemented by other sources. They are truly earmarked.

As Slack and Bird (1991) note, however, the existence of both a benefit rationale and tight earmarking by no means implies that development charges are calculated accurately. For one thing, the basis for the required estimates is not really good enough to accomplish precisely the desired fiscal differentiation. Moreover, since new homeowners subject to development charges are also subject to property taxes and user charges, they are, in effect, also paying for the debt-financed portion of services benefiting existing residents – unless, as has sometimes been done, the development charge is reduced to offset this "double tax" element. Finally, it is open to question in any case whether it makes economic sense to, in effect, require many individual builders to borrow small amounts more expensively, which is really what happens with development charge financing, rather than to finance through (cheaper) municipal borrowing.

Along similar lines, the province has encouraged "innovative financing," which could dramatically increase earmarking at the municipal level. The motivation here is the same as that inspiring development charges – to make beneficiaries of urban infrastructure investments bear their costs, or at least a large portion thereof. Some options examined to date include value capture and build, operate, and transfer (BOT).[29] Value capture – for example, special property tax assessments for owners of properties whose value is enhanced by new infrastructure investments – has recently been discussed for the proposed Sheppard subway extension in Toronto. Under BOT, private-sector investors would build community facilities such as arenas and golf courses, charge a user fee that would make the investment attractive, and later transfer ownership to the municipality after costs had been recouped. Both methods contain a strong benefit link between the tax or user charge and use of those funds for infrastructure purposes. This is pure earmarking.

Other Canadian Experience

Perhaps the most surprising thing about earmarking, broadly defined, in Canada is how important it appears to be in fiscal terms. A recent survey (Hickling Corporation 1991) concluded that, in 1990, as much as $50 billion of federal revenues could be considered earmarked, if one included both payments to special-purpose fund such as the Canada Pension Plan and revenues from the public received by crown corporations. This analysis suggests that over 36 per cent of federal budgetary revenue is earmarked (or almost 25 per cent, if one excludes enterprise revenues). The same study estimated that 20–25 per cent of total provincial receipts (including specific-purpose transfers from other governments) were earmarked and that the proportion of earmarked local revenues, even leaving out utility revenues, might be as high as 40–45 per cent.[30] Large as these figures are, there appears to have been little growth in earmarking over the last twenty years.[31]

The very broad definition of earmarking, which extends to such extremely loose varieties as "announcements associating taxes with certain spending programs," used in such calculations is not very useful, however. Much of this earmarking is more "notional" than "effective," let alone "pure." This subsection simply considers briefly a few of the more important provincial and local experiences with earmarking.

Most provincial earmarking is, as in Ontario, notional, except for the recent special funds in British Columbia discussed below. Since health services appear to be the most popular government program with taxpayers, notional earmarking seems most widespread there. British Columbia, like Alberta and Yukon, levies health insurance premiums to help finance the program, while Quebec and Manitoba, like Ontario, levy employer payroll taxes. All the revenue from Nova Scotia's retail sales tax (the Health Services Tax) and half of the revenue from the same tax in Saskatchewan are earmarked for health programs.[32] In none of these cases, however, does the earmarked tax supply more than a fraction of the expenditure on health services, and in none is there any indication that the earmarking has been in any way effective.

In contrast, British Columbia has recently introduced pure earmarking in three new funds. First, the Health Special Account (HSA) announced in the 1992 budget receives one-half of all net provincial lottery proceeds. These funds are lodged in a special account of the general revenue fund to be used for "urgent health priorities." Bill 10-1992 spells out these priorities as health research, health promotion, and health education services, in addition to simple "health care." Although it is too early to assess the HSA's expenditure impact, the breadth of designated uses makes it unlikely that the HSA will amount to much.

Second, the 1992 budget also announced the Natural Resource Community Fund (NRCF), to be financed from 0.5 per cent of all natural resource revenue, other than fines, collected by the province. The purpose of this fund is to assist natural resource–dependent communities to "ride out," and adjust to, changes in their economic fortunes.[33] Expenditures may be made for training and retraining unemployed workers, for job creation and maintenance, for worker relocation, and for assistance to local governments in covering their operating costs. Any money, in excess of $25 million, not spent by the end of the fiscal year, however, is to be transferred to general revenues.

Third, the Sustainable Environment Fund (SEF) was initiated earlier, in 1990. A large part of the expenditures from this program will be dedicated to a ten-year reforestation program. Besides reforestation, the fund will finance a hodgepodge of environmentally related activities: municipal solid waste programs, a Hazardous Waste Management Corporation, energy conservation, environmental protection and research, vehicle emission inspections in the Lower Mainland, and acquisition of parklands and natural habitat. An initial injection of $50 million was provided by the lottery fund. Continuing funding is to be secured by earmarking proceeds from government sales of tree seeds and seedlings and a host of environmental levies, including $3 for each new pneumatic tire sold in the province, $5 for each lead-acid battery sold, and, in a rather trendy gesture, all revenues from taxation of disposable diapers for babies.[34] In addition, all the revenue collected from fees, permits, and approvals under the Waste Management Act will flow into this fund. All fines and penalties under this act and other environmental and wildlife acts will likewise be captured by the SEF.

In contrast to the provinces' relatively small and constant use of earmarking, user fees, all of which can potentially be earmarked, have grown at the municipal level in Canada. As shown in Table 5, user fees rose from 7 to 12 per cent of total municipal revenue between 1975 and 1990.

In practice, however, very little, if any, of the revenue produced by local user charges is earmarked to pay for the public services whose purchase gave rise to it. As a rule, the revenue is simply paid into general revenue accounts.[35] Moreover, pricing practices differ widely among municipalities. Most tried – inappropriately, if understandably – to apply some sort of average cost formula, but specifications of the formula ranged from a notion of average variable costs to average

TABLE 5
User Charges in Canada as a Source of Local Government
Revenue, by Province, 1975 and 1990

	1975	1990
Newfoundland	8.3	10.9
Prince Edward Island	4.8	7.0
Nova Scotia	5.3	8.1
New Brunswick	13.3	17.4
Quebec	7.0	8.5
Ontario	5.7	12.9
Manitoba	5.3	9.0
Saskatchewan	7.1	10.1
Alberta	10.7	15.4
British Columbia	8.9	13.6
Yukon	14.1	14.6
Northwest Territories	10.8	29.2
Canada (weighted averaged of all provinces/territories combined)	7.0	12.0

SOURCE: Calculated from data in CANSIM, Statistics Canada, Ottawa, 1991, by H. Kitchen, "Efficiency of Delivery of Local Government Services under Alternative Organizational Modes," Peterborough, unpublished, 1992.

total cost.[36] On the whole, most municipal user charges in Canada, when not earmarked, are in effect consumption taxation. Even when they are earmarked – as when there is a separate municipal public utility enterprise – the way in which prices are set makes them generally, at best, poor instruments for signalling consumers' preferences.

U.S. Experience

Earmarking, both pure and notional, is more common in the United States than in Canada.[37] Around 28 per cent of federal government revenues were earmarked for specific expenditures in 1990. Payroll taxes are imposed on both workers and employers to cover social security payments (old age pensions, disability payments, and survivors' benefits) and medicare expenditures incurred by the elderly. For many low-income workers, these social security taxes are now a much greater burden than personal income taxes; although it can also be argued that, unlike the latter, this burden may be somewhat justified on benefit grounds.[38]

The other major federal taxes that are earmarked are those financing the highway and airport trust funds and the "Superfund."[39] Motor fuel excise taxes are earmarked to the highway trust fund to pay for maintenance and expansion of the interstate highway system. As is also true in Canada, airfare ticket taxes are earmarked to pay for airport facilities. In total, around 75 per cent of the expenditure of the U.S. Department of Transport is financed by earmarked taxes and user fees. The highway and airport trust funds in general represent appropriate use of earmarking and have drawn little criticism.

The same cannot be said about the Superfund, set up in 1980 to repair the environmental damage caused by toxic dump sites and to pay compensation to injured parties. Nearly 40 per cent of the revenue accruing to this fund is derived from excise taxes on petroleum stocks and 42 chemical feedstocks. Because all firms owning taxed feedstocks pay the same rate of tax regardless of their past, current, or prospective behaviour, the Superfund levies have only a weak relationship to the environmental costs attributable to the present or previous actions of individual firms.

Moreover, all firms involved in development of a waste site are jointly and severally liable for the costs of cleaning up. Such collective liability, while superficially attractive as reaching "deep pockets," may, in practice, have been counterproductive. Private insurance companies have revoked their environmental liability coverage for individual companies, premiums for which previously acted to "internalize" the external damage costs.

Such earmarking for new expenditures may in fact stimulate too much spending on environmental clean-up. A recent study, for instance, argued that the 1175 sites already on the National Priority List for clean-up have a price tab that may reach $30 billion and that a further $55–74 billion will be required for new sites added to the list.[40] The goal of restoring every site to its "original condition" is not sensible, and there should be procedures for identifying sites that impose an immediate threat to human health and those that do not. At the moment, there is little correlation between risk levels and decisions to restore a site. The role of earmarking in financing environmental programs is discussed further below.

Earmarking is also common at the state and local level, although there is wide variation in degree.[41] Between 1953 and 1983, earmarking at the state level, however, fell by more than half, from 51 to 21 per cent (see Table 6). At the local level, where revenues from user fees are normally earmarked, user charges have increased (from 26

TABLE 6
Earmarked Taxes as a Proportion (%) of Total U.S. State Tax Revenues,
by State, Selected Years, 1953–54 to 1983–84

State	Fiscal year			
	1953–54	1962–63	1978–79	1983–84
U.S. average	51	41	23	21
New England				
Connecticut	26	23	0	1
Maine	46	39	19	20
Massachusetts	56	54	41	40
New Hampshire	53	54	31	24
Rhode Island	6	4	0	1
Vermont	42	39	23	23
Mid-Atlantic				
Delaware	0	3	0	5
Maryland	47	40	34	24
New Jersey	7	2	25	39
New York	13	10	0	6
Pennsylvania	41	63	15	15
Great Lakes				
Illinois	39	43	14	18
Indiana	49	39	43	33
Michigan	67	57	38	39
Ohio	48	48	21	18
Wisconsin	63	61	n.a.	12
Plains				
Iowa	51	44	19	13
Kansas	77	66	29	25
Minnesota	73	74	12	13
Missouri	57	40	20	29
Nebraska	55	53	41	29
North Dakota	73	43	29	21
South Dakota	59	54	33	32
Southeast				
Alabama	89	87	88	89
Arkansas	41	36	21	18
Florida	40	39	28	28
Georgia	29	22	11	9
Kentucky	46	29	n.a.	16
Louisiana	85	87	5	4
Mississippi	40	37	n.a.	30
North Carolina	38	30	20	8

TABLE 6 (*concluded*)

State	Fiscal year			
	1953–54	1962–63	1978–79	1983–84
South Carolina	69	62	56	55
Tennessee	72	77	60	26
Virginia	39	32	27	24
West Virginia	57	39	21	21
Southwest				
Arizona	47	51	31	29
New Mexico	80	31	36	44
Oklahoma	62	59	n.a.	43
Texas	81	66	54	20
Rocky Mountain				
Colorado	75	51	17	25
Idaho	51	44	38	32
Montana	61	53	55	60
Nevada	55	35	34	52
Utah	74	62	52	48
Wyoming	61	64	54	69
Far West				
Alaska	n.a.	6	1	2
California	42	28	12	13
Hawaii	n.a.	7	5	5
Oregon	47	36	23	19
Washington	35	30	29	26

SOURCE: R. Ebel, ed., *A Fiscal Agenda for Nevada*, Reno and Las Vegas: University of Nevada Press, 1990, pp. 152–53
n.a. = not available.

per cent of own-source revenue in 1961 to 34 per cent in 1989). State and local user charges over this same period rose only from 19 to 22 per cent.[42]

Some states practise pure earmarking, even when there is no benefit rationale. Nevada, for example, logically earmarks its gas tax for highway construction and maintenance; but it also earmarks cigarette taxes to finance grants to counties and taxes on slot machines and estates to pay for higher education. Similarly, taxes on alcoholic beverages are earmarked to pay for grants to counties and cities as well as, more plausibly, for drug and alcohol rehabilitation.

California often uses referenda to pass tax measures. In 1988, it

adopted Proposition 99, called for a 25-cent-per-pack tax on cigarettes to be used for a variety of programs, including state aid to
public libraries, health care for the indigent, and health and education generally. Initially, a large portion of the revenue was targeted
to tobacco-related health care programs, such as cancer research
and anti-smoking campaigns. A year later, however, use of these
funds to subsidize hospital trauma care was authorized. Since it
seems rather unlikely that smokers are more likely than others to be
involved in automobile crashes, this redirection of the funds suggests perhaps that there was never really any benefit rationale for
this earmarking.

Also in 1988, Indiana approved a half-cent increase in state cigarette taxes to be earmarked to paying for a new program of subsidized child care for school-age children. Children 5 to 14 years old,
with working parents or whose parents are enrolled in a training program, are offered care both before and after school hours. There is no
charge for poor families, and a sliding scale for others. One sponsor
of this tax remarked that the "nice thing about this money is we can
count on 'it' every year until 1993."[43] About the same time, the city of
Chicago imposed its own earmarked tax on cigarettes to pay for
accommodation for the homeless. On the whole, there is clearly no
benefit rationale for such earmarking.

Finally, New Jersey provides an example of notional earmarking.
The state dedicates a portion of its personal income tax to education
and local property tax relief, but, as is common in Canada, there is no
evidence that educational spending has been stimulated by this earmarking, in part because the earmarked revenues contribute only a
portion of the expenditure in question. This point is discussed further
below.

Earmarking: Pros and Cons

The Case against Earmarking

Earmarking is frequently criticized because it allegedly shields
expenditure programs from the critical assessment that they would
otherwise receive from budgetary authorities. The concern is that earmarking will build rigidities into the expenditure allocation process
and prevent authorities from efficiently reallocating funds whenever
spending priorities change.

For a number of reasons, however, this fear of budgetary rigidity may be exaggerated. First, the earmarking constraint on expenditures may be more apparent than real. Changes in the rate of an earmarked charge or tax, for example, permit a degree of freedom to adjust the expenditure flows in the earmarked area in either direction – although experience suggests that such "prices" may tend to be rather "sticky." Moreover, if earmarking is notional, budgetary authorities always hold the final card in deciding by how much to "top up" the amount of earmarked revenue.

If, in contrast, pure earmarking is employed, and it passes a benefit test, the inability of expenditure authorities to redirect earmarked revenues may bar inefficient reallocations. Finally, the rigidity hypothesis assumes implicitly that, if expenditures were made from general fund financing, they would receive closer scrutiny. While this may be true for new expenditure proposals, it is not characteristic of most established programs, where expenditure levels are mandated by previous legislation.

Pure earmarking of new projects may increase accountability, because everyone can understand where the revenue is coming from and how it is being spent. However, with notional earmarking – the most prevalent form in Ontario and the rest of Canada – and also to some extent with effective earmarking, tracing the impact of earmarking on the fiscal system is very difficult.

This problem has its roots in the fungibility of funds – the fact that money not used for one purpose is available for others. Suppose a province imposes new environmental taxes (or "user fees") that are earmarked to pay for reforestation, as British Columbia has recently done. Suppose, further, that, without earmarking, exactly the same amount of reforestation would have been undertaken. In this situation, the earmarked revenues dedicated to reforestation permit funds that would otherwise be spent on that objective to be directed to financing other expenditures. The same fiscal outcome would have ensued if the environmental taxes were earmarked to underwriting these other expenditures and there were no diversion of funds from the reforestation budget.

Substituting pure earmarking for general fund financing of existing programs creates the same problem. Determining the impact of earmarking requires accurate assessment of the situation that would have occurred in the absence of any earmarking. Given the fungibility of funds, the only general conclusion that can be reached is that earmarking will probably expand the range of expenditure options available to governments. Accurately pinpointing how these options are exercised will be difficult, if not impossible. This point is discussed further below.

From a normative standpoint, the contribution of earmarking to public welfare clearly depends on how the additional fiscal resources are used. If the earmarked revenues finance some otherwise unexploited opportunities to expand the public sector in areas where marginal benefits exceed marginal costs, earmarking will enhance economic efficiency. If, however, there are no such opportunities left, further expansion of the public sector is inefficient and the most efficient use of the extra funds would be to return them to taxpayers in the form of a tax cut. If the extra resources were used instead to finance redistributive transfers, the incidence of the earmarked taxes would have to be compared with the benefit incidence of the transfers to determine the effectiveness of earmarking in meeting equity objectives.

Earmarking is thus like any other fiscal instrument: it can be applied well or it can be applied poorly. Pure earmarking, for example, has little appeal as a budgetary process when the benefit link between tax and expenditure is completely severed. When the revenue source earmarked and the expenditure function supported are totally unrelated, the amount of spending is not based on measure of demand for the service but instead is determined by an arbitrary and irrational funding procedure. Under these conditions, there is almost certain to be either "too much" or "too little" of the public service when the amount supplied is evaluated on efficiency grounds. Unless there is a clear benefit link between tax payment and service provided, pure earmarking will probably result in an efficiency loss rather than an efficiency gain in comparison with general fund financing.

As an example of ill-considered earmarking, cigarette excise taxes could be earmarked to finance education. Some U.S. states, such as California, have adopted earmarking practices of this type. One problem with such practices is that the thirst for knowledge has little to do with the craving for nicotine. Worse, a successful anti-smoking campaign would have dire implications for the level of literacy. Nor would it make sense to earmark cigarette tax revenues to pay for sewers or environmental control. The absence of any complementarity between smoking and learning, or between smoking and waste generation, means that the excise tax conveys no useful information about the demand for public services.

For similar reasons, the earmarking of general revenues for a specific expenditure purpose as a rule has no compelling fiscal logic. For example, for some years, the Canadian federal government earmarked a share of the personal income tax, the corporate income tax, and the federal sales tax to pay for the old age pension. The amounts raised from these tax sources, however, were related only loosely to the amounts spent (or promised) as pensions. Such earmarking makes no economic sense and serves no useful budgetary purpose. Earmarking a fraction of general revenues to particular expenditures serves no function in signalling demand for public services.

Since there is so much earmarking for which no benefit rationale exists, we must seek another explanation of why earmarking enhances efficiency. The obvious one is, of course, simply the "halo effect" of making tax increases or charges more acceptable by attaching them, in name or in fact, to desired expenditures. This is discussed further below. The public choice literature offers another political explanation, in which earmarking becomes an offshoot of rational rent seeking by those determined to use the public sector to advance their private interest. In this view, earmarking is promoted by those groups that expect to benefit from the expenditures in question as a means of obtaining a more secure source of funding.

As an example of such "rent seeking," consider the fact that about one-third of Canadian adults smoke. If politicians offered to increase the tax on cigarettes and earmark the proceeds for increased educational spending, presumably at least two-thirds of the voters might, from a self-interested perspective, be expected to support this proposal. Even some smokers might approve if they placed a high value on more educational services. Nonetheless, the essence of this earmarking proposal is that it permits a majority of non-smokers to "gang up" on a minority of smokers and force them to pay for expenditures that are of general benefit to everyone.

Earmarking may also allow a minority to exploit a majority, rather than the reverse. For example, a modest increase in fuel taxes may be earmarked to pay for new subway construction. A majority of road users would be burdened by this tax, the proceeds of which would be used for the benefit of non-users. Those living close to the new subway, or who own property near it, would become noticeably better off. As before, however, this example is complicated by the fact that some road users might favour this earmarking if they felt that the subway would persuade some households to leave their car at home and help reduce road congestion.[44]

Moreover, what is earmarked for one use today can be diverted to some alternative use tomorrow as competing rent seekers struggle to twist earmarking in their favour. It may not even be necessary to do this overtly if it can be accomplished covertly by manipulating expenditure categories. For example, if the gas tax were earmarked to pay for highways, groups interested in raising safety standards and reducing speeding might urge inclusion of highway patrol costs in the expenditures made for "highways."

The Case for Earmarking

As already emphasized, the case for earmarking is strongest when there is a close benefit link between payment of the earmarked tax and use of the tax to finance additional expenditures. When such a link exists, taxpayers are supplied with public services that are of particular benefit to them. When, for example, taxpayers pay the excise tax imbedded in the price of a litre of gasoline, they indicate at least some willingness to pay for provision of road services, and it is not inappropriate to earmark such excise taxes for provision and maintenance of road services. Given the high degree of complementarity between gas consumption and road usage, the excise tax is a close substitute for levying a direct user fee on road service consumption.

Such benefit-related earmarking reveals the preferences of taxpayers for public services and thus sends a clear demand signal to the public sector about how much of the service should be supplied. Under these conditions, earmarking assists in providing an efficient level of public goods to households, since supply automatically adjusts to demand. To the extent that earmarking thus implements the benefit principle of taxation, it solves the two most important problems in public finance: deciding how much of a public good to supply and who should pay for it.

Besides satisfying the economic efficiency criterion, rational (that is, benefit-related) pure earmarking may also meet some of the demands for fair taxation. If taxpayers pay for identifiable, publicly provided services that they consume, and no one either receives a service without paying for it or pays without receiving service, this outcome is as consistent with the accepted canons of fairness as charging everyone the same price for a loaf of bread.

Of course, for earmarking to be efficient, it must be restricted to where it works best. Earmarking is appropriate if the public sector offers services that resemble privately supplied services in that each taxpayers's consumption of the service can be accurately monitored (or at least satisfactorily approximated) and if the marginal costs of extending public services to taxpayers can be measured reliably. Under these circumstances, it is efficient to charge each taxpayer a user fee geared to the marginal cost of providing the service in question.

Establishing a benefit rationale for earmarking is only a necessary, not a sufficient condition for achieving economic efficiency. Benefit-based pure earmarking will not work well unless the tax rate (or user charge) is set appropriately. In principle, the tax rate (or user charge) should closely approximate the short-run marginal cost of providing the public service. For publicly provided private goods, this pricing procedure also contains an investment guideline: invest in more capacity if the appropriately set price exceeds long-run marginal cost. Where the public sector provides "lumpy" public goods such as uncongested roads, a two-step investment and pricing procedure is necessary. First, total benefits must be compared to total costs if the project is undertaken and if price is set equal to short-run marginal cost. Second, if the investment decision is favourable, the price should be equated to short-run marginal cost.

Failure to get prices "right" and to consider the interdependence of pricing and investment decisions can easily steer earmarking off the efficiency tracks. For example, if price is set in excess of short-run marginal cost, the surplus accumulated in an earmarked fund could be inefficiently invested and wasted under earmarking. In the United States, for example, it has been alleged that earmarked taxes on airline passenger tickets and aviation jet fuel (for the Airport and Airways Trust Fund) have been set at too high a level in comparison to short-run marginal costs and have resulted in an enormous surplus of investible funds that dwarfs the set of aviation projects displaying attractive benefit-cost ratios. This example illustrates the more general proposition that inappropriate public-sector prices will inevitably distort public-sector investment decisions. Under general fund financing, for instance, failure to impose any price for a publicly provided service will normally result in overinvestment in the service's capacity.

Earmarking may also be appropriate even when transaction costs make assessing user fees impractical, provided that it is possible to attach an excise tax to consumption of private goods that is a close complement to consumption of the public service. In the case of the

Figure 3
The Case for Partial Earmarking

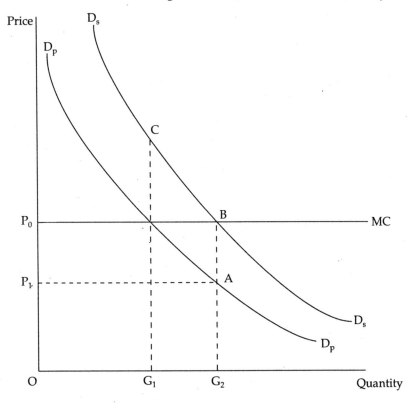

earmarked gas excise tax, for example, road users as a group are made to pay for the road services that they consume.

Partial earmarking may be appropriate if consumption of the public service generates external benefits for other households. (See Figure 3.) The public service – immunization, for example – can be provided at constant marginal cost MC. Private demand for this service as D_PD_P The difference in height between this demand curve and the "social" demand curve D_SD_S measures the benefits that accrue to the rest of society when an individual is immunized. If individuals paid the full cost of immunization and were charged a user fee of DP_0, only G_1 of the service would be demanded, an inefficiently small amount, since the value to society of more individual consumption (the vertical distance G_1C) exceeds the marginal cost of greater consumption.

The socially efficient level of consumption is the amount shown as G_2, where the value to society and the marginal cost of further consumption are equated. To achieve this efficient level of provision, individuals should be charged the fee OP_1, which is less than marginal cost, and the proceeds from this payment, the area OP_1AG_2, should be earmarked to help pay for the service. The balance of the cost of this service, the area P_1P_0BA, should be financed from general revenues. As can be seen from the figure, the larger the gap between the private and social demand curves, the less scope there is for earmarking. In the limit, where the public service is a pure public good, such as national defence, the marginal cost of extending service to another household is zero, and there is clearly no role for either user pricing or earmarking in financing provision of this type of service.

Besides helping to achieve efficiency in public-service provision of private goods, earmarking, if appropriately designed, may also enforce intertemporal agreement on expenditure actions (Teja 1990). Suppose, for example, that the federal government enacted an earmarked excise tax on chemical stocks to finance the clean-up of toxic chemicals. Unless the proceeds of this tax were earmarked for this purpose, taxpayers in "clean" areas might resent having to pay for improved amenities of those residing in "dirty" areas. Residents of dirty areas could of course say that they would, in their turn, be willing to pay for any future clean-up of clean areas that subsequently became contaminated, but there is no way in which current voters can bind the decisions of future politicians facing such a decision. Earmarking may offer a way around this impasse to the extent that it guarantees that funds will be available for clean-up no matter when such funds may be needed in future.[45]

Finally, there are other political reasons for considering earmarking. There is little doubt that many Canadians feel overtaxed and would reject higher levels of general taxation. Nevertheless, many might endorse a variety of new earmarking initiatives, with varying degrees of enthusiasm, for several reasons. Some might see earmarking as the rational choice mechanism that it can be under certain conditions and would welcome the opportunity to exert greater control over how their tax dollars are spent. Others may perceive new opportunities to engage the public sector in redistributive activities favourable to themselves.

Still others may support earmarking, not knowing that it is chimerical. Notional earmarking, in particular, lends itself to deception of taxpayers. Governments may succeed in "selling" new expenditure programs by giving the public the illusion that funds will be earmarked from various sources to these programs. In fact, the earmarked revenues may be funnelled into general revenues or, if channelled into a separate fund, may be matched by reduced funding from non-earmarked revenue sources. In either case, taxpayers may end up not getting what they thought they would.

As noted above, it is inherently difficult to determine what would have happened without earmarking. Clearly, however, if spending levels under earmarking are roughly the same as they would be with no earmarking, earmarking effectively siphons off any new revenues for purposes other than those for which it was "sold." To the extent that taxpayer-voters are unable to discern just how their earmarked taxes are being spent, they are victims of fiscal sleight-of-hand. Such earmarking may appeal to politicians as an easy source of new revenues in tough times, but it is nothing but an empty promise.

Alternatively, earmarking may not deliver to politicians what they expect in the form of new revenues. A considerable amount of experimental work suggests, for example, that tax compliance depends, in part, on use made of tax revenues. Other studies have suggested that uncertainty about the tax system on the whole tends to increase tax compliance and hence tax revenues.[46] If some revenues are earmarked to provide certain public goods, however, it turns out that uncertainty on the revenue side may reduce tax compliance in contrast to the general-funding case, in which taxpayers' uncertainty about enforcement and tax policies would generally be expected to increase compliance by risk-averse taxpayers.

Suppose, for example, that there is initially a certain degree of uncertainty, intended or unintended in the operation of the tax system because of such features as frequent changes in laws, imprecision on various points, and uneven administration. If now some revenues are strongly earmarked, thus strengthening the link between payment of taxes and receipt of expenditure benefits, tax compliance may actually decline, and hence tax revenues will fall. Earmarking, in effect, makes the individual taxpayer's decision about compliance depend partly on his or her perception of how likely others are to comply. If others are expected to pay more, the individual may be tempted to "free ride" and pay less by underdeclaring taxable income; if others are expected to pay less, the same temptation to pay less arises because now the individual receives less value for the tax dollar. In contrast to general funding, with earmarking, the more uncertain a person is that others will pay their taxes, the less likely he or she is to pay his or her own.

Assessing the Evidence

To this point, the argument in this section may lead the reader to sympathize with the apocryphal politician who told his colleagues that he wanted a one-armed economist as an adviser because he was tired of being told "on the one hand this, but on the other hand that!" Actually, however, the conclusion to which this argument leads is clear: properly designed earmarking can be not only useful but even essential in leading governments to do the right things in the right quantities. In particular, earmarking is appropriate when there is a strong benefit connection between the expenditure financed and the revenue tapped – that is, when the latter is, in effect, a "tax price" for the former. In such instances, not only should the revenue be earmarked, but except for the "partial" case discussed above, the earmarking should be "strong" – the amount spent should be tightly related to the amount collected. A related, though weaker case may be made for earmarking in some instances on the grounds of taxpayers' likely acceptance and intertemporal binding. In practice, however, most earmarking in Canada appears to fail these tests and, hence, have little to be said for it.

Moreover, even the strong, rational case for earmarking rests on the proposition that earmarking actually affects both how much revenue is collected and what it is used for. In fact, it is exceedingly difficult to test these propositions empirically. Early attempts to do so were very crude. Deran (1965), for example, found no relationship between the extent of earmarking and the level of expenditures in U.S.states. Eklund (1972, 1980), in a cross-section study of highway expenditures in developing countries, found that earmarking of funds to highways was associated with higher expenditures on highways. The evidence on this question reported for various countries in Johansen (1989), however, may best be described as "mixed" – and is, in any case, based at best on casual empiricism. In a more systematic recent U.S. study, Borg and Mason (1988) found that increasing lottery revenues earmarked for school aid actually resulted in a decline in such aid, as general-fund spending for this function was cut back more than proportionately.

More recently, Dye and McGuire (1992) considered fairly rigorously the following question: "When taxes are earmarked for a particular purpose, does spending for that purpose increase by the amount of the earmarked revenues?" Their results, based on U.S. state data, suggest that "it depends." Changes in the level of earmarked revenues per capita appeared to have no effect on the level of total state expenditures per capita, as Deran (1965) had also found. And spending on education did not change when more taxes were earmarked for education – a result similar to, though less strong than, Borg and Mason's (1988). As suggested above, the fungibility of revenues, of course, explains these results. When state taxes, however, were earmarked to highways, although general-fund support for highways fell somewhat, total spending on highways rose – as Eklund (1972, 1980) had suggested – though by only a fraction of the earmarked revenues. Nonetheless, Dye and McGuire (1992, 554) conclude: "Taken as a whole, the results suggest that a greater reliance on earmarking may be associated with lower spending. We found *no* evidence to support suggestions that a greater reliance on earmarking will result in higher expenditures."

Finally, another recent study by Kimenyi, Lee, and Tollison (1990) similarly casts doubt on the effects of earmarking in practice.[47] This evaluation took a different tack and focused on the revenue side of earmarking, not on spending. It argued that introduction of earmarking should result in an increase in the revenue of the earmarked tax, essentially because earmarking provides an incentive for interest groups to lobby for increases in the earmarked tax rather than for a larger share of a fixed total budget. Their study of the effects of earmarking the U.S. federal fuel tax to the Highway Trust Fund in 1956 lent some support to this "rent seeking" view of earmarking.

The Potential for Earmarking in Ontario

"Green" Taxes and Expenditures

External effects have long been discussed in economics, as have proposals to offset their influence through application of "corrective" excise taxes and subsidies. Recently, however, this theoretical discussion has moved into public policy as a result of the "greening" of the budget, in which countries are turning to such fiscal instruments to assist in the war on pollution. We looked above at some recent environmentally motivated fiscal initiatives in Ontario, British Columbia, and the United States. The present section briefly reviews the major principles of environmental pricing, refers even more briefly to some recent European experience, and then addresses the issue of whether the proceeds from environmental taxes should be earmarked.

Private market activity frequently produces unwanted by-products or wastes that impair the quality of the environment and inflict external costs on society generally. The role of an environmental tax or subsidy is to make producers aware of these external costs and to create an incentive to scale back these costs to the "proper" level.[48] But what is the "proper" level of pollution? Clearly, it cannot be zero, because the costs of attaining lower levels of pollution must be balanced against the resulting benefits.

Consider first the simplest case – a fixed relationship between amount of pollution and level of output produced. At an optimum level of pollution, producers would be subject to an excise tax (or environmental user fee) such that their prices reflected the marginal social costs of production. The price-increasing effect of the excise tax would deter consumption of pollution-emitting products.

However, often it is not the output that is the source of pollution, but, rather, use of particular inputs such as coal. In these cases, the excise tax goes appropriately on emissions resulting from use of these inputs, and the optimum amount of emissions would be realized when the per unit tax rate equals both marginal abatement costs and marginal pollution costs for each producer. An excise tax at this rate would make it profitable – cost saving – for producers to restrict emissions until these two marginal costs were equated.[49]

The more closely a tax instrument can be targeted to its pollution objective, the better the results concerning its regulation function. For example, if sulphur dioxide is the primary source of acid rain, it is more efficient to tax such emissions directly than to do so indirectly by taxing use of coal as an input or consumption of coal-based products. A given reduction in acid rain pollution may be accomplished at smaller cost if firms install emissions-reducing scrubbers than if they are inducted to switch to an alternative energy source.

As an illustration of such targeting, Dobbs (1991) has argued that a user charge on rubbish collection is less desirable than a user subsidy (or refund), because the latter gives a stronger incentive to dispose of litter by recycling. A user fee, by contrast, encourages littering. A deposit on returned pop bottles, for example, encourages their return rather than their careless destruction. It is targeted more tightly to the anti-littering objective. Similarly, if less lead-laden smog is the goal, a tax on use of leaded gasoline is better targeted than an alternative tax on large, fuel-using cars.

Use of such "green" taxes on emissions has grown rapidly in Europe in recent years. Finland, Holland, and Sweden tax carbon dioxide emissions. Sweden also taxes nitrous oxide emissions from power plants and plans to tax discharges of heavy metal waste. Norway taxes CFC emissions; Denmark, rubbish production; and Germany, cars, on the basis of their exhaust emissions and noise levels. None of these taxes, however, is earmarked.

More generally, a recent survey found widespread deployment of a variety of fiscal instruments to curb environmental abuse in OECD-countries.[50] Effluent charges are levied on discharges of air and water pollutants in most countries. User charges are imposed for treatment of waste products in public-sector facilities. Product taxes based, for example, on the sulphur content of the item or on use of lead-acid batteries are common. Excise taxes are frequently employed to discourage use of environmentally damaging products such as leaded gas. Subsidies in the form of grants, soft (subsidized) loans, and tax deductions and credits are also available for a long list of environment-conserving investments. Finally, extensive use is made of deposit refunds to reduce waste and littering and elicit more recycling.

Despite this proliferation of fiscal instruments, direct regulation remains clearly the dominant method for dealing with most pollution problems (certainly the major ones) in Europe, as elsewhere. This extensive arsenal of fiscal tools is a supplement to regulatory action or a second line of defence. Indeed, since the taxes and charges are often set at levels too low to be significant incentives, they appear to be motivated more by the desire for revenue than for their environmental effects. Although much of the resulting revenue is directed towards alleviating the environmental problems on which the charges and taxes are based, European earmarking is generally notional rather than pure. As a rule, the revenue from these sources is generously supplemented with funds drawn from other sources.

That polluters should bear the cost of any environmental damage for which they are responsible seems eminently consistent with the benefit theory of taxation. This correspondence with equitable outcomes may be more apparent than real, however. Pollution taxes and charges, like any others, may be shifted onto other taxpayers, making their effective incidence quite different from their formal incidence. A disproportionately large share of such levies may, for example, be borne by low-income households once the effects of these costs on relative product prices is taken into account. Still, on efficiency grounds, it is clearly always desirable, if not always practical, to price environmental effects through taxes and charges.

However, there is no logical argument for designating the proceeds of such taxes for new environmental expenditures. In particular, the costs and benefits from increasing such expenditures should be compared with the costs and benefits of other uses of these funds, including reducing other taxes. There are clearly non-environmental benefits to be had from substituting an essentially "costless" revenue source for the costly, distorting taxes that would otherwise have to be used. If, for example, the social cost of raising another dollar of tax revenue from non-environmental taxes is $2.00, it would be inefficient to earmark a dollar of environmental revenue for expenditure on the environment if the social benefits from doing so are only $1.50. It would be even worse if the environmental expenditure of a dollar yielded benefits worth less than a dollar.

None of this is to deny that environmental clean-up projects may be socially worthwhile. But, if they are, it should be possible to demonstrate their desirability on the usual benefit-cost grounds, and they should not receive approval simply because "the money is there" from earmarked funds. In general, the optimal amount of expenditure on environmental clean-up bears no direct relationship to the amount of revenue that may be raised from an efficient environmental levy. As Oates (1991) has argued, an efficient environmental tax not only curbs environmental damage but also delivers the windfall benefits of extra revenue whose best use is likely to be less reliance on other kinds of distorting taxes. The impact of such a tax on economic efficiency is therefore virtuous twice over.

In principle, pollution taxes should be either raised or lowered from their efficient level, ignoring revenue effects, depending on whether higher tax rates raise or lower total revenue (Lee and Misolek 1986). For example, if a higher tax rate increases total revenue, pollution taxes should ideally be raised until the marginal net cost from further abatement of pollution – the difference between marginal abatement costs and marginal pollution costs – exactly balances the marginal efficiency benefits derived from substituting pollution tax revenue for general revenues.

What should be done with revenues from environmental charges and taxes? From the point of view of environmental regulation, such revenues should clearly not be used to compensate the victims (Oates 1991, 3). In cases where the "victims" have already been compensated by being able to pay lower rents, there is no persuasive equity argument for further compensation. Apart form the matter of previous recompense, the argument is simply that, if compensation were paid, the victims would no longer have any incentive to undertake offsetting actions – for example, by moving away from sources of pollution. Paying compensation for environmental damage is similar in many respects to providing subsidized insurance for property damage for people who wish to reside on a flood plain. Too many people will live in areas subject to flooding, and unnecessary charges on the public purse will arise when the flood comes, followed shortly by the swollen damage claims.

But provisional compensation may, nonetheless, be needed either to ensure political support or to satisfy equity concerns. If it is, a case can be made for linking any compensation to the form of harm that a policy choice inflicts – for example, road improvements to remedy congestion, or dedication of dollars or land for local amenities such as parks to bolster property values reduced by operation of a given facility.[51]

More and Better User Charges

The strongest case for earmarking clearly concerns user charges. Persuasive arguments for greater reliance on them by both provincial and municipal governments may be made. At the provincial level, there is considerable scope for applying new earmarked user fees in higher education. Failure to charge full-cost university tuition fees, for instance, clearly results in an "upside down" subsidy to the rich from the poor. Because university students are drawn disproportionately from upper-income families, and university costs not covered by tuition are financed from general revenues, numerous studies have shown that spending on universities significantly redistributes income from the poor to the rich. To make the rich pay a fairer share yet keep the doors open to the poor, properly structured charges could produce substantial revenue for educational institutions (presumably largely in replacement of general revenue financing). Moreover, if supported by an appropriate program of student loans, they can do so without reducing (and they may even facilitate) access for lower-income students.[52]

Even in health care, where user charges are less obviously attractive, a most promising approach might be one currently being considered in Quebec. That proposal would require Quebec residents to include in their taxable income an imputed element equal to the estimated value of the health care benefits consumed (presumably up to some "catastrophic" limit to avoid impoverishing the ill). The result would be, in effect, a variable user fee geared to income levels. Low-income users with no, or low taxable income would pay no, or a modest user fee and continue to be subsidized by the health care system. Others would be charged at rates varying by income and amount of services used. Such schemes are not novel, of course, having been proposed some years ago in both the United Kingdom and in Ontario.[53] The increasing need to control health care costs suggests that it is perhaps time to consider again the possible role of user charges even in this sector.

Undoubtedly, however, the greatest scope for more and better use of user charges is at the local level, where various studies have suggested that much more could be done.[54] Such charges could be used not simply vis-à-vis provision of the obvious services provided to individuals, such as water and sewage, but also to some extent even in such unlikely areas as fire protection, by, for example, levying fees on companies (and perhaps even households) that have a higher risk of fire. When no such fees are assessed, potential victims of fires are less likely to invest in safety measures that reduce these risks. Failure to levy user fees where they are applicable results in government spending that is not only higher than it should be but also targeted in ways that do not reflect the real needs of society – as determined by citizens, rather than bureaucrats.

Of course, it is not enough simply to impose user fees. What is critically important is to "get the prices right," to charge the correct user fee, and to earmark the proceeds. Even where such fees are commonly levied, there are often clear defects in their design. Water rates, for example, are frequently applied as fixed charges independent of the volume of water consumed. Consequently, the marginal costs of consumption is zero, leading to over-consumption of water and over-investment in water capacity. Even when metering of water consumption is applied but declining block rates are used, prices are less than marginal cost for large consumers, favouring those with big lawns and swimming pools. The fact that sewer charges are usually pro-rated on the amount of the water bill only compounds this pricing error.

Distance from the source of supply, for example, should matter in setting an appropriate user fee, as should seasonal peaks in demand. Generally, user fees should correspond to the marginal costs of providing service to each consumer. To cover capital or fixed costs, a connection or admission fee should be charged. Such two-part pricing is a more efficient instrument than a user fee set at the level of average total cost. On the whole, Ontario municipalities should clearly be encouraged to adopt an "appropriate fee for services" approach to program delivery wherever possible. Many municipal waste management facilities and parking lots, for example, are seriously underpriced.

Other Possibilities

Smoking, like drinking alcoholic beverages, is commonly thought to create adverse external effects. These effects are both real and financial. It has been argued, for example, that "second-hand smoke" may kill people; drunk drivers certainly do. In addition, innocent bystanders are also at financial risk under Ontario's health care system, since they must pay for the health care costs incurred by those who abuse their bodies by smoking and drinking.

In principle, so-called sin taxes are intended to make smokers and drinkers aware of the real and financial costs inflicted on the rest of society by their consumption choices. Excise taxes on cigarettes and alcoholic beverages may, therefore, be viewed as a form of "user" fee, and the policy issue becomes one of determining whether the user fee is set at an appropriate rate to reflect these external costs.

Pogue and Sgontz (1989) try to answer this question for alcoholic beverages in the United States using an optimum tax framework. Their purpose is to see not whether tax collections match measurements of external costs[55] but what the most efficient tax rate is when benefits of higher tax rates (fewer external costs) are balanced against costs (distortion in the consumption pattern of beverage consumers). For 1983, they calculate the external cost as $127 per gallon of pure alcohol. The optimum tax rate is estimated to be 51 per cent, more than twice the actual rate of 24 per cent in 1983.

For Canada, Raynauld and Vidal (1992) focus instead on the redistribution of welfare between smokers and non-smokers resulting from tobacco taxes. Ignoring the problem of "second-hand smoke," they calculate the net external cost of smoking to be $207 million in 1986, of which $143 million is estimated to be borne by non-smokers. These external costs consist of extra health care expenditures minus health cost savings arising from premature death. These costs pale in comparison to the benefits enjoyed by non-smokers in the form of lower pension contributions and their share of the public expenditures financed by tobacco taxes. In 1986, the authors suggest, perhaps $4.34 billion was transferred to non-smokers from smokers. Penance for the sin of smoking seems to outweigh vastly the cost of the sin.

Sumptuary taxation of tobacco and liquor products satisfies the benefit criterion, because users of these products are required to pay at least some of the costs imposed on third parties. Although it is not necessary to earmark the proceeds of such taxes to pay for the adverse health consequences of smoking and drinking, the rates for excise taxes on products with important external effects clearly need to be set with these consequences taken into account.

Much the same can be said for taxation of motor vehicles and motor fuel. In this case, however, there are really two separate aspects that need to be taken into account. First, such taxes can to some extent be considered "road user charges" and may properly be earmarked through a device such as a road fund to construction, maintenance, and operation of a road system. A particularly interesting example of such a road fund is Switzerland's.[56] Traditionally, such road funds have been financed by earmarked vehicle and fuel taxes, supplemented, where feasible, by tolls. Second, however, recent improvements in technology have made it possible to price road use more effectively and efficiently than ever before, including the external costs imposed by congestion and automobile-generated air pollution.[57] As with environmental pricing in general, however, while there is a sound economic case for "pricing out" such externalities through taxes and charges wherever feasible, there is no good case for earmarking the proceeds of such environmental taxes to road uses.

Another possible role for earmarking studied of late is use of payroll taxes to finance worker training. Assessment of the desirability of such a scheme requires answers to many questions. Who provides the training – the employer or the public sector? What kind of training – general or specific – is to be provided? Who ultimately pays for the training – the worker – by accepting lower wages – or the consumer – who faces higher prices?

More generally, why should a general payroll tax be used to pay for specific training benefits? One argument in favour of such a scheme is similar to "reverse social security" (Whalley and Ziderman 1989). Workers receive the benefits of training when they are young or unemployed, and they pay taxes for it when they are working. Over their lifetimes, it probably balances out.

Although this argument is ingenious, the more developed the labour market, and the more specific the skills for which training is wanted, the stronger the argument for "firm-based" rather than "government-based" training, however financed. To the extent that public intervention is needed at all (for example, because of liquidity constraints facing workers needing training), it would seem preferable to use a better-targeted instrument such as subsidized loans to workers or an employer tax credit if certified training is provided.[58]

Another instance where some earmarking may be indicated is taxes on tourists and tourist promotion expenditures. As Dwyer and Forsyth (1992, 20) show, if tourist taxes are earmarked for such expenditure, the results will probably promote welfare. Nonetheless, such a link may not be advisable: "If taxes can be levied on tourism without fear of retaliation, they should be levied at the optimum level no matter what promotion is undertaken. Such revenues should be used for the best available purpose, possibly to reduce other taxes if they are distortionary. In evaluating the case for promotion, the marginal cost of government funds, whether or not greater than their nominal value, should be used, since the funds, even if they are raised cheaply from tourism taxes, can be put to other uses." This is, of course, exactly the same as the argument made above concerning environmental taxes. Once again, there may be a good case for both the tax and the expenditure, but there is no good economic case for linking them.[59]

Notes

The first draft of this paper was prepared for the Ontario Fair Tax Commission and completed in February 1993. The authors are grateful to Juliana Sonneveld for research assistance.

1 Webber and Wildavsky (1986, 29).
2 Presumably, risk of arbitrary expenditure changes arising from such factors is considered greater than the budgetary instability that may result from tying expenditures to a particular revenue source. See, for example, the extensive discussion of earmarking in Colombia in Bird (1984) and McCleary and Uribe Tobon (1990).
3 Public Administration Service (1962, 39). Similarly adverse assessments may be found in such standard works on budgeting as Burkhead (1956) and Premchand (1983), although the latter, perhaps reflecting the more favourable view of earmarking common in the theoretical literature since the "Buchanan revolution" discussed below, is less sweeping in its condemnation. For other general critiques of earmarking, see McMahon and Sprenkle (1972) and Brazer (1985).
4 See Hickling Corporation (1991) and Postner (1992), respectively. The

main previous study of this question in Canada, and still by far the most extensive, is Bird (1976).

5 See, for example, Buchanan (1963, 1967); Goetz (1968); Browning (1975); Brennan and Buchanan (1980, 150–52); Oakland (1985, 1989); Teja (1990); and Wagner (1991).

6 Musgrave (1992, 15). His basic argument goes back to Wicksell and Lindahl (see Musgrave and Peacock, 1958). Musgrave is, as always, careful in specifying precisely the assumptions underlying his advocacy of earmarking and the substantial limitations that he envisages in practice. Nonetheless, the remarkable agreement on the theoretical superiority of earmarking by the two intellectual "fathers" of modern public finance, Buchanan and Musgrave, is noteworthy in view of the very different philosophical stances that they have adopted on most issues.

7 This characterization is common in the literature: see, for example, the recent fascinating study of the evolution of federal taxation in Canada by Gillespie (1991), in which the basic model assumes that the task of tax policy makers is to minimize the political cost of raising "required" revenues.

8 See, for example, Johansen (1989) and Heggie (1991). As these authors (and Bird 1976) note, there are many qualifications that must be borne in mind in setting prices for use of road services – or any of the other publicly provided private services for which user charge financing should, in principle, be employed – such as substitutability of other transport modes. It is obviously not possible, in the present paper, to explore the details of how charges should be set for particular services. Our concern is rather simply to establish the case for earmarking such charges once they are set.

9 See the discussion in Perret (1991). Other experiences with road funds, by no means all of them good, are discussed in Johansen (1989) and Heggie (1991).

10 This situation is changing, however, as new techniques of electronic vehicle identification, "smart cards," and so on are developed. See Hau (1991a) for an interesting review of over a dozen experiments with different road pricing techniques (most related to congestion pricing) now taking place around the world.

11 The argument, but not the figure, is based on Bird (1976); this source should also be consulted for much more extensive treatment of most of the points touched on in this brief exposition.

12 If MC is decreasing over the relevant range, the service has the characteristics of a public good, and charging a full cost price for it would be inefficient. If MC is increasing, the analysis is more complex, but not fundamentally altered.

13 For a review of some of the evidence, see, for example, Mushkin (1972)

or Bird (1976). Of course, even if the poor do benefit substantially from lower charges, giving away the service to everyone is a singularly wasteful and inefficient method of redistribution. It would be better to charge full cost prices and provide offsets to the poor through tax transfers or through some "credit card" device, as set out in Mushkin. Such matters cannot be explored further here, however. Our point is simply to establish that it is neither sensible nor necessary to subsidize provision of public services for distributive purposes.

14 Subject, of course, to a de minimis condition, to avoid the obvious problem that the cost of setting up numerous small, earmarked funds may outweigh the benefits of doing so.

15 Net revenues from the GST by law are supposed to be used solely to reduce the public debt and related debt charges. The mechanism employed to accomplish this aim is to exclude GST revenues from general budgetary revenue and to direct it to a special account, which then pays public debt charges. At present, this fund itself is in considerable deficit, since the expenditures with which it is charged greatly exceed the revenues accruing to it.

16 The first of these dimensions is stressed in McCleary (1991) and the second in Bird (1984).

17 For a detailed examination of Colombian earmarking, see McCleary and Urbie Tobon (1990) and Bird (1984).

18 As mentioned earlier, this "tight" a linkage is, strictly speaking, correct only when MC is constant. The analysis becomes considerably more complicated when MC is increasing or decreasing. For further discussion, see any text on public utility pricing (for example, Crew and Kleindorfer 1991).

19 For example, if area OGPC in Figure 1 is contributed by an earmarked tax. The federal deficit-reduction fund mentioned above also illustrates the point, at least for the foreseeable future.

20 Actually, as Raynauld and Vidal (1992) argue, they may not so benefit because they die sooner.

21 This procedure may have some advantages in terms of predictability for both granting and recipient governments, but it has no benefit rationale.

22 See also Bird (1976) for a related argument with respect to public housing.

23 See, for example, Winch (1962), Haritos (1973), Johansen (1989), and Heggie (1991).

24 In terms of Figure 1, for example, if the amount of earmarked revenues flowing to the indicated expenditure, as represented by the shaded area OPCG, is much less than the amount that would be spent in any case, the earmarking is meaningless.

25 The levy is also called a feebate ("fee" plus "rebate") because it both imposes a higher tax on less fuel-efficient cars and offers a subsidy to more fuel-efficient cars.

26 In addition, information from Ontario Treasury officials indicates that the Liquor Control Board of Ontario (LCBO), which collects the dispenser disposal fee, reaped about $11 million from it in 1990–91. The amount was expected to rise to about $45 million in 1992–93.

27 See Statistics Canada (1992).

28 Much the same result could be achieved, in a fiscally less conservative fashion, by borrowing for capital projects and, over time, paying off the debt thus incurred.

29 For a more extensive discussion of other "public-private partnership" schemes, such as density bonuses, linkage fees, parkland dedication, and public equity in private ventures (such as Toronto's Skydome), see Bird and Slack (1993).

30 Hickling Corporation (1991), supplemented by calculations based on Canadian Tax Foundation (1992).

31 See Bird (1976, 4–5), which estimates the total of charges, benefit taxes, and earmarked revenues as 36 per cent of federal revenues, 45 per cent of provincial own-source revenues, and 16 per cent of local own-source revenues. (These figures do not mean that all the benefit taxes identified, such as motor fuel taxes, are earmarked.) The reason for the big differences in the proportions shown for the provincial and local governments appears to be that the ratios in Hickling Corporation (1991) relate to total revenues, including intergovernmental transfers, most of which they assume to be earmarked, especially at the local level.

32 As Robinson (1986) notes, the Saskatchewan tax is called the Education and Health Tax. Although similar names are used in some other provinces (such as Social Services and Education Tax in New Brunswick and Social Service Tax in British Columbia), there does not appear to be even notional earmarking in these cases. Incidentally, Prince Edward Island levies its taxes on tobacco and alcohol in the name of the Health Tax Act, although again there appears to be no explicit earmarking.

33 This fund appears to be similar to the Mining Community Research Fund in Manitoba, which receives 3 per cent of provincial mining royalties and can be used to aid the economic development and diversification of mining communities and to supplement the municipal tax base in times of adjustment for such communities; Hickling Corporation (1991, 11).

34 British Columbia imposed its tax on disposable diapers by cancelling the previous sales tax exemption. Manitoba has now copied this approach, earmarking the proceeds to an environmental innovation fund.

35 See Sproule-Jones and White (1989). These authors suggest that the Statistics Canada data on which Kitchen (1992) based the figures shown in Table 5 actually understate the role of user fees. They argue for excluding the property tax revenue raised to finance school boards and for including business taxes and special assessments as user fees. Statistics Canada considers the latter property taxes rather than user fees. When these adjustments are made, Canadian municipalities collected 20 per cent of total revenue and 31 per cent of own-source revenue from user fees in 1981. In contrast, in 1951, user fees represented only 4 per cent of own-source revenue. Much of this increase can be traced to the growth in the sale of municipal services, which accounted for 28 per cent of total user fees in 1951 and 61 per cent by 1981.

36 See Sproule-Jones and White (1989), as well as Bird (1976) for an earlier examination of municipal pricing. Sproule-Jones and White err in arguing that the appropriate user fee should be geared to average total cost. As bird (1976) shows, if a public project is worth building, its services should, in principle, be priced according to short-run marginal costs.

37 For comparisons, see Hickling Corporation (1991) and Bird and Slack (1983). Although no one appears to have explored systematically the reasons for this difference, Bird and Slack suggest that, at least at the state/province and local level, user charges are invoked less in Canada because of the more general use of intergovernmental transfers.

38 This is a complex argument, which cannot be gone into here. For different views on the link between social security taxes and benefits, see, for example, Pechman, Aaron, and Taussig (1968); Pesando and Rea (1977); and Burbidge (1987).

39 Of lesser importance are earmarked payroll levies on coal companies, to finance the black lung disability fund, and earmarked user fees for inland waterways and for aquatic resources. The federal pipeline safety program is also financed exclusively by a levy on oil and natural gas transmission lines.

40 See Travis and Doty (1989); for a review of a wide range of U.S.studies on this and related issues, see Cropper and Oates (1992).

41 See Ebel (1990), Downing (1992), and Netzer (1992) for recent surveys of the use of earmarking at the subnational level in the United States.

42 These figures come from Netzer (1992) and include utility revenues in both the numerator and the denominator. Downing (1992), who excludes such revenues, finds an even more striking increase in local reliance on user charges, with the proportion of current charges within general own-source revenue rising from 18 to 48 per cent from 1967 to 1987; he

attributes this increase both to fiscal stress and to citizens' preference – as shown by surveys, 525–26 – for user charges over general taxes.

43 State legislator Dan May, as reported in the *New York Times*, 24 October 1988.

44 Strictly speaking, the example works only if it is assumed that roads are already optimally priced and used. In the real world, in which roads are generally underpriced, there may often be a "second-best" argument for taxing road users and subsidizing mass transit users (see Bird 1976).

45 Of course, since no Parliament can bind a future Parliament, even earmarking cannot guarantee this outcome but at least makes it perhaps both more plausible and more probably.

46 For citations, see Alm, Jackson, and McKee (1992), on which the following argument is based.

47 See also the more or less identical study reported in Wagner (1991).

48 See Cropper and Oates (1992) for a review of much of the extensive literature on environmental economics. See also Dewees (1992) for a review of environmental taxation in Canada.

49 Regulation that was sufficiently adept at equalizing these two marginal costs would also be an optimal policy response, as might a combination of "standards" and taxes (Baumol and Oates 1988) or a system of marketable permits. While a tax on pollution and an equal-valued subsidy for not polluting can both potentially achieve the optimal amount of pollution in the short run, the tax instrument is the preferred alternative in the long run because any subsidy has the perverse effect of enticing entry into the industry and hence encouraging a larger volume of emissions. The present discussion, however, focuses solely on the tax instrument.

50 See OECD (1989).

51 See Burtraw (1991).

52 For the most recent proposal along these lines, see Stager (1989).

53 See Houghton (1968) and Ontario Economic Council (1976).

54 See especially Bird (1976) and Kitchen (1992). The present discussion is very abbreviated. For more extensive treatment of local user charges, see these references.

55 For an early study of this question in Canada, see Johnson (1973) and more recent work by Raynauld and Vidal (1992).

56 See the extensive discussion in Perret (1991) as well as the more general discussions of road pricing and road funds in Johansen (1989) and Roth (1990, 1991).

57 See Faiz (1990), Hau (1991b), and Heggie (1991) for thorough reviews of these questions.

58 Although this general question has not been explored in the present

paper, clearly such a credit would be "earmarked" in the same sense that any other specific "tax expenditure" (for example, for charitable donations) is earmarked.

59 However, as Bird (1992) argues, when tourist facilities are not optimally developed and there is a shortage of public savings, a stronger case can be made for assigning tourist tax revenues to finance such (fiscally productive) facilities. Moreover, where the impact of tourism is geographically concentrated and to some extent adverse for local residents (as when wildlife parks take away hunting land), some compensation may be appropriate.

Bibliography

Alm, J., B. Jackson, and M. McKee. 1992. "Institutional Uncertainty and Taxpayer Compliance." *American Economic Review*, 82: 1018–26

Baumol, W.J., and W.E. Oates. 1988. *The Theory of Environmental Policy.* 2nd ed. Cambridge: Cambridge University Press

Bird, R.M. 1976. *Changing for Public Services: A New Look at an Old Idea.* Toronto: Canadian Tax Foundation

– 1984. *Intergovernmental Finance in Columbia: Final Report of the Mission on Intergovernmental Finance.* Cambridge, Mass.: Law School of Harvard University

– 1992. "Taxing Tourists in Developing Countries." *World Development*, 20: 1145–58

Bird, R.M., and E. Slack. 1983. "Urban Finance and User Charges." In *State and Local Finance*, ed. G.F. Break, 211–37. Madison: University of Wisconsin Press

– 1993. *Urban Public Finance in Canada.* Rev. ed. Toronto: John Wiley & Sons

Borg, M.O., and P.M. Mason. 1988. "The Budgetary Incidence of a Lottery to Support Education." *National Tax Journal*, 41: 75–85

Brazer, H.E. 1985. "Some Observations on Earmarking." In National Tax Association–Tax Institute of America, *Proceedings of the 77th Annual Conference 1984*, 269–73. Columbus, Ohio

Brennan, G., and J.M. Buchanan. 1980. *The Power to Tax.* New York: Cambridge University Press

Browning, E.K. 1975. "Collective Choice and General Fund Financing." *Journal of Political Economy*, 83: 377–90

Buchanan, J.M. 1963. "The Economics of Earmarked Taxes." *Journal of Political Economy*, 71: 457–69

– 1967. *Public Finance in Democratic Process.* Chapel Hill: University of North Carolina Press

Burbidge, J. 1987. *Social Security in Canada: An Economic Appraisal.* Toronto: Canadian Tax Foundation

Burkhead, J. 1956. *Government Budgeting.* New York: John Wiley & Sons

Burtraw, D. 1991. "Compensating Losers when Cost-Effective Environmental Policies Are Adopted." *Resources,* 104: 1–5

Canadian Tax Foundation. 1992. *Provincial and Municipal Finances 1991.* Toronto: Canadian Tax Foundation

Crew, M.A., and R. Kleindorfer. 1991. *Economics of Public Utility Regulation.* Cambridge, Mass.: MIT Press

Cropper, M.L., and W.E. Oates. 1992. "Environmental Economics: A Survey." *Journal of Economic Literature,* 30: 675–740

Deran, E. 1965. "Earmarking and Expenditures: A Survey and a New Test." *National Tax Journal,* 18: 354–61

Dewees, D. 1992. "Environmental Taxation." In *Taxation to 2000 and Beyond,* ed. R.M. Bird and J. Mintz, 29–60. Toronto: Canadian Tax Foundation

Dobbs, I. 1991. "Litter and Waste Management: Disposal Taxes versus User Fees." *Canadian Journal of Economics,* February: 221–27

Downing, P.B. 1992. "The Revenue Potential of User Charges in Municipal Finance." *Public Finance Quarterly,* 20: 512–27

Dwyer, L., and P. Forsyth. 1992. "The Case for Tourist Promotion: An Economic Analysis." Discussion Paper No. 265, Centre for Economic Policy Research. Canberra: Australian National University

Dye, R.F., and T.J. McGuire. 1992. "The Effect of Earmarked Revenues on the Level and Composition of Expenditures." *Public Finance Quarterly,* 20: 543–46

Ebel, R.D. 1990. *A Fiscal Agenda for Nevada.* Reno and Las Vegas: University of Nevada Press

Eklund, P. 1972 "A Theory of Earmarking Appraised." *National Tax Journal,* 25: 223–30

– 1980. "Benefit Taxation Revisited – a Study of Collective Decision-Making in Developing Countries." Washington, DC. Unpublished

Faiz, A. 1990. "Automotive Air Pollution: Issues and Options for Developing Countries" WPS 492, PRE Working Paper. Washington, DC: World Bank

Gillespie, W.I. 1991. *Tax, Borrow and Spend: Financing Federal Spending in Canada, 1867–1990.* Ottawa: Carleton University Press

Goetz, C.J. 1968. "Earmarked Taxes and Majority Rule Budgetary Processes." *American Economic Review,* 58: 128–37

Haritos, Z. 1973. *Rational Road Pricing Policies in Canada.* Ottawa: Canadian Transport Commission

Hau, T. 1991a. "Congestion Charging Mechanisms: An Evaluation of Current Practice." Infrastructure and Urban Development Department. Washington, DC: World Bank

- 1991b. "Economic Fundamentals of Road Pricing: A Diagrammatic Analysis." Infrastructure and Urban Development Department. Washington, DC: World Bank

Heggie, I.G. 1991. "Improving Management and Charging Policies for Roads: An Agenda for Reform." Infrastructure and Urban Development Department, Report 92. Washington, DC: World Bank

Hickling Corporation. 1991. "Earmarking of Revenues and Program Management." Prepared for Royal Commission on Passenger Transportation. Ottawa. Unpublished.

Houghton, D. 1968. *Paying for the Social Services*. London: Institute of Economic Affairs.

Johansen, F., ed. 1989. "Earmarking, Road Funds and Toll Roads: A World Bank Symposium." Infrastructure and Urban Development Department, Discussion Paper 45. Washington, DC: World Bank

Johnson, J.A. 1973. "Canadian Policies in Regard to the Taxation of Alcoholic Beverages." *Canadian Tax Journal*, 21: 552–64

Kimenyi, J.S., D.R. Lee, and R.D. Tollison. 1990. "Efficient Lobbying and Earmarked Taxes." *Public Finance Quarterly*, 18: 104–13

Kitchen, H. 1993. "Efficient Delivery of Local Government Services." Discussion Paper 93-15. School of Policy Studies, Queen's University, Kingston, Ont.

Krashinsky, M. 1981. *User Charges in the Social Services*. Toronto: Ontario Economic Council

Lee, D.R., and M.S. Misolek. 1986. "Substituting Pollution Taxation for General Taxation: Some Implications for Efficiency in Pollution Taxation." *Journal of Environmental Economic Management*. 13: 338–47

McCleary, W. 1991. "The Earmarking of Government Revenue: A Review of Some World Bank Experience." *World Bank Research Observer*, 6: 81–104

McCleary, W., and E. Uribe Tobon. 1990. "Earmarking Government Revenues in Colombia." Policy, Research and External Affairs Working Papers WPS 425. Washington, DC: World Bank

McMahon, W., and C. Sprenkle. 1972. "A Theory of Earmarking." *National Tax Journal*, 23: 255–61

Musgrave, R.A. 1938. "The Voluntary Exchange Theory of the Public Economy." *Quarterly Journal of Economics*, 53: 213–37

- 1992. "Separating and Combining Fiscal Choices: Reflections on the Wicksellian Model." Paper prepared for International Seminar in Public Economics. Tokyo. Unpublished

Musgrave, R.A., and A.T. Peacock, eds. 1958. *Classics in the Theory of Public Finance*. New York: St Martins Press

Mushkin, S., ed. 1972. *Public Prices for Public Products*. Washington, DC: Urban Institute

Netzer, D. 1992. "Differences in Reliance on User Charges by American State and Local Governments." *Public Finance Quarterly*, 20: 499–511

Oakland, W.H. 1985. "Earmarking and Decentralization." In *National Tax Association–Tax Institute of America, Proceedings on 77th Annual Conference 1984*, 274–77. Columbus, Ohio

– 1989. "Principles of Earmarking." In *Earmarking, Road Funds and Toll Roads: A World Bank Symposium*, ed. F. Johansen, 1–19. Infrastructure and Urban Development Department Discussion Paper 45. Washington, DC: The World Bank

Oates, W.E. 1991. "Pollution Charges as a Source of Public Revenues." University of Maryland Working Paper No. 91-22, University of Maryland, Department of Economics, College Park, Md

Ontario. Ministry of Treasury and Economics. 1992. *1992 Ontario Budget: Meeting Ontario's Priorities, Presented ... April 30, 1992*. Toronto: Queen's Printer for Ontario

Ontario Economic Council. 1976. *Issues and Alternatives, 1976: Health*. Toronto: Council

Organisation for Economic Cooperation and Development (OECD). 1989. *The Application of Economic Instruments for Environmental Protection*. Paris: OECD

Pechman, J.A., H.J. Aaron, and M.K. Taussig. 1968. *Social Security: Perspectives for Reform*. Washington, DC: Brookings Institution

Perret, F.L. 1991. "The Swiss Road Accounting System: Evolution towards a Better Transparency." Ottawa. Unpublished

Pesando, J.E., and S.A. Rea. 1977. *Public and Private Pensions in Canada: An Economic Analysis*. Toronto: University of Toronto Press

Pogue, T.F., and L.G. Sgontz. 1989. "Taxing to Control Social Costs, the Case of Alcohol." *American Economic Review*, 79: 235–43

Postner, H. 1992. "Earmarked Taxes: Analytical Review." Prepared for Government and Competitiveness Project. Kingston, Ont. Unpublished

Premchand, A. 1983. *Government Budgeting and Expenditure Controls*. Washington, DC: International Monetary Fund

Public Administration Service. 1962. *Modernizing Government Budget Administration*. Washington, DC: Agency for International Development

Raynauld, A., and J.P. Vidal. 1992. "Smokers' Burden on Society: Myth and Reality in Canada." *Canadian Public Policy*, 18: 300–17

Robinson, A.J. 1986. *The Retail Sales Tax in Canada*. Toronto: Canadian Tax Foundation

Roth, G. 1990. "Perestroika for U.S. Highways: A Bold New Policy for Manag-

184   Wayne R. Thirsk and Richard M. Bird

ing Roads for a Free Society." Reason Foundation, Policy Insight, No. 125, November
- 1991. "Pricing, Financing and Ownership of Roads in a Free Society." Paper at 2nd International Conference on Privatization and Deregulation in Passenger Transportation, Tampere, Finland, 20–21 June
Slack, E., and R.M. Bird. 1991. "Financing Urban Growth through Development Charges." *Canadian Tax Journal*, 39 (5): 1288–1304
Sproule-Jones, M., and J. White. 1989. "The Scope and Application of User Charges in Municipal Governments." *Canadian Tax Journal*, 37: 1477–85
Stager, D. 1989. *Focus on Fees: Alternative Policies for University Tuition Fees.* Toronto: Council of Ontario Universities
Statistics Canada. 1992. *Public Finance Historical Data, 1965/66–1991/2.* Ottawa
Teja, R.S. 1990. "The Case for Earmarked Taxes." *International Monetary Fund Staff Papers*, 35: 523–33
Travis, C., and C. Doty. 1989. "Superfund: A Program without Priorities." *Environmental Science and Technology*, 23: 1333–34
Wagner, R., ed. 1991. *Charging for Government: User Charges and Earmarked Taxes in Principle and Practice.* London: Routledge
Webber, C., and A. Wildavsky. 1986. *A History of Taxation and Expenditure in the Western World.* New York: Simon and Shuster
Whalley, J., and A. Ziderman. 1989. "Payroll Taxes for Financing Training in Developing Countries." Policy, Planning and Research Working Paper 141. Washington, DC: World Bank
Winch, D.M. 1982. *The Economics of Highway Planning.* Toronto: University of Toronto Press

Notes on Contributors

Richard M. Bird is Professor in the Department of Economics, University of Toronto.

G. Bruce Doern is Professor in the School of Public Administration, Carleton University, Ottawa.

Evert A. Lindquist is Assistant Professor in the Department of Political Science at the University of Toronto.

Wayne R. Thirsk is Professor of Economics at the University of Waterloo.

Commission Organization

Chair*
Monica Townson

Vice-Chairs
Neiol Brooks**
Robert Couzin**

Commissioners
Jayne Berman
William Blundell
Susan Giampietri
Brigitte Kitchen**
Gérard Lafrenière
Fiona Nelson
Satya Poddar**

Executive Director
Hugh Mackenzie

Director of Research
Allan M. Maslove

Assistant Director of Research
Sheila Block

Executive Assistant to Research Program
Moira Hutchinson

Editorial Assistant
Marguerite Martindale

* Chair of the Research Subcommittee
** Member of the Research Subcommittee